The Fiction of
Paule Marshall: Reconstructions
of History, Culture, and Gender

The Fiction of
Paule Marshall

RECONSTRUCTIONS OF
HISTORY, CULTURE, AND GENDER

Dorothy Hamer Denniston

The University of Tennessee Press • Knoxville

Frontispiece: Paule Marshall. Photograph by Jerry Bauer.

Selections from *Praisesong for the Widow* reprinted by permission of the Putnam Publishing Group. © 1983 by Paule Marshall.

Selections from *Daughters, The Chosen Place, The Timeless People, Reena and Other Stories, Brown Girl, Brownstones,* and *Soul Clap Hands and Sing* reprinted by permission of Paule Marshall. All © by Paule Marshall.

Parts of chapters 2 and 4 have previously appeared as "Early Short Fiction by Paule Marshall" in *Callaloo* 6, no. 2 (Spring–Summer 1983): 32–45, reprinted in *Short Story Criticism* (Gale Research Co., Fall 1990).

The paper in this book meets the minimum requirements of the
American National Standard for Permanence of Paper for Printed
Library Materials. ∞ The binding materials have been chosen
for strength and durability.

Library of Congress Cataloging-in-Publication Data

Denniston, Dorothy Hamer, 1944–
    The fiction of Paule Marshall: reconstructions of history, culture, and gender/Dorothy Hamer Denniston.—1st ed.
        p.   cm.
    Includes bibliographical references and index.
    ISBN 0–87049–838–X (cloth: alk. paper)
    ISBN 0–87049–839–8 (pbk.: alk. paper)
    1. Marshall, Paule, 1929– —Criticism and interpretation. 2. Women and literature—
United States—History—20th century. 3. Afro-Americans in literature. 4. Caribbean Area—
In literature. 5. Sex role in literature. 6. Africa—In literature. 7. Women in literature.   I. Title.
PS3563.A7223Z64   1995
813'.54—dc20   94–18767
                                                                                                    CIP

To my parents,
Irma and Rev. James Hamer

Contents

Acknowledgments

For assistance in completing this book, I am indebted to many people. Professors Barbara Christian, Coppèlia Kahn, and Thadious Davis read the working draft in its vaguely defined form and offered invaluable suggestions for its revision. I am especially indebted to Thadious Davis, who subsequently read and commented on a second draft. Her incisive, constructive criticism as well as her suggestions for restructuring the study contributed greatly to further precision in my thinking and writing. Whatever shortcomings remaining are most certainly my own.

A special note of thanks is extended to Paule Marshall, who graciously granted me several personal interviews. She continues to inspire my life with her warm presence and powerful vision.

To Professor Michael Harper, I shall always be grateful. Like a seasoned griot, he shared with me those wonderful stories and anecdotes which helped sustain the work and the worker. I am grateful also to the participants in the 1993 Ford Foundation Summer Seminar, "History, Content and Method in Afro-American Studies." This seminar, directed by John W. Roberts, of the Center for the Study of Black Literature and Culture at the University of Pennsylvania, brought together several new friends and colleagues who helped to refine my introduction: Lillian Ashcraft-Eason, Dianetta Bryan, Frank Dobson, Alma Freeman, Aaron Gresson, Pearlie Peters, and Hoda Zaki. Others who read and critiqued portions of the original manuscript include my colleagues at Brown: Paget Henry, Elizabeth Kirk, George Monteiro, and Mark Spilka.

For financial support to continue my research and writing, I am pleased to acknowledge grants from the University of Tennessee, Knoxville, and Brown University. The offices of the Associate Provost and the Dean of Faculty at Brown also provided monies for computer services. Many thanks to Alan Renear and Shannon Miller for the critical reformatting of the original disks and to Jane Simmons and Jennifer Campbell for keyboarding the final copy. Throughout this protracted affair I have been motivated and encouraged by the love and faith of my family—both nuclear and extended. They are too numerous to name individually, but special mention goes to my sisters, Dr. Norvell Jackson and Miki Winder and to my brothers, James Hamer Jr. and Elmer Hamer. Without their love and support, I could not thrive. Special mention also goes to my closest friends: Dee Ann and Bill Clark, Marlene Godfrey, Dr. Samuel Johnson and Ben Swan. Their presence in my life is a blessing.

Introduction

Anatomy of an Aesthetic— The African Cultural Base

We [as people of African descent] must accept the task of "reinventing" our own images and the role which Africa will play in this process will be essential.

Paule Marshall

During the 1970s and 1980s, fiction by African-American women achieved critical prominence. Novels by Toni Morrison, Alice Walker, Gloria Naylor, Ntozake Shange—to name a few—directed a generation of readers to the diversity of black women's creativity and the richness of their vision. The popular appeal of such writers has fostered an interest in new black women artists. J. California Cooper, Marita Golden, Terry McMillan, and Xam Cartier come to mind. It has also revived an interest in writers who have enjoyed critical acclaim without widespread recognition. Paule Marshall is one such author.

Marshall is perhaps best known in academic circles for her work on the experiences of West Indians within African-American culture in the United States. In her fiction as a whole she is concerned with the experiences of African peoples throughout the diaspora. Scholars have commented in books and literary journals on her treatment of the impact of colonization on the psyche of American and Caribbean blacks. Barbara Christian, Hortense Spillers, Eugenia Collier, John McCluskey, and many others, whom I will cite as I proceed, provide engaging essays on Marshall's artistry and important themes. All agree that the author's fiction represents an attempt to identify, analyze, and resolve the conflict between cultural loss/displacement and cultural domination/hegemony. Correctly assessing the cultural differences that accrue from place to place, Barbara Christian states that "the shape of [Marshall's] characters can scarcely be detached from the space around them."[1] I argue in this study that the cultural space surrounding Marshall's characters also includes her imaginative reconstruction of African history and culture to establish an underlying unity that links all peoples of African descent. Indeed, the chronology of Marshall's publications suggests her intentional design to reverse the "middle passage"; that is, she examines the experience of blacks not in transit from Africa to the New World but from the New World back toward Africa. Simultaneously, she combines forms of written narrative that are Western in origin with the style and function of traditional African oral narrative. She thus revitalizes an ancient aesthetic within a modern construct and develops a unique literary voice. True to the spirit of African art, Marshall's finished creations go beyond the mere objet d'art to become composite images that resonate within and without the text. Those images reflect stratified, sometimes superimposed worlds, but worlds that can be encompassed in patterns of traditional African belief, thought, and form.

Née Valenza Pauline Burke, Marshall was born on April 9, 1929, in Brooklyn, New York. The daughter of Ada and Samuel Burke, emigrants from Barbados, she grew up in a tightly structured West Indian–American community listening to stories about "home" (Barbados). Marshall first visited Barbados when she was nine years old, and she recalls writing a series of poems after that visit which reflected her impressions. That visit may well have been significant for instilling within her the value of her Barbadian ethnicity as different from her African-American identity in New York. That visit also may have informed, if only subliminally, her sense of the immediacy of her African heritage. However, it was not until she began to write serious fiction that a distinct cultural pattern began to emerge. She also began to focus on female characters as subjects and preservers of African cultural practices.

Marshall had been attending Hunter College, majoring in social work, when illness necessitated a one-year stay in a sanatorium in upstate New York. There, in a tranquil lake setting, she wrote letters so vividly describing the surroundings that a friend encouraged her to consider a career in writing. After her recuperation, she married psychologist Kenneth Marshall in 1950, transferred to Brooklyn College, changed her major to English literature, and graduated Phi Beta Kappa in 1953. In 1959, she gave birth to her only child, Evan-Keith Marshall, who is a naval engineer residing in London. Divorced in 1963, she wed Nourry Ménard, a Haitian businessman, seven years later.

Marshall resisted teaching and social work, the prescribed professional goals for educated black women of her day, and eventually found work in New York City as a researcher and staff writer for a small black magazine, *Our World,* edited by John P. Davis. As the only woman on the staff, she was initially relegated to the food and fashion section. Later she was assigned more challenging feature writing, which took her to Latin America and to the West Indies. Her fiction writing, however, started off with short vignettes, composed at the end of her working day. From these exercises came her first published short story, "The Valley Between" (1954). Under similar circumstances, she completed the first draft of *Brown Girl, Brownstones,* and with its publication in 1959, her career as a fiction writer was established. Her subsequent fiction includes *Soul Clap Hands and Sing* (1961), "Reena" (1962), "Some Get Wasted" (1964), "To Da-duh: In Memoriam" (1967), *The Chosen Place, the Timeless People* (1969), *Praisesong for the Widow* (1983), and *Daughters* (1991).

Marshall combines a writing career with teaching and is a professor of English and creative writing at Virginia Commonwealth University. Previously, she held teaching appointments at the University of California, Berkeley, the Iowa Writers' Workshop, the University of Massachusetts, Boston, Columbia University, and Yale. She has received the Guggenheim Fellowship, 1960; the Rosenthal Award (American Academy of Arts and Letters), 1961; the Ford Foundation Grant for Poets and Fiction Writers, 1964–65; the National Endowment for the Arts and Humanities Award, 1967–68 and 1978–79; the CAPS Awards, 1974–75; the Tribute to Black Womanhood Award (Smith College), 1983; the American Book Award, 1984; the Langston Hughes Medallion Award, 1986; the New York State Governor's Arts Award (literature), 1987; and the John Dos Passos Award for Literature, 1989. In 1990, Marshall was a *PEN/Faulkner Award* Honoree, and in 1992, she received the prestigious John D. and Catherine T. MacArthur Fellowship.

Like Toni Morrison, Gloria Naylor, and other literary artists concerned with ethnic and cultural history, Marshall faces the problem of interpreting reality from a dual consciousness. This two-ness of selves was identified by W. E. B. DuBois in *Souls of Black Folk* (1903). However, even DuBois did not observe sufficiently the *three-ness* of those who were black and Caribbean and American. Marshall's uniqueness as a contemporary black female artist stems from her ability to write from these three levels of awareness. To be sure, her cultural identity as both African American and African Caribbean allows her to understand how the two cultures alternately diverge and coalesce. Furthermore, she is aware that both cultures reflect a distinct reality that has no direct equivalent in the Anglo-American way of life. To reconcile this three-part existence in her fiction,

Marshall compromises neither her African-American nor her African-Caribbean identity. Rather, she brings both back to their original source in traditional African culture.

It is important to add here that Marshall's imaginative return to traditional African culture is certainly critical to her uncovering of "hidden continuities" between peoples of African descent. But her artistic vision is forward-looking, suggesting change and possibility. She clearly acknowledges what Stuart Hall describes as "critical points of deep and significant *difference*," which constitute black cultural identities in the New World. Given the displacement and dispersal of African peoples, cultural identities cannot remain static.

> Cultural identities come from somewhere, have histories. But, like everything which is historical, they undergo constant transformation. Far from being eternally fixed in some essentialist past, they are subject to the continuous 'play' of history, culture, and power. Far from being grounded in mere 'recovery' of the past, which is waiting to be found and which, when found, will secure our sense of ourselves into eternity, identities are the names we give to the different ways we are positioned by, and position ourselves within, the narratives of the past.[2]

In her fiction, Marshall "positions" herself in an "imagined community,"[3] and that community, though undergoing transformation, privileges and allegorizes a history and culture that stems from a single source.

My own interpretive discourse takes into consideration only selected aspects of traditional African culture to illustrate my thesis that, in nearly all of her fiction, Paule Marshall reclaims African culture for black diasporan peoples. I do not intend to suggest totalizing formulations for indigenous African cultures which, of course, vary from region to region. Nor do I intend to utopianize the African past. Rather, I wish to outline specific cultural components of traditional African culture as practiced primarily in the western and central regions of the continent. These components inform Marshall's subject matter as well as provide the essential framework for her artistry. Many of these cultural components also sustain a continuing influence upon the several black societies thriving in the world today.

Certainly, the African influence can be readily discerned in black music where syncopation, repetition, and improvisation are common features. African survivals are also apparent in black religions (Christian and tribal), in dance patterns, and perhaps even in mannerisms. Scholars Geneva Smitherman, J. L. Dillard, and Joseph E. Holloway are among those who argue convincingly that the speech of black Americans, with its intonations, rhythms, and grammatical syntax, is derivative of West African communication patterns.[4] Marshall vividly describes these cultural elements in her fiction. In her written reconstruction of the spoken word, especially, the language of her characters sways with the beat of Caribbean and, by extension, African rhythms. Marshall's skill with language stems from a legacy which she proudly proclaims—a legacy which, in the finest of African traditions, was passed on to her orally by her West Indian mother and female kinfolk (and here the term *kinfolk* is intended to connote a cultural collective). Writing about their narrative abilities, Marshall credits these Barbadian women as the source of her inspiration:

> It wasn't only what the women talked about, the content; but the way they put things, the style. The insight, irony, wit and their own special force which they brought to everything they discussed; above all, the poet's skill with words. They had taken a language imposed upon them, and infused it with their own incisive rhythms and syntax, brought to bear upon it the few African words and sounds that had been retained. In a word, transformed it, made it their own. I was impressed without being able to define it, by the seemingly effortless way they had mastered the form of story-telling. They did not know it, nor did I at the time, but they were carrying on a tradition as ancient as Africa, a centuries old oral mode by which the culture and history, the wisdom of the race had been transmitted. Theirs was the palaver in the men's quarter and the stories the old women told the children seated outside the round houses as the sun declined. They were, in other words, practising art of a high order, and in the process revealing at a level beyond words their understanding of and commitment to an aesthetic which recognizes that art is inseparable from life, and form and content are one.[5]

Marshall's notion of art as inseparable from life is integral to African cultural traditions, and it may help us to understand the unique perspective from which Africans and, to a large extent, their descendants interpret the world.

In "From the Poets in the Kitchen," Marshall writes of how her parents always talked in antilogical terms: "nothing, no matter how beautiful, was ever described as simply beautiful. It was always 'beautiful-ugly': the beautiful-ugly dress, the beautiful-ugly house, the beautiful-ugly car." She goes on to explain that they "were expressing a fundamental dualism in life: the idea that a thing is at the same time its opposite, and that these opposites . . . make up the whole."[6] This dualism forms the core of traditional African thought and is expressed through an acceptance of paradox as a means of achieving equilibrium. In other words, to separate one category from its opposite can only lead to chaos. Good and evil coexist as do the physical and the spiritual. According to Levy-Bruhl, "Philosophy, theology, politics, social theory, land, law, medicine, psychology, birth and burial all find themselves logically concatenated in a system so tight that to subtract one item from the whole is to paralyze the structure of the whole."[7] The same may be said of the arts. Basil Davidson remarks that the arts were "the corporeal rendering of otherwise inexpressible unities between the known and the unknown. They were shared links with ancestors and gods who had shaped the world and laid down rules for its progression."[8]

Many of those rules, we know, were transmitted through the oral tradition that recorded history and preserved folk traditions (tales, proverbs, riddles, topical songs). My emphasis here, however, is on the nature of oral narrative as a form of literary expression. Since oral literature is centered on the same ideas as written literature (the ideas, beliefs, hopes, and fears of a people), its purpose is to create and maintain a group identity, to guide social action, to encourage social interaction, and simply to entertain. Oral art is equally concerned with preserving the past to honor traditional values and to reveal their relevance to the modern world. These seem to be Marshall's objectives in nearly all of her fiction, but critical to my central thesis for this study is the identification of specific components from the African oral narrative form that Marshall adopts and adapts in her written art.

One component is the use of proverbs, which may be interspersed throughout a piece to establish an illustrative, didactic pattern. As rhetorical devices in both written and oral literatures, they may further serve to introduce, supplement, or conclude a story. Marshall follows this format as she inserts, in summary fashion, short quotations that characterize particular figures or personalities in *Brown Girl, Brownstones.* She achieves a similar effect in other novels by the use of secondary material (or subtales), which may be frequently employed in the oral delivery.[9] Whatever the approach, dramatic rendering is paramount. Vocal intonation, facial expressions, and body movements must be calculated to contribute to the impact of the recitation. But equally important are the occasion, musical accompaniment, and, in some cases, dance. The latter becomes especially significant in *Brown Girl, Brownstones, The Chosen Place, the Timeless People,* and *Praisesong for the Widow,* novels in which Marshall's craftsmanship is executed in such dynamic fashion as to elicit feelings and sensations usually reserved for the theater. As in the oral presentation, we *see* subtle and elaborate gestures and *hear* the pitch and intensity of the human voice. Further, the artist incorporates music and dance into these novels to describe events of cultural importance.

Marshall's love for ornate language is unquestionably Afrocentric, and as she portrays black peoples of the Caribbean and the Americas, her characters' love of words is equally apparent. Especially in her rendering of the rhythmic, lilting, colorful West Indian dialect, Marshall not only captures the essence of black language as a forceful tool of communication, but she also shows how speech itself can be a form of art. Even minor characters in her fiction seem able to reconstruct an event, without deliberation, raising it to a climax and mesmerizing the fictive listeners and the reader alike. Ingenious syntactical rearrangements bring about a poetry that compels imaginative associations and entertains with the sheer delight of sound. As author, though, Marshall suggests rather than transcribes living speech, for this approach "preserves the flesh and sting of it, without impeding the flow of her narrative."[10] She uses dialectal speech to separate the characters' views from those of the narrator, thereby broadening the readers' perspectives. At the same time, Marshall fuses biblical and literary allusions throughout her fiction to amplify thematic concerns.

Another component of the literary oral form is the audience, which functions both as spectator and participant. Ruth Finnegan tells us that the audience may affect the presentation: "The artist may tend, for instance, to omit obscenities, certain types of jokes, or complex forms in the presence of, say, children or missionaries (or even foreign students) which he would include in other contexts. And direct references to the characteristics, behavior, or fortunes of particular listeners can also be brought in with great effectiveness in a subtle and flexible way not usually open to written literature."[11] Yet Marshall manages to include in her written forms direct and subtle references as well as occasional risqué jokes. This is apparent again in *Brown Girl, Brownstones,* several short stories, and her most recent novel, *Daughters.* More importantly, the author gives her fictive audience an opportunity to challenge or to clarify portions of their own oral "performances."

The occasion certainly bears significance in an oral presentation. Be it a wedding or a funeral, a victory song or a work song, appropriateness dictates the content and the medium. Appropriateness may outweigh the content, says Finnegan, "but even when there is not this specific connection, a piece of oral literature tends to be affected by such factors as the general purpose and atmosphere of the gathering at which it is rendered, recent episodes in the minds of performer and audience, or even the time of year and propinquity of the harvest."[12] Again, Marshall adheres to this pattern in her novels when she inserts short tales at major events of ritual significance. The artist perfects this strategy to build suspense within the story at hand. Like the African oral performer, however, her first consideration is to tell an interesting story. By infusing the language with rhythms, symbols, and images reflecting African cultural traditions, she extends her purpose to include instruction.

The embellishment of language, the manipulative tactics of the narrator and speaker, the use of hyperbole and exaggeration, of simile and metaphor, the direct involvement of the audience—all contribute to a figurative mode of expression that reflects, at one and the same time, a social, cultural, and literary context. In Marshall's hands, form and content merge to foster unity in a personal, communal, and national sense. In her collection of novellas, *Soul Clap Hands and Sing,* and in her subsequent novels, that unity gradually expands to include an international or global sense.

Unity is further achieved through Marshall's manipulation of time, which, quite essentially, is expressed from an African perspective. Although not as evident in her early short works, Marshall turns to this African cultural concept in her longer fiction. As a vehicle of measurement, time for many African peoples moves not in a linear fashion but in a cyclic continuum. As opposed to "change and progress," it involves "recurrence and duration." In *African Religions and Philosophies,* John Mbiti explains: "Time is simply a composition of events which have occurred, those which are taking place now and those which are immediately to occur. What has not taken place, or what has no likelihood of an immediate occurrence falls in the category of "No time." What is certain to occur, or what falls within the rhythm of natural phenomena, is in the category of inevitable or *potential* time."[13]

Such a synchronic view of time might suggest the abolition of history as Westerners ordinarily understand it, but it does not negate a sense of history. The orientation is simply different. Time from an African perspective must be experienced in order for it to become reality, and experience suggests the past and the present. Through the oral tradition, Africans look back to their origins and, like peoples of all civilizations, they make use of various myths to explain such things as the existence of God and other deities, the creation, et cetera. The immediate and remembered past, which goes back several generations, affirms that the rhythms of life remain continuous and intact. Marshall incorporates this idea in *The Chosen Place, the Timeless People* and in *Praisesong for the Widow.* She later reconfigures time in *Daughters.*

Of course, the cycle can be broken by natural disaster or by the actions of individuals who threaten the harmony of continued communal existence. However, traditional African communities embody political, social, and moral force and have the power—indeed, the duty—to restore functional order. And here is where the often misunderstood efficacy of rites and rituals comes in. The propitiation of the gods; ceremonies attending birth, puberty, marriage, death; festivities associated with a major event, such as the harvest—these ensure the physical, emotional, and spiritual well-being of the population and are aimed, as Davidson observes, at re-stating "the comforting assurances of . . . tradition. In them, human action moves symbolically with the rhythms of the natural world around them, recreating that rhythm in moral terms."[14]

In Marshall's fiction, time moves in a circular fashion to reinforce the structure and content of her art. It becomes, in other words, a functional device for reviewing the lives of her characters to help clarify their present dilemmas. Simultaneously, it reveals the cultural perspective that most of her characters of African descent bring to their varied environments. Most dramatically in *Praisesong for the Widow,* the artist symbolically manipulates historical and fictional time to re-create the universe in African ontological terms. In *The Chosen Place, the Timeless People* and *Daughters,* she also manipulates time to establish recurrent historical and social patterns.

In pivoting existence around and in response to earthly and cosmic environments, Africans made religion essential to virtually every facet of daily living. That is, religion was not institutionalized so as to separate secular and spiritual life; rather, it informed, directed, and became the very fabric of secular living. Furthermore, traditional African life necessitated moral involvement with and responsibility to the entire community. This, of course, is related to the notion of the extended family. Since the community included ancestors, the individual's commitment to shared beliefs and practices took on even greater significance. "To be human is to belong to the whole community," writes Mbiti, "and to do so involves participating in beliefs, ceremonies, rituals, and festivals of that community."

> A person cannot detach himself from the religion of the group, for to do so is to be severed from his roots, his foundation, his context for security, his kinship and the entire group of those who make him aware of his own existence. To be without one of these corporate elements of life is to be out of the whole picture. Therefore, to be without religion amounts to a self-excommunication from the entire life of society.[15]

Marshall allows us to glimpse this cultural phenomenon through the rites and rituals she describes in her fiction, as well as through symbolic presentations of the Calypso tradition, the Ring Shout, and mysterious tales of obeah. Importantly, however, such rites are almost invariably intermingled with traditional Christian imagery, in part to reflect syncretism with the dominant religion wherever peoples of African descent have landed. In fact, Marshall plays upon the interchange of deities by portraying characters who, while adopting Western religion, remain faithful to indigenous beliefs and suffer no disintegration of personality.

Since Marshall's central characters are most often women, it is important to comment on the role of women in traditional African societies.
Obviously, African women could physically ensure the continuation of
cyclic time through procreation. The significance of their biological function cannot be overemphasized. In addition to guaranteeing a particular
genealogical line, a child became another link in the extension of the ex-
isting community. As Mbiti puts it, "a child cannot be exclusively 'my
child' but only 'our child.'"[16] This concept of communal parentage may
provide an important reference for an appreciation of the extended family.
For the African woman in particular, the birth of a child symbolizes the
embodiment of a life force that enables her own personal relationship to the
larger community. The birth of a child further authenticates the woman's
eternal relationship to time. It is a relationship that Bonnie Barthold
terms "metaphysically independent of men . . . and generally only to be
enhanced by childbirth."[17] And since age is revered in traditional African
societies, it is not surprising that when a woman becomes elderly, her status rises. Old age further "signal[s] her approaching entry into the world
of the ancestors."[18]

As is commonly known, many traditional societies practiced polygamy.
Thus, the burden of bearing and rearing a large family was not placed on
a single woman. As indicated in the passage quoted above, parenting itself became communal. This is not to suggest that traditional African societies ignored separate roles for women and men, but, consistent with
their ontology, separate activities complemented or paralleled each other.
Niara Sudarkasa points out:

> In most African societies, as elsewhere, the division of labor along sexual
> lines promoted a reciprocity of effort. If men were farmers, women were
> food processors and traders. Where men and women were engaged in the
> same activity (such as farming or weaving), they produced different items.
> Among the Ibo, females and males grew different crops; among the
> Yoruba, the female and male weavers produced different types of cloth on
> different types of looms. Where both females and males traded, there was
> usually a sexual bifurcation along commodity lines. Normally, too, men
> predominated in long-distance trade, and women were predominant in
> local markets.[19]

African languages may also provide "linguistic clues into the 'neutrality'
of gender in many African societies":

> The absence of gender in the pronouns of many African languages and the
> interchangeability of first names among females and males . . . [are] possi-

bly related to a societal deemphasis on gender as a designation for behavior. Many other areas of traditional culture, including personal dress and adornment, religious ceremonials, and intragender patterns of comportment, suggest that Africans often deemphasize gender in relation to seniority and other insignia of status.[20]

Given these observations, then, the woman in traditional African societies was not seen as assuming an inferior or subordinate role. Rather, she maintained her own autonomy in economic, social, and political spheres. Sudarkasa comments that "except for the highly Islamized societies of Sub-Saharan Africa, . . . in pre-colonial times women were conspicuous in high places. They were queen-mothers, queen-sisters, princesses, chiefs, and holders of other offices in towns and villages; occasional warriors; and, in one well-known case, that of the Lovedu, the supreme monarch. Furthermore, it was almost invariably the case that African women were conspicuous in the economic life of their societies, being involved in farming trade, and craft production."[21]

While citing other female monarchs such as Nzingo, the sixteenth-century "Amazon Queen" of Angola, Lillian Ashcraft-Eason cautions that "despite the social and political prominence of some women in West Africa, there were culturally legitimate ways in which men ensured the subordination of women, particularly after the onset of Islam. Such subordination may have reflected an historical reaction by men against an earlier era when women's status was higher."[22]

Colonialism destroyed, or at least disrupted, the economic, political, and social autonomy of African women as well as African men. Under the patriarchal—and racist and capitalistic—system, both sexes were exploited; both were refused the honor and respect accorded them in their indigenous environments. But it is the heritage of a prototypical African woman that Marshall creates and celebrates in her fiction. She draws on the elements of female strength, independence, and ability to promote self-worth through communal empowerment. The author depicts how the position of contemporary black women has often been mandated by the disadvantages of the social, political, and economic situations in which they find themselves, and she depicts how the strength of black women has been too often misinterpreted as an emasculating power. The myth of the matriarchy (significantly, developed by white men and supported, to a large extent, by black men and white women) has wrought insidious effects upon the social and psychological well-being of black women. Having assimilated some of the attitudes and values of the larger Anglo-American society surrounding them, black women have suffered not only the frustrations associated with imposed standards of beauty and femininity but also those that define the very essence of responsible motherhood. As Marshall describes the "advantages" the larger society grants to white women, she exposes the painful limitations that black women face. But she also reveals how black women forge ahead—not always to transcend the barriers but most often to resist them. Thus, Marshall shows that black women have gained from their heritage the flexibility and resiliency to reshape their worlds and that of their immediate families and communities to survive with dignity, with purpose, and with pride.

In this brief introduction, I have suggested that the fiction of Paule Marshall, which concerns cultural history, be approached from a culturally specific perspective. Since African-American and other black cultures in the Americas and the Caribbean are sociopolitical and historical phenomena, these factors must be taken into consideration to arrive at a full appreciation of the thematic and structural design so vital to Marshall's craft. As Karla Holloway observes, "discovering context may also mean recovering consciousness." This can lead as well to a "critical recovery of cultural organization,"[23] which can restructure and restore the fragmented psyche. The chapters to follow provide close readings of Marshall's fiction as it illustrates her narrative journey back into history to retrieve and reclaim those cultural elements which have sustained African peoples throughout the diaspora. I often choose to rely on Marshall's own language so as to give proper prominence to her unique cultural expression. My emphasis on Marshall's craft, however, is intended to underscore her focus on cultural expression and history. Necessarily, she fuses Western images and allusions within her fiction; she is a product of both the Old World and the New. However, it is precisely because she prioritizes her identity as a woman of African descent that she looks back to Africa. I contend throughout my study that the issues, problems, and themes Marshall explores may indeed reflect her own personal odyssey. However, as an artist, she prepares her readers for a reevaluation of the African presence in the Western hemisphere. Most importantly, she offers a discursive model for change and possibility. As her artistic vision expands to include all peoples, Paule Marshall develops a sensibility that is faithful to her African heritage. She figures a cosmogonical wholeness by valuing cultural difference even as she celebrates the triumph of the human spirit.

Chapter One

Challenging the American Norm

The Gendered Sensibility in "The Valley Between"

The ideals grounding Marshall's early fiction are especially relevant to her first published work, "The Valley Between" (1954),[1] which is her only fictional piece to use white characters exclusively. Its publication in the fifties is significant. Marked as it was by the increasing momentum of the Civil Rights movement, the period had as a major concern the total integration of blacks into mainstream American society. In fact, the most resounding support for this objective came with the 1954 litigation *Brown v. the Board of Education,* in which the nation's highest court declared separate educational facilities "inherently unequal." For proponents of social equality, an obvious extension of that ruling was that the separation of the races in all arenas of American life would not be tolerated. As is evident, "The Valley Between" appears on the verge of social transformation and dramatic change.

Marshall may have deliberately selected white characters in an attempt to erase color distinctions in art—to show that a black artist need not confine herself to race issues alone, but could paint, and paint effectively, white middle-class portraits. Of course, her decision to use white characters may have been very practical: simply to appeal to the white readership of the magazine in which her story appeared. Furthermore, since this was Marshall's first published work, she may have been unsure of her literary domain. "The Valley Between," then, might well represent a launching point—a mapping out of the terrain that her later work would explore in considerably more depth. Equally speculative but perhaps more in keeping with the historical plight of many African-American writers, Marshall may have chosen to use white characters to disguise her own feelings. "We wear the mask," wrote Paul Laurence Dunbar, one of her favorite poets. It seems not unreasonable to suggest that Marshall, who was herself involved in "an early, unwise first marriage"[2] as she put it, was distancing herself from her own predicament through the story. Perhaps she was also attempting to show more inclusively that black women, as well as white, wrestled with the problems of sexism in their own personally and socially prescribed worlds. If we consider the fact that the fifties also represented for women in general a period of forced role reassessment, Marshall's choice to use white characters becomes even more complex. Striving to become more middle-class, blacks began to imitate standards set by white society: men were to be the sole economic provider for the family; women were to be passive and subordinate. bell hooks explains that in order to reverse the effects of World War II, when black and white women were compelled to be independent workers, mass media strongly influenced gender roles:

> White and black women alike were subjected to endless propaganda
> which encouraged them to believe that a woman's place was in the
> home—that her fulfillment in life depended on finding the right man to
> marry and producing a family. If women were compelled by circum-
> stances to work, they were told that it was better if they didn't compete
> with men and confined themselves to jobs like teaching and nursing.[3]

Mass media may have indeed affected black and white women's consciousness of the "feminine ideal" but, as Marshall reveals, West Indian women of her generation were encouraged to be independent and find meaningful work—certainly better than the domestic work their mothers were forced to do. While West Indian–American women were expected to excel, to be self-sufficient and ambitious, they were "systematically programmed" to go the established American route: marriage, the 3.2 children, and, hopefully, the brownstone house. A conflict necessarily resulted, as Marshall points out about her own experience:

> So then you were caught, at least for me, personally—I was caught in a
> kind of dilemma: on the one hand, wanting to pursue whatever I wanted
> to pursue professionally; on the other hand, feeling the pressure from the
> community, from my mother, to find someone to marry—that no matter
> what you accomplished professionally, it really was not enough if you
> were not also married.[4]

Marshall did marry an intelligent and ambitious young man of West Indian descent. He did not oppose her "doing things professionally," but he did express ambivalence about her being a writer:

> On one hand, he was very pleased . . . and he was pleased because—and he told me this when we first met, maybe it was our very first date when I was age seventeen—but anyway, he let me know that he did not want to be married to an ordinary woman. He didn't even want to go out with an ordinary woman! This was age seventeen. . . . My first date with a person! There was on his part the insistence that if I was going to be involved with him, I had to be a sort of different, extraordinary kind of person because he considered himself that. And he was—very bright and very gifted in his way. And so when we married and I started writing, he was pleased because here was affirmation, confirmation that he hadn't married an ordinary person.[5]

"The Valley Between" clearly grows out of the frustration Marshall experienced once she realized that her husband could not understand that "I needed the support and the understanding to be this kind of multidimensional, sort of multitalented person—that I just found it difficult to be the writer, the housewife, the wife, the student (because I was still in school at the time). All of it was just so very difficult. And I used to get a little impatient with myself because it seemed to me, 'Why wasn't it manageable?' It seemed to me that others had managed it, didn't they? Well, of course they didn't!"[6] Here and in the story, Marshall describes the nature of marriage and gender oppression which, at best, discourages female personhood. It is an oppression so insidiously pervasive as to convince the woman herself that she is somehow selfish, deficient, and unworthy of love and respect. Controlled as it may be, though, female anger and resentment are the emotions that simmer below the surface. The author sorts out this dilemma through writing. Additionally, the short story she creates foreshadows the significance of gender issues to her creative vision. It also signals her further exploration of the possibilities for the female to combat imposed social, political, and cultural constraints.

Marshall states in her prefatory comments to the 1983 Feminist Press edition of "The Valley Between" that the story is "a flawed, first effort, something from the early days of my apprenticeship." Be that as it may, she instinctively knew that a good short story usually makes its point by building on the cumulative details of everyday existence. Close analysis of "The Valley Between" also reveals a message that, nearly a quarter of a century later, was to dominate the thought of women and propel them toward renewed levels of feminist consciousness.

The story opens with the main character, Cassie, warming milk for her infant, Ellen. The serene kitchen, warmly insulated against a drizzling rain, presents to us the familiar feel of comfortable, though not extravagant, middle-class American life. The chipped pink and white cup marked "baby," the child's toys, even the breakfast of coffee, juice, and stewed prunes— all contribute small details to the reader's image of mainstream American family life. The setting seems ordinary, commonplace, unexcitingly quotidian, but the very lack of newness disturbs Cassie's security and warmth. "Yes, warm, that was the word. It was the suffocating warmth of the afternoon in the park, having to listen to the unceasing gossip of the other mothers."[7] We discover through flashback that Cassie has desperately sought for something other than "the ritual of seven o'clock dinners and having the same people over to play cards." She desires something different that will give her life and perhaps that of her husband, Abe, a freshness and vitality. She recalls that as a child "the library had been her sanctuary, not only against the rainy world, but against all that was incomprehensible and ugly in life." It was there that she discovered the "joy of reading" and grew in her "desire to learn—to have all the muddled ideas clear, defined in words and images, and thus made a part of her." Here Marshall suggests that the act of reading is empowering to the self. Cassie, however, additionally needs validation from a man. She remembers how Abe had once given her life significance, but her life is now "being spent in one compressed, limited space." Somehow she has to change the routine to find new meaning and fulfillment.

The young woman finds a partial solution to her predicament by returning to college for two years to complete her degree. Her husband, though, resents the time she must spend away from home and openly defies her need for something other than familial responsibilities. The increasing tension drives a wedge between them, creating "a wide untraceable valley" and making them "two proud mountains, unwilling to even look at each other, incapable of coming together." Marshall describes here the problem of the American construction of gender. Its traditional emphasis on female subordination renders female autonomy virtually unattainable.

The story is thoroughly integrated in its theme of everydayness, for it climaxes with yet another ordinary occurrence. During the young woman's classes, the child is attended by her maternal grandmother, who lives in an upstairs apartment. On this particular day (the story covers less than twenty-four hours), little Ellen slips out into the rain to play and subsequently develops a fever. Cassie is later than usual in returning home; she has stopped for "coffee with some of the girls." How good it has been to talk to someone "without being tense!" But the tension returns. "I should have been here," is her immediate reaction. We know that this is not the guilt of a negligent mother. Nor is it blame ascribed to the aging grand-mother. It is the forced reaction of a woman in defeat, a woman oppressed by conditions she cannot combat. "'He's won,' she sighs."

Abe does, in fact, emerge as the conqueror, and the ensuing argument reflects his unyielding domination. But Cassie responds with new strength and insight:

> "Yes, I'm selfish and self-centered, just as you are bull-headed and blind. It's not so much school or even Ellen—it's just us—two people who should never have met each other. You would have been much better off with some other girl from your home town. . . . I should have just fin-ished up one phase of my life before starting another. I wasn't ready for the kind of life you have to offer me, and I couldn't give you very much."

What is at stake here is Cassie's right to selfhood as well as her right to challenge and reject social constructions made for her by a patriarchal cul-ture. She is disappointed with her position as a female, yet she cannot or will not defy conventional middle-class standards. When confronted by her husband with the option of staying home or leaving altogether, she finds that the decision, in effect, has already been made for her. With sadness and resignation, Cassie states: "I only pity both of us for having lost so much simply because you want me to be happy on your terms. I haven't got the strength to defy you anymore—you and your male strength. Let's not talk."

As indicated in Cassie's response, Marshall is obviously concerned with something more than the surface issue of a resumed education. In this in-stance, Cassie's education is but a symptom of the much larger disease of assumed gender roles, which, because they remain unquestioned, poison male-female relationships. In her careful choice of words and phrases, Marshall describes the debilitating effects upon the woman whose self-fulfillment is denied. For example, as Cassie goes through her morning ritual of preparing breakfast, she glances "nervously at the clock." She "timidly" opens the bedroom door to check whether her husband is awake. At the kitchen table, she watches Abe "furtively, fearful that if their eyes met they would have to say something decisive and final to each other." During idle conversation with Abe, she "fidgets" with their child's doll, "trying consciously to fit its broken head back into the socket of the neck." This symbolic gesture represents Cassie's conscious desire to repair her own broken life.

Abe is not given the detailed attention that Cassie receives; after all, this is not his story. But the reader is made to understand his position. He, too, is a victim in his blind acceptance of a system of cultural values that assigns fixed gender roles, a system he has never seen fit to question. He is well intentioned in his attempts to reconcile their differences, but, ultimately, his way is best. Abe has absolutely no conception that there might be a better way.

The story ends with Cassie uttering the appropriate "feminine" line: "Your supper's ready by now, Abe." Though it strikes a hollow note, Cassie's capitulation remains. She can be wife and mother, but not person. The forces of history and tradition that have molded the respective responses of female and male have led to the fragmentation that now characterizes their relationship. The author suggests that traditionally in American society it has been the woman who has had to sacrifice that part of herself which craves fulfillment and that, traditionally, the woman has accepted that fate. Her resignation to a status secondary to that of the male has not only been expected but demanded by all social patterns of acceptance. In "The Valley Between," however, we see that simmering beneath this forced acceptance is a dormant, rebellious spirit, which, if vented in a supportive atmosphere, can bring creative and useful dimensions to the lives of both men and women.

And herein lies Marshall's feminism. It is not a political platform that simply attempts to equalize the power of an inherently oppressive system. It seems apparent in the development of the storyline that the system has already gone awry. Marshall searches for new values, new modes of thought that enhance gender distinctions by extending priority to individual human needs. She suggests in "The Valley Between" that we must first define gender roles as they are operative in contemporary American society. Then we must evaluate them according to the limitations imposed by such definitions. Finally, we must redefine them to suit more comfortably our personal preferences and individual abilities. This conclusion seems reasonable considering the lingering question that remains a part of the story: On whose terms must individual value be determined and at what costs?

Two lingering questions remain outside the story itself. In view of Marshall's notions of female independence, is the immigrant dream of a middle-class, American life tantamount to a nightmare in disguise? How can she situate her own life and the lives of others like her within conventional American race and gender constructs? Marshall's unquestionable inclusion in an Afro-American/African-Caribbean culture necessitates first an acknowledgment of her *other-ness.* It also necessitates a movement toward and a concentration in her immediate West Indian heritage. It is consistent, then, that in her next work, *Brown Girl, Brownstones* (1959), the author turns to a black community to reconsider some of the issues raised in "The Valley Between." From this vantage point, "The Valley Between" represents Marshall's challenging of American values and signals the first leg of her examination of cultural and gender paradigms.

Chapter Two

Beyond
Bildungsroman

Constructions of Gender and Culture in *Brown Girl, Brownstones*

In her first novel, *Brown Girl, Brownstones* (1959), Marshall explores the coming of age of Selina Boyce contextualized in the struggle for survival of a black immigrant family and community. Significantly, the novel also foregrounds Marshall's consciousness of moving beyond the construction of identity prevalent in the United States. On one level, then, *Brown Girl, Brownstones* is a *Bildungsroman*. On another level, it is a *Künstlerroman*. On still another, more comprehensive level, the novel chronicles African-Caribbean culture thriving in an environment hostile to its mores and beliefs. Because it prioritizes—indeed, celebrates—a black community as empowering to the individual, the novel moves beyond Western literary paradigms to unveil a distinctly African orientation. *Brown Girl, Brownstones* becomes, first and foremost, a text about individual development that is inseparable from the development of the collective body.

Several critics have already commented on *Brown Girl, Brownstones* as a *Bildungsroman*. Barbara Christian, Susan Willis, Susan Stanford Friedman, Mary Helen Washington,[1] among others, discuss the protagonist's growth particularly in relation to the several distinct communities with which she interfaces. While I devote some attention to this important aspect of the novel, my focus is primarily on Silla and Deighton Boyce. For my purposes, these two characters constitute the dominant, conflicting forces that shape the novel's heroine, and they are central to my consideration of gender roles in transition. However, I wish to emphasize in this chapter the author's use of language to reflect West Indian culture and her treatment of women as oral transmitters of that culture. Though Marshall may not have been consciously aware at the time, with *Brown Girl, Brownstones* she embarks on her artistic destiny to depict the black woman in fiction not simply as "a product of America, but one whose story is equally tied and bound to the West Indies as it is to its source—Africa."[2]

As the title suggests, the imagery of architecture especially cements the novel together. In fact, the novel is built upon blocks (books) that are tiered. Book One, "A Long Day and a Long Night," introduces the major characters. Book Two, "Pastorale," engages us with the girl becoming woman. Book Three, "The War," describes the battle between Selina's parents within the larger battle of World War II. Book Four, "Selina," portrays Selina's growth toward her own personal and cultural identity. From the very first paragraph to the last, Marshall's architecture is so carefully wrought as to elicit with seeming effortlessness an imposing metaphor for the novel itself.[3] The buildings, the rooms, the streets, the very silences cry out in sympathy with the exigencies of the black immigrants' plight in America. The title of the novel, which was suggested by her husband, also signals the setting in urban New York even as it promises to focus upon a brown girl, a subject which until recently had rarely been treated in African-American fiction. What little that had been published by the time *Brown Girl, Brownstones* appeared was long out of print or in such limited editions that an aspiring young black woman writer had few, if any, models by which to gauge her talent. But Marshall tells us that she had to write.

Interestingly enough, even as Marshall describes the growth and development of Selina, the young heroine generally remains in the background until the last book of the novel. While her presence is felt throughout the novel and we gain important insights through her limited perceptions, Selina's characterization as the brown girl lends only superficial unity to the whole. Firmly guiding the novel is the presence of an omniscient narrator who controls and modifies our responses so that we delve into the minds and hearts of equally complex personages. Important to West Indian and African-American cultures and important to the author's ultimate objective, Selina observes from an appropriate distance: "A child is to be seen, not heard." Thus, Marshall provides the reader with information to help us see more than any single character and to understand the conflicting forces at hand. In the process, she unveils her broad insight into the development of the African-Caribbean/African-American psyche. Hers is an insight not marred by the acknowledgment of American racism but rather enriched by its unabashed honesty and deliberate confrontation of cultural values in conflict with personal desires and ambitions. It is through Marshall's exploration of this conflict, figured especially through Silla and Deighton Boyce, that a new vision evolves and an ancient aesthetic is revitalized.

Marshall starts the novel from an essentially personal base, but as we have already seen in "The Valley Between," personal need not be strictly autobiographical. *Brown Girl, Brownstones* presents in realistic detail the Barbadian or Bajan-American community in which the author grew up. The characters, however, are composites of people she knew. Silla, for instance, is not a portrait of Marshall's real mother, who, divorced from her husband and forced to live on welfare, felt defeated by the circumstances of her life.[4] The fictional Silla, to the contrary, represents the personality and perseverance of many West Indian women whom Marshall knew as a child—examples of self-propelled, assertive women active in controlling their own spheres of meaningful existence. Of Selina, whom many critics believe to be Marshall as a young girl, the author comments: "If anything, she's a kind of idealized image of myself. The kind of person I would have liked to have been: assertive, forthright, taking life in hand. Those marvelous qualities she has were not me at all. I was always so retiring, with my books all the time, and terrified of life. But that force Selina has is, I suppose, a kind of wishful thinking on my part.[5]

Wishful thinking notwithstanding, the novel seems to represent another type of thinking—perhaps functionally therapeutic for the author—as she narrows down the cultural values (American, African-American, African-Caribbean) that influence her. *Brown Girl, Brownstones* is, in large part, the artistic rendering of personal issues paramount to the author's internal and external dilemma of connecting her identity, without shame or apology, to its proper source. Marshall admits that as a child, she tried to deny her West Indian heritage: "I went through torture as a girl growing up in Brooklyn, going to school with those heavy silver bangles on my wrist, and when we went to the West Indies and came back with heavy West Indian accents, the kids used to laugh at us. It was dreadful. So I went through a whole period of rejecting that part of myself."[6] *Brown Girl, Brownstones* provides the opportunity for the author to explore some of those feelings within a "manageable landscape." Ultimately, this exploration speaks to the conflicting message a young black girl receives as she attempts to define herself in a multicultural context. It speaks as well to the complexity of the psychological and cultural displacement that blacks in many parts of the world experience.

That displacement becomes apparent in the novel as we travel through the world of the Bajan-American community in Brooklyn. Working night and day, saving every penny to purchase property, seemingly undaunted by racial slurs and prejudice, the Barbadian immigrants band together in tightly knit neighborhoods to form a formidable social and economic power of their own. They, like other immigrants, chose to leave their homelands to escape poverty and exploitation. But, unlike other immigrants, they also left their native land to escape the historical effects of slavery and colonialism. America, especially New York, symbolized wealth and opportunity, and Brooklyn became the nesting spot for most of these pioneering black immigrants.

Marshall's parents were a part of the wave of Caribbean immigrants who came to the United States after World War I. And we know that during the 1940s another influx occurred. Always mindful of the poor economic conditions of their homelands, the West Indians believed that with persistent determination and close management of even a limited income, anyone could eventually "buy house." The Barbadians, especially, "who had never owned anything perhaps but a few poor acres in a poor land, loved the houses with the same fierce idolatry as they had the land on their obscure islands."[7] In New York neighborhoods once dominated by Jews and Italians, "the West Indians slowly edged their way in. Like a dark sea nudging its way into a white beach and staining the sand, they came" (4). By 1939, when *Brown Girl, Brownstones* begins, the white exodus is nearly complete, and the neighborhood of Stuyvesant Heights (now Bedford-Stuyvesant) takes on a colorful, distinctively African-Caribbean dimension.

One aspect of that emerging West Indian community was language—the sound of the voices and the stories that reflect specific cultural elements. Most important to my consideration of the novel is the juxtaposition of contrary terms, which suggests that in the West Indian view of the world, like that of the African, opposites or contradictions make up the whole. African-Americans may be familiar with the adage, "God don't like ugly, and He ain't stuck on pretty." In the Caribbean a similar construction of contrarieties describes both situations and people as "beautiful-ugly" or "poor-great," to underscore the integrity of both characteristics. In keeping with the belief that the body and spirit are one, given names may be replaced or followed by such terms as *faith* or *soul*. "Silla-soul," for example, not only becomes a name of address but further indicates a merging of the physical, visible self with the spiritual.[8] In such examples, woven throughout the novel, we see the importance of language in defining an epistemology that has a dialectic nature.

In many ways, this dialectic is similar to the African-American notion of "signifyin'," which also has oppositional, rhetorical levels. As Henry Louis Gates, Jr., illustrates in his seminal work, *The Signifying Monkey,* the term defies simple definition. For my purposes, Claudia Mitchell-Kernan's summary works best:

> The Black concept of *signifying* incorporates essentially a folk notion that dictionary entries for words are not always sufficient for interpreting meanings or messages or that meaning goes beyond such interpretations. Complimentary remarks may be delivered in a left-hand fashion. A particular utterance may be an insult in one context and not another. What

pretends to be informative may intend to be persuasive. The hearer is thus constrained to attend to all potential meaning carrying symbolic systems in speech events—the total universe of discourse.[9]

The "total universe of discourse" is certainly engaged in *Brown Girl, Brownstones,* and the language especially challenges us to "understand the characters and their stories with reference to the very words that give them life."[10] To make a statement emphatic, characters may frequently use double adjectives. Someone who is deceased is "dead-dead," or when the temperature is high, the sun is "hot-hot." Deighton, Selina's father, describes Barbados as "poor-poor but sweet enough." The language is also peppered with proverbs that succinctly express an idea. Referring to the disciplining of children, one character cries, "Hard ears wun hear, own ways you'll feel." This may be interpreted as a loose equivalent of "Spare the rod, spoil the child." No explanation seems necessary for the following proverb: "Two head bulls can't reign in the same flock." And we can easily understand what Silla means when she exhorts: "You see, that's what you get for putting yourself up in things before you know what you're up against. I tell you, you's like David without a sling!" Later she mumbles, "Judas smile! Judas words! I deserve to spend the rest of muh days in sackcloth and ashes." Biblical allusions abound in the speech.

Hyperbole and metaphor also help us to visualize a given image. Miss Mary, the aging white tenant in the brownstone, is not merely old but has "been down here since they said, 'Come let us make woman.' She might of passed on and pass away and make room in the world for somebody else" (19). At one point, Silla discusses the hypocrisy of some churchgoers: "Lemme tell you . . . , you don see God any better by being sanctified and climbing the walls of a church and tearing off your clothes when you's in the spirit, or even when you's up in the so-called High Church, choking on the lot of incense and bowing and kneeling for hours and singing in various tongues. Not everyone who cry 'Lord, Lord' gon enter in" (68–69).

All of the above confirm Marshall's unmistakable immersion in the sounds and meanings of the Barbadian vernacular, and we conclude that before the words were even transcribed to the page, she had learned about the potency of the spoken word. Verbal articulation, Marshall came to understand, so vividly activated human experience in all its moods and expectations that the expression became inseparable from the experience. This oral legacy was passed on to her by her mother (to whom the novel is dedicated) and the women friends who shared her special flair for language:

> They *created poetry* as they sat around a table talking. It wasn't that they read. There weren't books of poetry around the house as such, and no one read poetry. But their ability to recreate scenes, to talk about people, to

dissect character, that was the stuff of poetry and literature. It was just there in the most natural kind of way, as Africans see art, as an integral part of life and not something you set apart in a museum or theatre or what have you.[11]

This speaking tradition is carried on in *Brown Girl, Brownstones* through the implementation of African oral narrative techniques. And, appropriately enough, in building her story, Marshall makes use of these "kitchen poets" both to advance the drama and to supplement her themes. Silla is especially adept in expressing ideas. In fact, Marshall repeats Silla's words and phrases to introduce whole chapters or segments of the novel. "Talk you, talk," applauds one of her friends. "Be-Jees, in this white man world you got to take yuh mouth and make a gun." Indeed, spoken words are so powerful that they become "living things" to Selina. "She sensed them bestriding the air and charging the room with strong colors" (71).

Movement and color in the novel help to form image clusters which, in conjunction with water imagery (especially the sea), build multiple levels of seeing, feeling, and meaning. "The sea ain't got no back door," for example, meant "that it wasn't like a house where if there was a fire you could run out the back. Meaning that it was not to be trifled with. And, meaning perhaps in a larger sense, that people should treat all of nature with caution and respect."[12] "It don do no good to reef up," says one character to suggest it does no good to bring up or dig up something from the past. Here, however, images of the tropics specify and define the context. *Yam*, itself an African word, is used as an infinitive meaning "to eat." *C'dear*, a familiar form of address in Barbados and spoken with a hard *C*, means "good Lord" or "for heaven's sake." *Wha'lah*, with the primary stress upon the second syllable, is a creolized form of *voilà*.

Barbadians also arrange words in a distinctively descriptive fashion. A woman who is pregnant, for example, is said to be "tumbling big." Or a woman who is too free with her sexual favors might be called a "thorough-fare" or a "free-bee."[13] Taking their image from the belly band that is tied around the stomach of a newborn baby to keep the navel pressed in, they often use the expression "tie up you belly" to mean one had to hold in the pain when dealing with adversity.[14] Marshall shows that the women in *Brown Girl, Brownstones* refuse to be made powerless by their condition of being black, female, and foreign; they use language as one means of exercising some measure of control over their lives and the events that shape them.

The language of the women also exposes us to West Indian cultural mores and beliefs. Florrie Trotman, for example, continues to wear a piece of coal tied around her waist, and she carries finny and goat foot as amulets against Obeah, a form of sorcery. As the others laugh at her superstitiousness, she retorts: "Oh, wunna laughing cause I got sense enough to protect muhself against all the evil people does try to do yuh. But I know what I doing" (71). We are reminded of the traditional African religious practice of accepting numerous gods to ward off potential harm from one who may have been overlooked. Included here is Florrie's testimony of the deadly effects of Obeah. I quote at length to emphasize the art with which the tale is delivered and the narrator's description of the audience's participation:

> ". . . When I was a girl home I did see obeah work on somebody and the person is dead-dead today. . . . You did know Affie Cumberbatch?" Her slit eyes swept them, reaching out to include [the listeners] in her question. "A good-looking clear-skin girl from Cane Garden with hair down she back? You know who I talking 'bout?"
> They nodded reluctantly.
> "That girl die when she was only twenty and in perfect health. Now tell what she die from?" She pointed to Silla.
> "Woman, how could I remember and that thing happen donkey years?"
> "Then, lemme tell you and listen and believe. . . . She [dear-aunt Do-Da] took me with her to the obeah man. I hear she tell him she want to work obeah on Affie and she pay him good-good money. And I see the bag of the obeah man. . . . "
> "Florrie, yuh lying now!" Iris gasped with fear.
> "Who tell you I lying? I see the bag! It had in some rusty nails and feathers and broken glass and thing so. He took some out and put in a bottle and bury it, and all the time he chanting. He give muh dear-aunt Do-Da duppy dust to put in muh uncle food so that he would pass it on to Affie when he was in the bed with she. He told muh dear-aunt not to worry, that Affie Cumberbatch was as good as dead. And I kiss my right hand to God." Florrie kissed both sides of her right hand and raised it. "When you hear the shout, Affie Cumberbatch took in sick. Her people throw 'way money enough on doctors and still cun find what was wrong with the girl. They even boil lizard soup and give she, but it din do no good. Affie said she felt like a crawling under she skin and she continue cry for a pain. She said she heard the duppies walking 'pon the roof at night and a hand cold as death 'pon she body. And Be-Jees before the year out Affie Cumberbatch was in she grave. Now tell me that's some game-cock bring ram-goat story!" She glared at them triumphantly. (71–73)

The use of double adjectives for emphasis, the references to duppies (ghosts) and to items used in traditional practices of witchcraft, the rhythmic, polyphonal speech, the dramatic gestures—all confirm Florrie's immersion in the art of oral narrative. As if to underscore her own familiarity with the tradition, Silla adds a proverb: "Florrie, I gon tell you like the old people home did say. What you believe in, you die in. If you believe there's a duppy walking 'pon the roof, then one is there" (73).

Later in the novel, we are privy to another marvelous example of the African narrative tradition as Florrie tells the story of a wedding "back home." The reader not only experiences the response of the fictive, listening audience but also participates firsthand as she is drawn into the bawdy humor and the fast-paced action. We begin to appreciate, on quite a different level, the power of words as sheer entertainment; and we understand how the images born of the Barbadian experience contribute to the movement and flow of the lives of the characters.

Marshall, all the while, develops a story about how a first-generation African-American girl interprets the world of her immigrant parents and community and how she comes to terms with her ethnic inclusion. Selina Boyce is ten years old as the novel begins. In contrast to her older sister, Ina, who grows gracefully and passively into adolescence, Selina is an awkward, truculent tomboy of sorts facing head-on the problems of her racially, economically, and politically circumscribed world. Because of her romantic and imaginative bent, the young girl is often associated with her father. In fact, she is repeatedly referred to as "Deighton's child." Selina is drawn to her father, who represents springtime and sunshine, not only in terms of his affable and carefree personality but also in terms of his favorite room, the sun parlor, importantly connected with his idyllic memories of "home" (Barbados). Silla, on the other hand, is a stern pragmatist, and Selina associates her with winter and darkness. She is a formidable and tenacious woman, who, because of her far-from-idyllic life in Barbados, is determined at any cost to "make it" in America. She recognizes, all too painfully, the realities of racist exploitation in their new environment and, unlike her husband, is willing to sacrifice pleasure for security and economic advancement. Also, unlike her husband, she *believes* in her ability to succeed, to provide a better life for herself and her family in America where "at least one has a chance."

We are alerted early on in the novel to a difference between Silla's and Deighton's approaches to the larger white world surrounding them. Deighton, for example, pauses uneasily before the kitchen, "shaken as always by the stark light there, the antiseptic white furniture and enameled white walls. The room seemed a strange unfeeling world which continually challenged him to deal with it, to impose himself somehow on its whiteness." Silla, on the other hand, "stands easily amid the whiteness . . . in the relaxed unselfconscious pose of someone alone" (22). Similar reactions by minor characters augment the story line and help to strengthen Marshall's thematic concern with the confusion of a people trying, as G. O. Bell says, "to establish a precarious foothold in an alien land."[15] But the conflict between Silla and Deighton Boyce makes up the core of the novel.

Looming in the background, almost as a subtale, is the issue of the land—the "piece of homeground"—that Deighton has recently inherited. He plans to return to Barbados and build a magnificent dream house "just like the white people own; a house to end all houses." His wife insists that he sell the land and use the money to purchase the brownstone that they currently lease. This difference in opinion not only provides the fuel for the developing controversy between the parents but also creates a clear demarcation between land and home, between Barbados and New York, between humanism and materialism. The question of where to live turns into the more penetrating question of how to live,[16] and Marshall begins her critique of both the "American Dream" and the "Dream of the Return." As the complexities of personality, culture, and psychological motivation unfold, we are hurled into a world of fluctuating tensions: violence and calm, turmoil and peace, practicality and romanticism, conformity and rebellion. To these, Marshall adds black and white (with the attendant associations of light and darkness), silence and sound, blindness and vision (with the implications previously explored by Richard Wright and Ralph Ellison).[17] Much like the antonymic adjective *beautiful-ugly,* the author does not privilege one as more realistic or nobler than the other. Instead, she leaves Selina to establish her own values, her own traditions, her own homeplace. Before her destiny can be named, however, she must understand the cultural conflict that shapes her in an almost allegorical way as her parents battle each other in their contrasting responses to America.

As indicated earlier, Silla has clear expectations of her new life in America, and she sets about with dogged determination to be successful. For artistic purposes, Silla figures most prominently in the novel to represent all the Bajan women. It is significant, then, that Selina never refers to Silla as "my" mother; rather, she is "the" mother:

> It was always the mother and the others, for they were alike—those watchful, wrathful women whose eyes seared and searched and laid bare, whose tongues lashed the world in unremitting distrust. Each morning they took the train to Flatbush and Sheepshead Bay to scrub floors. The lucky ones had their steady madams while the others wandered those neat blocks or waited on corners—each with her apron and working shoes in a bag under her arm until someone offered her a day's work. Sometimes the white children on their way to school laughed at their blackness and shouted "nigger," but the Barbadian women sucked their teeth, dismissing them. Their only thought was of the "few raw-mout' pennies" at the end of the day which would eventually "buy house." (11)

These women are unquestionably strong, capable, independent, assertive. In fact, they seem so invincible in the novel that critics have erroneously charged that Marshall perpetuates the myth of the emasculating or castrating black woman. Although the author is concerned with the sexist nature of fixed gender roles, it is clear that the crucial issue for her in *Brown Girl, Brownstones* is to describe the difficulties of establishing an *individual* identity within a cultural matrix where the problems of race and gender supersede those of one's humanity. She shows plainly that it is the white world that castrates black men—not their wives. She chooses to highlight the female struggle because it is the one with which she is most familiar. Her choice to give the female prominence is also to establish her worth as an independent, active force. Further, Marshall chooses to make the black woman representative of the larger collective black struggle for survival. Finally, Marshall wishes to reexamine perspectives of the black woman by correcting her usual presentation as a one-dimensional sexual being. Perhaps with the exception of Suggie Skeete's portrait, Marshall minimizes the black woman's sexuality in order to emphasize her concern with the day-to-day issues of survival.

Those day-to-day issues, we come to understand, are so consuming for Silla that, like the Scylla of Greek mythology, she is metamorphosed into a monster. However, Marshall paints a compassionate portrait, for Silla is clearly motivated by the noblest of human concerns—love and survival with dignity. Unfortunately, the materialistic values she comes to accept spell the destruction of both. To help us understand this complex woman, whom we alternately admire and despise, the author provides the necessary background information. Very importantly, the passages devoted to Silla are almost invariably given in Selina's presence or in the presence of "the women." This fact suggests that early on, without the young girl's knowledge, Selina is joined in a sacred pact that will later define her indisputable inclusion in a powerful black sisterhood.

Silla's initiation into this sisterhood was especially harsh. She tells of her membership in the "Third Class" in the hills of Barbados. Contrary to Selina's innocent assumption, the "Third Class" had nothing to do with school. Rather it was "a set of little children picking grass in a cane field from the time God sun rise in heaven till it set. With some woman called a Driver to wash yuh tail in licks if yuh dare look up. Yes, working harder than a man at the age of ten" (45). The picture of the slave driver or overseer comes to mind, and as the mother continues her explanation, the exploitation of plantation workers in the Caribbean parallels that of the slaves in North America. "And when it was hard times," the mother goes on, "I would put a basket of mangoes 'pon muh head and go selling early-early 'pon a morning. Frighten bad enough for duppy and thing 'cause I was still only a child" (45–46).

Alluding to the commonality of Silla's experience, Marshall writes in summation: "She became the collective voice of all the Bajan women, the vehicle through which their former suffering found utterance" (45). And that suffering remains in the forefront of Silla's mind. Speaking to one of her friends, she recalls the poverty and exploitation of her homeland:

> "Iris, you know what it is to work hard and still never make a headway? That's Bimshire. One crop. People having to work for next skin to nothing. The white people treating we like slaves still and we taking it. The rum shop and the church join together to keep we pacified and in ignorance. That's Barbados. It's a terrible thing to know that you gon be poor all yuh life, no matter how hard you work. You does stop trying after a time. People does see you so and call you lazy. But it ain laziness. It's just that you does give up. You does kind of die inside." (70)

Silla comes to America to keep from dying and, given the backbreaking work she has already experienced, nothing in America seems insurmountable. It is with tragic awareness that she admits to her daughter: "I come here and pick up with a piece of a man and from then on I has read hell by heart and called every generation blessed" (46).

The hell to which Silla refers is a combination of a deep and complex love countered by an equally deep and complex resentment toward her husband. If she is to achieve her dream, she needs the help of an equally ambitious mate. Deighton, however, refuses to concede to her expectations of him, leaving Silla to assume the dominant role—even at the expense of her femininity. The rapaciousness of American society only exacerbates her predicament: "It's not that I's avaricious or money mad . . . or that I's a follow-pattern so that everything they do, I must do. But c'dear, if you got a piece of a man you want to see yourself improve. Isn't that why people does come to this place?" (174) Silla admits that black people "catch H— in this man's country," but it is still a place where working diligently together, she and Deighton could at least make headway.

Deighton, we know, often takes Selina into his confidence to share the joys of his boyhood as well as his dreams for the future. It is important that the narrator tells us that Selina, vaguely but surely, carried the impression that the differences between her parents stemmed from their very dissimilar childhood experiences. Deighton himself explains: "I's a person live in town and always had plenty to do. I not like yuh mother and the 'mounts of these Bajan that come from down some gully or up some hill behind God back and ain use to nothing. 'Pon a Sat'day I would walk 'bout town like I was a full-full man. All up Broad Street and Swan Street like I did own the damn place" (9–10). While certainly not well-to-do,

Deighton lived a life of relative middle-class comfort. According to Virgie Farnum, who was raised near him, his mother was a kind and forbearing woman who went beyond her means to raise her children. Deighton, the only boy, was gladly indulged. "And what she get for it?" Virgie scowls. "I know he land she in she grave with the lot of worry and aggravation. She cun do nothing with him" (33). Deighton's mother financed his college education with the hope that he would become a schoolmaster, one of the few professional options available to blacks, but Deighton sought the prestige and glamour of the white world. When his mother died, he left for Cuba as his father had done, then jumped ship to America where he met and married Silla.

Although Deighton, too, wishes to acquire property as an important sign of personal and economic independence and as an indication of upward social mobility, two important distinctions guide his thinking. First, he wants to build his dream house on "home ground." He thinks of Barbados as "poor, poor, but sweet enough." Through such descriptions, Barbados takes on an uncomplicated, relaxed, and romantic image both in contrast to Silla's memory of the island and in contrast to the fast-moving, competitive pace of New York. This consideration is directly related to the second distinction: Deighton will not be made to sacrifice all of his pleasures to work. "A man got a right to take his ease in life and not always be scuffling" (85). Part of that ease is reflected in his stylish, meticulous dress (he loves the feel of silk) and in his extramarital affair. It is significant that his wife's objections stem not so much from sexual jealousy as from economic factors. "Who in the bloody hell cares how many women he got," she grumbles. "Those women got nothing but a man using them. But his own got to come first" (31). Here, Silla hints at the West Indian woman's "tolerance" of extramarital affairs, a topic Marshall develops more explicitly in *Daughters* (1991). More specific to *Brown Girl, Brownstones,* however is Silla's voicing of the Bajan immigrants' attitude toward thrift. Whatever extra money one earns should be set aside to "buy house." And that house, for her, is in Brooklyn. Deighton is by no means disdainful of work; in addition to his correspondence studies, he holds down a full-time job in a mattress factory. His sense of style, however, his culturally derived definition of manhood, dictates something more lavish and a life that is certainly less restrictive than his fellow Barbadians accept in America.

A minor character speaks for the black immigrant community when she says of Deighton: "I tell you those men from Bridgetown is all the same. They don't know a thing 'bout handling money and property and thing so. They's spree boys. Every last one of them. . . . There ain nothin wrong with wanting piece of ground home but only when you got a sufficient back prop here. I tell you, he's a disgrace!" (55). Here Marshall may be comparing class attitudes toward labor as they exist between the city (town) folk and those who have a rural (country) background, but more important seems to be her exploration of how personal and cultural values may become subsumed or obliterated in the push toward assimilation. Deighton not only refuses, but perhaps is unable, to submit to a devaluation of his Bajan male identity. Of course, he is aware that racism exists back home. Fleetingly he recalls "those white English faces mottled red by a sun in the big stores in Bridgetown and himself as a young man, facing them in his first pair of long pants and his coarse hair brushed flat, asking them for a job as a clerk—the incredulity, the disdain and indignation that flushed their faces as they said no" (39). Although he dreams of a different answer, they also said no in America.

The author's consideration of how others perceive blacks is penetratingly insightful, but she is equally concerned with describing how that perception may sometimes influence the sense of self. Deighton has come to hold a "frightening acceptance . . . which sprang, perhaps from a conviction hidden deep within him that it was only right that he should be rejected" (83). We are reminded of DuBois's conception of "double-consciousness" in *The Souls of Black Folk:* "the peculiar sensation of always looking at one's self through the eyes of others, of measuring one's soul by the tape of the world that looks on in amused contempt and pity."[18] Deighton not only becomes invisible to whites but, because he scorns the demands of his new environment, he also becomes invisible to his own.

The "glitter and tumult" of Fulton Street on a Saturday night becomes for the author an avenue to describe Deighton's zest for life and to explore his invisibility from yet another point of view. It provides as well a vehicle through which Marshall can explore, if only momentarily, "the beauty and desperation and sadness" (still more contradictions) of the African-American experience. Fulton Street was

> a whirling spectrum of neon signs, movie marquees, bright-lit store windows and sweeping, yellow streamers of light from the cars. It was canorous voices, hooted laughter and voices ripping the night's warm cloak; a welter of dark faces and gold-etched teeth; children crying high among the fire escapes of the tenements; the subway rumbling below; the unrelenting wail of a blues spilling from a bar; greasy counters and fish sandwiches and barbecue and hot sauce; trays of chitterlings and hog maws and fat back in the meat stores; the trolley's insistent clangor; a man and woman in a hallway bedroom, sleeping like children now that the wildness had passed; a drunken woman pitching along the street; the sustained shriek of a police car and its red light stabbing nervously at faces and windows. (37)

This snapshot of black American poverty reflects precisely what the black immigrant population wishes to avoid. Deborah Schneider comments: "As blacks, they have been forced by white society to live in restricted ghetto neighborhoods; as Barbadians with a middle-class tradition, such as Deighton came from, which they are eager to defend, they wall themselves off from contacts with American blacks, contacts which would mean to them a drop in status as well as a blurring of their special ethnic identity.[19] For those like Silla who have come to America from an economically lower-class background, the poor living conditions of many black Americans is a vivid reminder of what the immigrants left behind. As Rosalie Riegle Troester says, they shun those black Americans "whose lives mirror conditions [they] dare not bring to consciousness"[20] Deighton himself is both "envious and respectful" of the men in the bars whose gestures have a violent yet playful aspect. "For somehow, even though they were sporting like boys, there was no question that they were truly men; they could so easily prove it by flashing a knife or smashing out with their fists or tumbling one of the whores in the bar onto a bed" (37–38). Deighton's cultural exclusion from the dominant black American population becomes apparent as the narrator questions: "But what of those, then, to whom these proofs of manhood were alien? Who must find other, more sanctioned ways? It was harder, that was all" (38).

Only his dream of returning to Barbados to live in high style allows Deighton to suffer the indignities of gossip and isolation. Consequently, when his wife betrays him by fraudulently selling his piece of "home ground," he is left with virtually nothing. He enacts his revenge by squandering the proceeds from the land on gifts for himself and his family, but his eyes the narrator describes as "eloquent": "They spoke of the hollow places inside him and the grief which underlined his high glee" (125). Silla, livid with angry contempt, becomes even more determined to buy the Brooklyn brownstone. An almost satanic presence fills the room when she vows to get not only the house but Deighton as well.

The "beautiful-ugly" wedding scene foreshadows Deighton's destruction. Marshall describes the extravagant wedding in miniscule detail to show the success of the Bajan community in their total imitation of white America, but she also criticizes this success by revealing that no real joy accompanies the occasion. The bride (forced to marry a West Indian instead of the southern American black whom she loves) walks toward her groom "like Iphigenia to her death at Aulis." With the guests of the bride and groom seated on either side of the center aisle of the church "like two warring camps," the mood of combat is created.

This mood, of course, reflects the growing tension between the major characters. It also serves to underscore the community's disapproval of Deighton. Everyone has heard of his shameful waste of the money; they alternately commiserate with Silla, then praise her stamina. "Soul, you has got your crosses to bear in that man," says Gatha Steed. "But I hear you still buying the house despite him" (128). (Silla has borrowed money from a loan shark.) Marshall illustrates in this scene the notion of communal support operative in African and, by extension, West Indian societies. In making Silla the center of attention, the sense of corporate life so deeply engrained in the community is assured. Since the social order and peace are "conceived of primarily in terms of kinship relations," any offense against an individual member of the community becomes an offense against the whole group.[21]

Communal support for the individual is symbolically rendered through the ritual of dance, which becomes both a form of entertainment and a form of social commentary. With the lilting sounds of the calypso, everyone is caught up in an infectious wave of movement and flow. The dancers form a tight, symbolic circle that, with centrifugal force, holds the participants together. Selina, pressed to the edge, glimpses her father at the door of the reception hall and, as she tries to pull away to greet him, the dancers keep her bound to the group. They are all singing loudly, "Small island, go back where you come from," a refrain that strikes a parallel with the West Indian community's attitude toward Deighton. Eugenia Collier rightly observes: "In this scene Selina sees herself first as an integral part of the community, reveling in a new sense of wholeness, then imprisoned by that same community, helping it to persecute her most beloved person. She has experienced two poles of belonging: the community as completion of the individual self, the community as control."[22] Deighton is symbolically excommunicated from the circle as Marshall goes on to describe the dancers closing "protectively around Silla and Ina; someone pulled Selina back. Then . . . the dancers turned in one body and danced with their backs to him" (150). The entire community condemns the offender and, with their song, drives Deighton away. Selina, on the other hand, is "initiated now into the group, is governed by its dictates, even against her will."[23]

As important as individual will may be, Marshall shows in the novel that empowerment from the collective body is still essential. Through her depiction of the Association of Barbadian Homeowners, she illustrates that the immigrant community embodies at least that potential. The association is a self-help organization committed to the cultural and economic advancement of its members. It is also a testament to the dawning political consciousness of a small black community determined to make its presence felt. One character refers to it as "the biggest thing since Marcus Garvey." Marcus Garvey, of course, was the West Indian leader who founded the widely supported Universal Negro Improvement Association in the 1920s. Convinced that America was unwilling to accept blacks on equal terms with whites, he advocated a "return to Africa" to establish a superior and independent black civilization. While Marshall deliberately includes this historical reference as a noteworthy contribution of the West Indian people to the progress of Africans all over the world, she also suggests the early influence this legendary black hero exerted over the formation of her own African sensibility. She remembers that during her childhood her mother's women friends spoke of Garvey with pride: "His name was constantly being invoked, for he had been their leader in the early twenties, the revolutionary who had urged the black and poor like themselves to rise up: 'Rise up you mighty race.' Who had declared Black is beautiful to women like themselves who had been brainwashed into believing they did not possess beauty. Garvey who had said economic self-sufficiency and Black nationhood. Who had said Africa."[24]

To illustrate the determination and cohesiveness of the West Indian community, the author permits us to eavesdrop on a closed meeting of the association. Our attention is immediately drawn to a banner that depicts "two black hands in a firm handclasp against a yellow background." Below the association's full name are the words:

IT IS NOT THE DEPTHS FROM WHICH WE COME
BUT THE HEIGHTS TO WHICH WE ASCEND.

Three or four hundred strong, the members listen attentively to the speaker as he describes the fund to which all members contribute and which, in turn, makes small loans. Then he turns to plans for a credit union and possibilities for involvement in local political and community affairs. Commenting briefly on the exclusive executive clubs that whites enjoy, he jests with frightening irony, "We ain white yet. We's small timers . . . but we got our eye on the big time" (221). The speaker articulates the drive, determination, faith, and hope of the Bajan people:

> "But tell me why we start this Association now when most of us gon soon be giving business to the undertaker? I gon tell you. It's because of the young people! Most of us did come to this man country with only the strength in we hand and a little learning in we head and had to make our way, but the young people have an opportunity to be professional and get out there and give these people big word for big word. Thus, they are our hope. They make all the sacrifice, all the struggle worthwhile." (221)

With the announcement of the scholarship that the association will soon offer to one of its young members, the audience pounds its applause, becoming a "single puissant force, sure of its goal and driving hard toward it" (222). Marshall here illustrates the black immigrants' belief in the American myth of assimilation and success despite, or perhaps in spite of, the racial discrimination imposed upon them. Simultaneously, she shows that the black immigrant experience is riddled with paradox. On the one hand, the Barbadian-Americans want and deserve economic success as their reward for hard work, and they strive collectively to reinforce their resistance to the hostility and resentment of those surrounding them. Such efforts call for a spirited and resolute conviction in the community's goals. On the other hand, to improve their economic standing, they adopt the same single-minded, selfish values of their detractors, thereby not only maligning the integrity of individual community members but also preventing them from relating their circumstances with those of the larger black American community. Marshall briefly touches on the notion of an African diaspora when the next speaker proposes that the banner be changed so that the word *Barbadian* will read *Negro*: "We got to stop thinking about just Bajan. We ain't home no more. It don matter if we don know a person mother or his mother mother. Our doors got to be open to every colored person that qualify. . . . I know it gon take time. Wunna gon have to ruminate long, but I ain gon return till I see that word *Barbadian* strike out and *Negro* put in its place. I thank you!" (222). To underscore the Bajans' eager defense of their identity, Marshall turns to tropical imagery: "As rain comes in the West Indies—without warning, to lash the earth in a helpless hysterical deluge—their indignation broke with the same fury" (222). The ensuing debate allows us to enter the minds of the Bajan women we met earlier.

All seem to agree that the business of renting rooms in their homes to gain income is a nuisance, and Iris feels sorry for the roomers who, in increasing numbers, are African Americans. "Even though they ain Bajans," she explains, "they's still our color." Florrie's response is harsh but real: "Sorry! . . . Sorry for roomers? Sorry? But Gor-blind yuh, Iris, who did sorry for you? I ain sorry for a blast. I had to get mine too hard. Let the roomers get out and struggle like I did. I sorry for all the long years I din have nothing and my children din have and now I got little something I too fat and old to enjoy it and my only son dead in these people bloody war and he can't enjoy it. That's what I sorry for" (224).

Silla helps to clarify these feelings when she says with painful awareness that Florrie's move to the more prestigious neighborhood of Crown Heights would not have been possible without the exploitation of others. "We would like to do different. That's what does hurt and shame us so. But the way things arrange we can't, if not we lost out" (224). Power, she explains, has nothing to do with color:

"It's true the roomers is our own color. But if they was white or yellow
and cun do better we'd still be overcharging them. Take when we had to
scrub the Jew floor. He wasn't misusing us so much because our skin was
black but because we cun do better. And I din hate him. All the time I
was down on his floor I was saying to myself: 'Lord, lemme do better than
this. Lemme rise!' No, power is a thing that don really have nothing to do
with color. Look how white people had little children their own color
working in coal mines and sweatshops years back. Look how those whelps
in Africa sold us for next skin to nothing." (224)

As she continues to talk about the nature of power, Silla concludes in proverbial fashion: "What's that saying 'bout the race is not to the swift? . . . I
tell yuh, *you best* be swift, if not somebody come and trample you quick
enough" (225).

While Marshall clearly supports self-determination for blacks in the
novel, she also cautions that in the climb toward upward social mobility,
blacks should avoid duplicating values that stifle compassion. Joining the
youth contingency, Selina listens to the discussion of the evening's proceedings and judges the group a "prim, pious, pretentious pack." When
asked her opinion of the associates, she hisses:

"I think it stinks. . . . And why does it stink? Because it's the result of
living by the most shameful codes possible—dog eat dog, exploitation,
the strong over the weak, the end justifies the means—the whole kit and
caboodle. Your Association? It's a band of small frightened people. Clan-
nish. Narrow-minded. Selfish. . . . Prejudiced. Pitiful—because who out
there in the white world you're so feverishly courting gives one damn
whether you change the word *Barbadian* to *Negro?* Provincial! That's your
Association." (227)

Selina clearly wants a different world, but it remains uncertain, undefined,
untried. Rushing from the room, she feels nothing but self-loathing because, as the narrator explains, "they had done nothing to deserve her in-
sults, nor had she come any closer to her own truth by maligning theirs"
(228).

The issue of changing *Barbadian* to *Negro* underscores once again
that the Barbadian community is culturally dissociated from the African-
American community surrounding it. It is clear, though, that the immigrants understand profoundly the effects of American stereotypes upon
blacks in general. Marshall candidly presents the reality of color as an im-
pediment to social and economic advancement, and she also shows that in
its umbrella-like dimensions, American racism makes no distinctions in

culture. The issue of Deighton's citizenship, for example, is never ques-
tioned as he seeks employment early in the novel. "These white people
here does think all colored people is from the South" (82). Later, when
World War II is in full scale, Selina fears her father will be drafted.
Deighton responds bitterly: "As far as the record goes I ain even in this
country since I did enter illegally. Y'know that's a funny thing when you
think of it. I don even exist as far as these people here go" (66). Ralph
Ellison's notion of invisibility readily comes to mind.

Throughout *Brown Girl, Brownstones,* Marshall draws on the concept of
invisibility to create a corrective lens through which the reader may view
the perceptions and sensibilities of the "other." In this regard, her consideration of the mother-daughter conflict within the context of race and culture is particularly compelling not only because the subject had received
little prior treatment in American or African-American literature but also
because Marshall avoids the "trivialization" of black female relationships.
She avoids as well the tendency (popular later in the 1970s and 1980s) to
idealize the mother-daughter relationship.[25] Silla and Selina, to be sure,
are not close friends, but they do hold a grudging respect for one another.
Silla, in her own inimitable style, refers to the young girl as a "force-ripe
woman," which implies a "worthy foe." Selina, in turn, is intrigued—perhaps even mystified—by her mother's strong will and tenacity. Even in
the several instances when Deighton, her beloved father, falls to defeat in
a contest with her Goliath of a mother, Selina, quite tellingly, wants
to be "out of the mother's way, but near her." As Marshall delves more
deeply into their relationship, she shows that Silla withholds affection in order to forge character in her daughter.[26] She also shows that
their mother-daughter conflict really camouflages deep-seated frustrations over the costs to the spirit in a racist, sexist, and materialistic
society.

That cost to the spirit is illustrated in a number of ways. We see it
subtly early on in the novel in the family photograph that captures Silla's
"shy beauty" and "the girlish expectancy in her smile" (8). Later, a flashback tells of the tenderness Silla comes to guard so cautiously. Deighton
comments:

> "Yuh see yuh mother there, lady-folks? That's the way she was when we
> was courting. Never a hard word. A look on her face that did make you
> think of Jesus meek and mild. Her head always down. I tell yuh, I never
> even knew what her eyes look like for the longest time. And then one day
> she raised them. Lord-God, I felt like Paul on the road to Damascus when
> the light of the Lord struck him and he fell down blind-blind! And lady-
> folks, I ain recover yet!" (118)

More poignantly, we see the cost to Silla's spirit when Selina observes her mother striding home from work through the park:

> Silla Boyce brought the theme of winter into the park with her dark dress amid the summer green and the bright-figured housedresses of the women lounging on the benches there. Not only that, every line of her strong-made body seemed to reprimand the women for their idleness and the park for its senseless summer display. Her lips, set in a permanent protest against life, implied that there was no time for gaiety. And the park, the women, the sun even gave way to her dark force; the flushed summer colors ran together and faded as she passed. (16)

Perhaps Marshall best describes Silla's loss when she engages her artistic imagination with the island of Barbados. In the wedding scene described earlier, the author briefly introduces an old man who remembers Silla as a young girl back home frolicking in a pasture. Selina tries to imagine her mother back then:

> The world had been when she [Selina] had not. Time stretched behind and beyond her small life. Years ago, on an island that was only a green node in a vast sea, the mother had been a girl who had danced till she had fainted once, and Selina had been nothing to her. Suddenly she yearned to know the mother then, in her innocence. Above all, she longed to understand the mother, for she knew, obscurely, that she would never really understand anything until she did. (145)

The land mass and traditions Marshall describes here are physically and emotionally distinct from the United States, suggesting a fusion between mother and country. That fusion is especially apparent when the author describes the mother's "dark, disquieting beauty":

> Silla had learned its expressions early from her mother and the other women as they paused in the cane fields and lifted their sun-blackened, enigmatic faces to the sea, as they walked down the white marl roads with the heavy baskets poised lightly on their heads and their bodies flowing in grace and restraint. They seemed to use this beauty not to attract but to stave off all that might lessen their strength. When a man looked at them he did not immediately feel the stir in his groin, but uneasiness first and then the challenge to prove himself between those thighs, to rise from them when he was spent and see respect and not contempt in their faces. For somehow their respect would mean his mastery of all life; their contempt his failure. (135)

This passage may hint of Deighton's relationship to Silla, but it also suggests Silla's culturally defined notion of what it means to be a woman. Instead of the passive female controlled and supported by a male protector, she has learned from her heritage an independence that enables her own personal relationship to her community. In her new environment, however, Silla's definition changes. She wishes to assume the role of a middle-class *American* woman. Marshall reveals that mutual misunderstanding of their separate gender roles contribute to destroying the individual dreams of both characters.

With the support of the Barbadian-American community, Silla remains undaunted. Excluded from that community, Deighton seeks another in the Father Peace Movement. In this section of the novel, Marshall makes an important historical reference to Father Divine who, during the 1920s and 1930s, spearheaded a social and religious movement that spread to many eastern and midwestern communities in the United States. Father Divine (his real name was George Baker) claimed to be God incarnate and, recognizing the spiritual as well as the physical needs of his followers, he espoused an ideology of peace in the here and now, as opposed to the more common religious theme of peace in the hereafter. He opened buildings which he called "heavens," and there he fed thousands of the dispossessed, the disillusioned, the disenchanted.[27] Black and white thronged to receive his blessings, and Marshall describes the "heaven on earth" which his followers, including her own father, found in the "kingdom of Harlem." Simultaneously, she portrays the powerful influence of indoctrination upon the weakened human psyche.

When Deighton joins Father Peace, he literally abdicates his responsibilities as husband and father. Love, combined with anger, guilt, and envy, leads Silla to initiate deportation procedures against him and shortly thereafter (on the day the war ends), she receives a cable announcing that Deighton has either jumped or fallen overboard and drowned within sight of the coast of Barbados. Although Selina reacts violently in a memorable scene in which she repeatedly calls her mother "Hitler," she later gives imaginary life to one of her father's boyhood activities of diving into the sea for coins. She pictures a tropical mist gradually dissipating to make way for the sun, which resembles a "brilliant coin." Her fantasy continues:

> When he saw the island, he emitted a low frightened cry, his hand rose to blot it out. For that low mound, resting on the sea like a woman's breast when she is supine, was Barbados. Time fled as the mist fled and he was a boy again, diving for the coins the tourists tossed into the sea, and he saw the one he wanted most in the bright disk of the sun. (190)

John Cooke suggests that "the idea of the return home is . . . a regression, the search for a woman's breast and the recapture of boyhood life." Through this image, Cooke continues, "Marshall rejects the homeland as forcefully as early Italian-American and Irish-American writers had before her."[28] True enough, Barbados is the homeland, and it may be reasonable to think of the sea as symbolically representing the womb. However, it seems more consistent with the design of the novel and its resolution to view this passage as an acceptance of the homeland. Selina imaginatively associates Barbados with the idyllic memories her father left her. Time, in this sense, becomes not a regression but a progression through living memory.

Selina's own personal progress becomes evident in the last book of the novel where Marshall focuses primarily on the young woman's sexual and emotional growth. Now eighteen years of age and in college, Selina thrives with activity. School, part-time work, Clive Springer on the weekends, the Association and, most importantly, dance—all these become a part of her. In many ways Clive resembles Deighton, but, significantly, Selina could be mistaken for Silla as she devises a scheme that will net enough money for her and Clive to go away together. If she is cunning enough, deceptive enough, willful enough, she can win the scholarship the Association plans to award. Selina's development as a performing artist becomes especially critical to Marshall's theme of individual empowerment through community.

Turning once again to dance as ritual, Marshall describes Selina's solo performance of the "Birth-to-Death Cycle." In this performance, significant to the structure of the novel, Selina brings consciously to mind the several characters in the novel with whom she interacts to depict the various stages of human development. It is important, though, that at this ritual no one from Selina's West Indian community is present. The earlier dance at the wedding was communal. In Eugenia Collier's words, "its essence united her not only with the New York Barbadian community but also with their ancestral home, and, on a more profound level, with the unknown ancestors across the Atlantic to whom song and dance meant life itself. At the recital, Selina dances alone."[29] And alone Selina must face the consequences of her deliberate emotional exclusion from this ancient community.

And so it is in a powerful scene following her performance that Selina is put in her "racial place"—forced, for the first time, to confront on a personal level the insidious effects of racism. Along with the white members of the Modern Dance Club at college, she is invited to celebrate her stellar performance at the home of one of the girls. We know that she has made a new friend in Rachel Fine, a somewhat defiant but sensitive personality who, in many ways, mirrors our young and energetic heroine. As a Jew, Rachel, too, is a minority female, and as a rebel, she, too, combats conventional standards that impinge upon her personal identity. Through her portrait perhaps Marshall suggests a potential sisterhood between "outsiders."[30] Marshall certainly suggests as much in her characterization of Miss Thompson, the African-American beautician who, though culturally "outside" Selina's immediate world, remains her mentor and confidante throughout the novel. As a product of the American South, Miss Thompson certainly understands the subtle and overt manifestations of racism. Without a doubt, she would understand the "funny silence" that occurred when Rachel first introduced Selina to the all-white dance troupe, that "abrupt drop in their animated talk when she entered, the subtle disturbance in their eyes before they said hello." The narrator explains that Selina's feelings included "the sudden awareness of danger that made her hastily scan the room, the momentary desire to leave and thus spare them her unsettling dark presence; then, just as strong, the determination to remain" (251–52). However, this same determination falters in the face of the hostess's mother, who subjects the starry-eyed Selina to every conceivable racial insult.

The inquisition that follows illustrates the thoughtless cruelty of whites who refuse to allow blacks their individuality. But Marshall is equally, if not more, interested in describing Selina's feelings of the moment, which culminate in her rushing from the apartment in a blind rage through the city streets. When Selina collapses in the entranceway of a vacant store, she sees the white woman's imposed image of her reflected in the window. But she also acknowledges that there was a part of her "which had long hated her for her blackness and thus begrudged her each small success like the one tonight" (289). This echoes Selina's muffled self-hatred at the beginning of the novel when, as a child, she fantasized about her vulgarity in a holy place. In the present episode, fantasy gives way to self-realization, for Selina understands that she has partially integrated the white illusion. The illusion will not vanish at will. Marshall describes it as "so powerful that it would stalk her down the years, confront her in each mirror and from the safe circle in their eyes, surprise her even in the gleaming surface of a table. It would intrude in every corner of her life, tainting her small triumphs—as it had tonight—and exulting at her defeats" (291). The reader sees in reflexive imagery that "along with the fierce struggle of her humanity, she must also battle illusions!"

After the debacle of her dance debut, Selina questions her lover, Clive:

> "What am I to do, curl up and die because I'm coloured? Do nothing, try nothing because of it?"
> "No," he responds, "you can't do that because then you admit what

some white people would have you admit and what some Negroes do admit—that you are only Negro, some flat, one-dimensional, bas-relief figure which is supposed to explain everything about you. You commit an injustice against yourself by admitting that, because, first, you rule out your humanity, and second, your complexity as a human being. Oh hell, I'm not saying that being black in this god-damn white world isn't crucial. No one but us knows how corrosive it is, how it maims us all, how it rings our lives. But at some point you have to break through to the larger ring which encompasses us all—our humanity. To understand that much about us can be simply explained by the fact that we're men, caught with all men within the common ring." (252)

Marshall clarifies the peculiar phenomenon of race by inveighing the symbols that Euro-American literature has instilled in the Western consciousness. Shakespeare and Hawthorne, for example, become the referents as Clive explains: "Who knows what they see looking at us? The whole damn thing is so twisted now, so deep-seated; the color black is such a hell of a powerful symbol, who can tell. . . . Some of them probably still see in each of us the black moor tupping their white ewe, or some legendary beast coming out of the night and the fens to maraud and rape. Caliban. Hester's Black Man in the woods. The Devil. Evil. Sin. The whole long list of their race's fears" (253).

Clive clearly understands the representation of race in the white world, but his argument is additionally grounded in the experience and texts of African Americans: "Maybe our dark faces remind them of all that is dark and unknown and terrifying within themselves and, as Jimmy Baldwin says, they're seeking absolution through poor us, either in their beneficence or in their cruelty." (253) His reference to James Baldwin emphasizes racial awareness as a heavy burden for the person of color. "But," he continues, "I'm afraid we have to disappoint them by confronting them always with the full and awesome weight of our humanity, until they begin to see us and not some unreal image they've superimposed. . . . This is the unpleasant and perhaps impossible job and this is where I bow out, leaving the field to you . . . and to the more robust of us" (253).

Clive, like Deighton, no longer considers himself among the robust; he has withdrawn from the field of battle. Selina, on the other hand, chooses to fight. It is her confrontation with the white woman, though, that catapults her into the recognition of the personal empowerment that her West Indian community affords. Susan Stanford Friedman correctly observes: "When [Selina] realizes that her mother and the Bajan Association created a powerful island in a sea of racism, then she is ready to shatter the cultural reflections of herself that nearly shattered her. In other words, the

illusion that she was a single individual who could make her way alone in
the white world nearly destroyed Selina. The lesson of the mirror is the
lesson of collective identity in both its alienating and transformative aspects."[31]

Marshall skillfully combines the earlier associations with blackness
with Selina's own inner darkness: "Her sins rose like a miasma from its
fetid bottom: the furtive pleasures with Clive on the sofa, her planned
betrayal of the Association, the mosaic of deceit and lies she had built to
delude the mother" (291). The color black takes on gradations of darkness
as the various images the author presents prompt both an emotional and
an intellectual response. For Selina, the darkness gradually dissipates as
she acknowledges the strength of her mother, "she who had not chosen
death by water," Miss Thompson, and all the others who daily bore the
brunt of similar humiliations yet endured. "Who are we to scorn them?"
was the question Clive had posed earlier.

The novel draws to a close on the evening of the scholarship presentation when Selina is predictably announced the winner. The faces of the
audience become "myriad reflections of [Selina's] own dark face." The imagery of the Caribbean serves well as the author continues by comparing
their smiling faces to a dark sea—"alive under the sun with the endless
mutations of one color. They no longer puzzled or offended her," the narrator tells us. "Instead, their purposefulness charging the air like a strong
current—suddenly charged her strength and underpinned her purpose"
(302–3).

The courage Selina shows cannot be fully appreciated by the fictive audience as she explains that she neither deserves nor wants the scholarship,
but the reading audience knows it is a measure of how far Selina has come
in her maturation and actualization: "My trouble maybe was that I wanted
everything to be simple—the good clearly separated from the bad—the
way a child sees things. But it's not simple or separate and children can't
understand it. Now that I'm less of a child I'm beginning to understand."
To the astonished mother, Selina confesses her intended plan and admits
that perhaps subconsciously she was trying to avenge Deighton's death.

Someone less stalwart, less committed, might have given in to Silla's
anguish over the sacrifices she had endured or the "final, frightening loneliness that was to be her penance." But Selina, though unsure of what she
wants, is sure that she wants to be her own person: "Everybody used to
call me Deighton's Selina but they were wrong. Because you see I'm truly
your child. Remember how you used to talk about how you left home and
came here alone as a girl of eighteen and was your own woman? I used to
love hearing that. And that's what I want. I want it!" (307). Appropriately, Silla ends the conversation with a benediction that reaches back in

time to her own mother and the African descendants before her: "G'long! You was always too much woman for me anyway, soul. And my own mother did say two head-bulls can't reign in a flock. G'long! . . . If I din dead yet, you and your foolishness can't kill muh now!" (307). The use of the appellation *soul* connotes both a physical and a spiritual kinship, and the proverb completes, in the traditional African style, a succinct summation of mother and daughter's personalities.

A final review of the portraits of Selina's loved ones brings the novel full circle and bequeaths to our heroine a small but uncertain strength. As she walks down Fulton Street, the "flickering lights" reflect her flickering hope of finding peace and the "things that shaped it: love, a clearer vision, a place" (308). With her telephone call to Rachel arranging passage aboard a ship to the Caribbean, we appreciate more fully the "journey" Selina must take to understand her heritage.

The novel ends with the architectural imagery that has been so integral to its structure and meaning. The brownstones, however, are no longer somnolent; they are now "ravaged," and "the staccato beat of Spanish voices," the "frenzied sensuous music" joined with "the warm canorous Negro sounds," replace the earlier calypso rhythms and sounds. As in the beginning, Marshall describes a neighborhood in transition. In one area, however, the brownstones have "been blasted to make way for a city project," and Selina observes "a solitary wall [standing] perversely amid the rubble, a stoop still [imposing] its massive grandeur, a carved oak staircase [leading] only to the night sky" (309). Selina emerges as the "sole survivor amid the wreckage" and, as a token of commemoration, she tosses over her shoulder one of the two silver bangles she has worn from childhood. The other bangle she retains as a sign of her acceptance of her West Indian heritage.

The resolution of the novel remains deliberately open-ended to suggest that Selina's journey to the Caribbean is a continuation of her search. Her cultural identity has not yet been firmly established. Her father and mother's images of the West Indies continue to intrigue, while vestiges of the American and African American confuse. But at last she is prepared—indeed, freed—to accept the challenge of defining herself in her own terms within a black cultural matrix. As we explore with Marshall the experiences of blacks of other cultures in different parts of the world, that identity becomes expansive enough to include all peoples of the African diaspora.

Chapter Three

Cultural Expansion and Masculine Subjectivity

Soul Clap Hands and Sing

I have travelled everywhere in your sea of the Caribbean . . . from Haiti to Barbados, to Martinique and Guadeloupe, and I know what I am speaking about. . . . You are all together, in the same boat, sailing on the same uncertain sea . . . citizenship and race unimportant, feeble little labels compared to the message that my spirit brings to me: that of the position and the predicament which History has imposed upon you. . . . I saw it first with dance . . . the meringue in the echo of calypsoes from Trinidad, Jamaica, St. Lucia, Antigua, Dominica and the legendary Guiana. . . . It is no accident that the sea which separates your lands makes no difference to the rhythm of your body.

Père Labat, 1743

Africans dispersed throughout the world necessarily adapted to their foreign environments and predicaments by assimilating some of the dominant features of the cultures in their new homelands. But as Marshall has shown in *Brown Girl, Brownstones,* cultural adaptations are often in conflict with indigenous customs and beliefs and frequently lead to ambivalence and confusion about one's place in society and in the larger world. Invariably, a complex configuration of problems evolves that includes the historical interaction between the colonized and the colonizer. Manifest also are personal and social problems within the colonized group itself, particularly within males whose experiences Marshall investigates in her collection of novellas, *Soul Clap Hands and Sing* (1961). This volume moves more deeply into the African diaspora and traces how black cultures reshape themselves in various lands.[1] Though each story may be read as a separate account, the collection as a whole suggests that Marshall's artistic vision expands from a restricted geographical area to a broader, more international scope. Her abiding concern, nonetheless, is with the ways in which confusion about and alienation from one's cultural groundings may bring into question the very meaning of New World existence.

In *Soul Clap Hands and Sing* Marshall reiterates concerns about materialism, oppression, and exploitation. She also explores the psychic and social forces that culminate in self-hatred, indifference, contempt for the masses. In view of her emphasis on female characters in her first two works of fiction, her shift to male characters in *Soul* merits some comment. In some respects the collection represents an exercise of sorts in preparation for her next novel, which delves more fully into the consciousnesses of several men and women of different nationalities, races, and cultures. But Marshall states that she deliberately selected male characters for her second major work of fiction to counter charges that in *Brown Girl* she portrayed a stereotypical image of black men as weak and emasculated.[2] Implied in such criticism was a question of Marshall's ability to develop realistically the vagaries of racism and oppression from the male perspective. Her treatment of male figures in *Soul* certainly illustrates her sensitivity to "masculine" concerns. Marshall, however, does not dismiss the female. In every selection, a female is a minor character who serves symbolically as the life-force as well as the avenue toward salvation. In most instances, it is a female character who prompts the male protagonist to make the decision which is crucial to the quality of his remaining life. Thus, women can be seen as the "catalyst for action" in *Soul Clap Hands and Sing*.

The title and the underlying idea for the collection are borrowed from William Butler Yeats's poem "Sailing to Byzantium." The well-known excerpt, quoted in the frontispiece, foreshadows the masculine condition at the center of the narrative:

> An aged man is but a paltry thing,
> A tattered coat upon a stick, unless
> Soul clap its hands and sing.

Thematic connections between Yeats and Marshall become obvious in the accounts of four men of four nationalities experiencing the inevitable decline of age. Both authors emphasize the decline and fall of Western values. Several lines from Yeats's poem take on added meaning when placed against the contents of *Souls Clap Hands and Sing.* The poet alludes to a voyage across "the mackerel-crowded seas." He evokes a sense of timelessness when he writes, "Of what is past, or passing, or to come." Related to timelessness is his reference to culture as "monuments of unageing intellect." Those monuments have their origins in "the holy city of Byzantium." Yeats further appeals to the "sages" to revive a sense of wholeness, to "be the singing masters of my soul."

Both poet and novelist express loss and dislocation from a sacred cultural source. But in *Soul* Marshall moves beyond the private musings of an individual to explore the ambivalent attitudes and conflicting values of several men facing decline. We move from Barbados to Brooklyn to British Guiana (Guyana) and, finally, to Brazil, and each locale becomes the title of the respective tales. With the exception of "Brooklyn," whose major character is a Jew, each story has a black male protagonist, and each story is set within surroundings so enigmatic as to invite complex readings. All of the stories concern the fragmented lives of men who have chosen to deny their origins. Their choices to live alone, their refusal to involve themselves in anything or with anyone to the extent which would require of them genuine sharing, has irrevocably shaped their long and unhappy lives. But Marshall stresses the values they have accepted as directly responsible for their separate predicaments. Caught up in the Western masculine/capitalistic credo of amassing wealth and prestige, the major characters develop hardened exteriors that are impervious to meaningful relationships. When the submerged need for love rises to the surface, they can only respond by reaching out to young women, who serve as "bringers of truth." Yet that reaching out stems from selfish motivations. Though the women "come to realize their own strength as a result of the encounter,"[3] the men are convulsed with pain and disillusionment as they face a moment of truth. The burden of responsibility, nonetheless, remains with the male figures whose separate tales embody what one observer calls "an enormously wide, almost mystic sense of the shimmering chiaroscuro of life in its mixed moods and human destinies."[4]

With its central theme repeated in different cultural and national settings, the collection gradually develops into what Ihab Hassan calls "the poetics of gerontology." But it is the poetics of *male* gerontology. Certainly the "lyrical brooding" in which the author engages re-creates the "sensual music" Yeats speaks of in his poem.[5] Unlike Yeats's persona, however, the men cannot "translate the harsh reality of aging into song"; instead, their dying moments sound the notes of lamentation and doom.[6] Yet Marshall's emphasis upon New World blacks suggests something other than her more apparent concern with age and aging. In the process of writing, she seems to have consciously developed a second motif: no individual progress is possible without a clear sense of who one is within a given community. Thematic repetition also illustrates the African narrative technique of projecting several different images to make a single instructive statement. It is an approach that for the author takes on an increasingly political dimension and emphasizes the diasporan connections she gradually makes. In fact, the closer she moves geographically to the continent of Africa, the more frequent and apparent African images become. The history of black people, she insists, is not "delimited to their presence in this part of the world. There are links and associations to a larger Black world."[7] That world has an essential unity born of struggle and resistance. While the individual experience must be confronted and ordered in its own peculiar national terms, it also comprises a portion of the collective experience of blacks all over the world. Such experience, as made clear through the story lines, must be shared in our respective communities to give our present and future lives meaning and direction. Further, Marshall argues in this collection that the realization of any vision of change lies in a profound and difficult confrontation of values—both latent and active—to transform human suffering into creative forms of responsive and responsible action.

Yet the Euro-American influence is ever present, as evidenced by Marshall's frequent allusions to Western literature. To a great extent, these Western allusions contribute to the "universality" of her art. More importantly, they help to illustrate that the tragedy of modern man who, as Darwin T. Turner states, "suffers from loneliness and uncertainty of his identity. The tragedy does not limit itself to one race or country; it affects all Western males."[8] In any case, the author who has already proven her predilection for opposites in *Brown Girl, Brownstones* reveals in *Soul* how the many differences between cultures and continents can fade to cancel out extremes.

Marshall reveals that the stories included in *Soul Clap Hands and Sing* were actually created in response to very personal concerns. She herself had a somber, retiring nature even as a child. Though she enjoyed ordinary play with other children, she tended to be solitary and withdrawn, seeking her company and comfort in books. She recalls her mother's frequent admonition: "Child, you're like someone who's living your last days first." And to some extent, she was. Having observed the painful experiences of many adults in her community—particularly those of her mother who, divorced and living close to poverty, believed herself to be a failure—Marshall was determined not to grow up. Yet she was intrigued with people who in their latter years seemed unfulfilled, and this fascination remained with her through her early adult life when she traveled on assignment for *Our World* magazine to Latin America and the Caribbean.[9] The characters in *Soul,* while clearly fictionalized, are based on such people. The old man in "Barbados," for instance, is a composite of the West Indian custodian who worked in Marshall's neighborhood library and the owner of the house in Barbados where she rented a room while revising *Brown Girl, Brownstones.*[10]

Marshall further reveals that the writing of the collection was her way of "questioning her commitment to the long-haul of being a writer. Was I really committing myself to all that being a writer involves?" Not wanting to be a one-book novelist, she certainly felt a sense of urgency to publish a second volume. But because of her increasing ability to write feature articles for *Our World,* with the necessary regularity publishing deadlines required, Marshall was also fearful of becoming a "hack writer." Her work with the magazine certainly taught her the importance of discipline, but it also increased her desire to become a serious writer of fiction. Given her protracted experience with the writing of *Brown Girl,* she knew that her second novel would take some time to complete, so she "drew from the hopper to write what was already there."[11]

What may already have been there might also have included Marshall's consideration of her own father's predicament. In *Brown Girl, Brownstones,* she approached the problems of the uprooted and displaced male who could not wholly identify with the oppressor but had no other way of proving his manhood.[12] Although she puts her questions to rest thirty years later in *Daughters* (1991), Marshall continually seeks answers. Her decision to use the shorter novella form for *Soul* may indicate her intermittent and differing responses. Far more feasible, however, is that Marshall became a mother in 1959, and the added responsibilities of caring for a child necessarily curtailed the time for writing complete novels. In an interview with Alexis DeVeaux she states that, despite her first husband's objections, she had to spend time away from home at a friend's apartment working on the collection. "I went ahead and did it. There were, he sensed it, I knew it, my need and determination to be my own woman. To do my own thing. I think this is something women have to acknowledge about themselves—their right to fulfill themselves."[13] Marital tensions and the responsibilities of motherhood notwithstanding, Marshall persisted and two years later *Soul Clap Hands and Sing* was published. Since so little critical attention has been given this collection, I provide below a close reading of each novella.

"Barbados"

The first, entitled "Barbados," takes place in Marshall's ancestral homeland. It concerns the life of Mr. Watford, a seventy-year-old West Indian man who has so deeply internalized the values of Western society that he has no space in his life for the very community he subconsciously longs to embrace. Having suffered the indignities of racism and neocolonialism, he has learned well the haughty condescension of powerful whites and takes a similar stance toward his own people. As the story unfolds, however, we see that the main character's actions reflect a deep and long-standing ambivalence. He is disdainful of Western ways, as can be seen in his attitude toward America where he has spent close to fifty years accumulating the wealth he now lords over his fellow islanders. Yet he is envious of the people of Barbados who, despite their poverty, are connected with a hopeful spirit and a new political consciousness. As Darwin T. Turner points out, however, Watford has "surrendered his humanity to the materialism of the American Dream."[14] In this novella, Marshall uncovers the dynamics of self-hatred as a learned process. She shows as well how self-hatred may be projected onto the masses in an expression of contempt—indeed, even of total apathy.

What is immediately striking about "Barbados" is the language, sensuous with its whispered sibilance and muted sounds of moans and murmurs. In fact, the imagery of throbbing is associated with Watford's own muffled passion. The narrator states that he is awakened each morning by the call of his Barbary doves, but it is the "feel" of the sound, rather than the sound itself, that stimulates him. His hands, though cracked and calloused, "had retained, from the many times a day he held the doves, the feel of their throats swelling with that murmurous, mournful note."[15] His muscular body, which "appeared to be absolved from time, still young," personifies an ongoing physical contest between nature and time.

Watford's strength seems full measure until we read of his desire to hide his exhaustion and weariness from the world and himself. Marshall describes him in minute detail, but it is his face which best reflects the ongoing struggle in which the old man engages:

> "His face was fleshless and severe, his black skin sucked deep into the hollow of his jaw, while under a high brow, which was like a bastion raised against the world, his eyes were indrawn and pure. It was as if during his seventy years, Mr. Watford had permitted nothing to sight which could have affected him." (5)

The narrator fills in the details of Watford's life through flashbacks, and we learn that he was the only one of ten children to survive childbirth. We also learn that since his boyhood in Barbados, he had always feared the night. He habitually closed his windows to the night air, fearing that "something palpable but unseen was waiting to snare him" (7). To protect himself against this threat, he lived a cloistered and cautious life. The

Protestant ethic of hard work, thrift, and moderation became his ruling principles. As for personal relationships, he seemed disdainful of all but occasional and superficial ties. By the time he was twenty and nearly "broken from work," his parents died, "leaving him enough money for his passage to America."

During his exile, Watford's life underwent no significant change. For fifty-five years, he worked in a boiler room of a Boston hospital and returned each evening to the basement apartment of the large rooming house he had managed to purchase. There he dressed in a medical doctor's *white* uniform and read the daily newspapers. The few acquaintances he made were of little consequence to him, as were the occasional women of whom he soon grew tired. "He had lived closeted like this," the narrator explains, "because America—despite the money and property he had slowly accumulated—had meant nothing to him. Each morning, walking to the hospital along the rutted Boston streets, through the smoky dawn light, he had known—although it had never been a thought—that his allegiance, his place, lay elsewhere" (7). Here the author hints of the depths of unarticulated feelings and unrealized wells of emotion that dwell within the main character. They reflect the dormant passion which, when finally released, is to be his undoing. A year before retirement, Watford resigns from his job, liquidates his assets, and returns to Barbados.

In Barbados, Watford continues to follow his daily routine of work and isolation, and in the evening he reads the Boston papers. Although they reach him several weeks later, he derives a curious joy from the "thought that beyond his world that other world went its senseless way" (6). Yet he identifies, in part, with America, for he has built a colonial house. With its solid stone columns, the house seems "pure, proud, a pristine white—. disdaining the crude wooden houses in the village outside its high gate" (3). Adjacent to the house is a grove of five hundred dwarf coconut trees, which Watford planted "because of their quick yield and because, with their stunted trunks, they always appeared young" (5).

As in *Brown Girl, Brownstones,* architectural design and the local scenery reflect something about the quality of life. In this story, the house provides a stark contrast to the poor living conditions of the native population and suggests the acceptance of values alien to their ways. Obviously, the gate symbolizes Watford's desire to wall others out, to keep himself apart. Though he seems content with what he feels is self-sufficiency, it is apparent that he still feels incomplete. His house, for instance, remains unfinished despite the fact that he has been in Barbados now for five years. Furniture from Grand Rapids crowds the room in no orderly fashion, and the walls remain "raw and unpainted." If it were not for his favorite piece, the "old mantle clock which eked out the time," it would seem that time had stood still.

In his self-imposed isolation, Watford expresses his disdain for the masses. As if to flaunt his good fortune, every evening he turns on the lights in the parlor and opens the doors to the portico so that passersby may glimpse him. But the author includes a brief description of the islanders to make the reader question Watford's arrogance. While he sits alone, outside his walls we hear the sounds of "the last hawkers caroling, 'Fish, flying fish, a penny my lady.'" We hear the "roistering saga-boys lugging their heavy steel drums to the crossroads where they would rehearse under the street lamp." In contrast to Watford's silent isolation, "the night sounds of the village welled into a joyous chorale against the sea's muffled cadence and the hollow, haunting music of the steel band" (6). The night, it seems, need not always presage a dreadful presence. For a fleeting moment, it becomes for Watford "like a woman offering herself to him . . . fragrant with the night-blooming cactus" (7). Before retiring, however, Watford returns to his hermetically sealed room, closing the windows against the night air.

Mr. Watford's usual routine is to change when the local shopkeeper, significantly named Mr. Goodman, sends a young boy to pick coconuts from Watford's grove. The coconuts are to be sold at the race track where customers would ritualistically cut off the tops and mix rum with the sweetened water. The narrator briefly takes us back to the time when Watford "had stood among them at the track as a young man, as poor as they were, but proud." Even then he was torn with ambivalence, for "he had always found something unutterably graceful and free in their gestures, something which had roused contradictory feelings in him: admiration, but just as strong, impatience at their easy ways, and shame" (10).

The shame has become the dominant feeling, and Watford's life of caution (a passion of another sort) is simply a rejection of all behavior that could even be vaguely associated with the common islander. Again suggesting his identification with the oppressor, he is pleased when the boy, standing "outside the back door" displays a respectful pose, "for the gestures were those given only to a white man in his time." Once more, the author takes us to the past to help us understand the present. Watford recalls

> the time when he had worked as a yard boy for a white family, and he had had to assume the same respectful pose while their flat, raw, Barbadian voices assailed him with orders. He remembered the muscles in his neck straining as he nodded deeply and a taste like alum on his tongue as he repeated 'Yes, please,' as in a litany. But because of their whiteness and wealth, he had never dared hate them. (8–9)

Watford's anger and hatred are displaced, for, as with other colonized peoples, the sense of hopelessness and of powerlessness in the face of the colonizer is often deflected onto those most like one's self. This hatred, while not always a conscious emotion, may virtually control human behavior to block out compassion or even the desire to appreciate the positive values that sustain the downtrodden.

Watford is particularly irritated with the boy who, despite his shabby appearance, carries a "natural arrogance like a pinpoint of light within his dark stare." It is an arrogance that seems to be bolstered by the political button the boy wears pinned to his patched shirt. Printed boldly on the button are the words "Vote for the Barbados People's Party," and below that, the motto of the party, "The Old Order Shall Pass." The double-entendre of the motto can hardly be missed, for we know the old order to be not merely those affected by age, but also those affected by the political states of colonialism and neocolonialism. Watford senses that the message is somehow directed at him, but secure in his belief that a little common sense and a lot of hard work ensures individual success, he feels no responsibility for others. He seems not to understand how his selfish actions contribute to the disparity between himself and his fellow countrymen. He says as much to Mr. Goodman, who pays him a visit later that evening: "Look that half-foolish boy you does send here to pick the coconuts. Instead of him learning a trade and going to England where he might find work he's walking about with a political button. He and all in politics now! But that's the way with these down in here. They'll do some of everything but work. They don't want work! . . . They too busy spreeing" (12). Going to England, of course, is a reference to the poor economic conditions of the island that force the people (especially the men) to emigrate to what is ironically termed "the mother country" to secure gainful employment. In *The Chosen Place, the Timeless People,* Marshall makes a similar reference to islanders who travel to Panama and sometimes to Canada and the United States to earn money, which they then send home for the support of their families.

The corpulent and openly concupiscent Mr. Goodman is introduced in the novella to establish a contrast with Watford and to serve as an intermediary between the old order and the new. His name is obviously symbolic of his character, and his physical description is clearly deliberate. Not only does Goodman smell of salt fish and rum, the common diet of the villagers, but his face with its "loose folds of flesh, the skin slick with sweat as if oiled, the eyes scribbled with veins and mottled" prove that his involvement with life and with people has been complete. It is Goodman's attitude, however, that the author wishes to emphasize. Responsive to the plight of his fellow villagers, "he owned the one shop in the area which gave credit and a booth which sold coconuts at the race track." The narrator lets us know that his generosity extended beyond business matters, for he also "kept a wife and two outside women, drank a rum with each customer at his bar, regularly caned his fourteen children, who still followed him everywhere (even now they were waiting for him in the darkness beyond Mr. Watford's gate) and bet heavily at the races, and when he lost he gave a loud hacking laugh which squeezed his body like a pain and left him gasping" (11). And Goodman has a marvelous sense of humor which the narrator captures: "Watford, how? Man, I near lose house, shop, shirt and all at races today. I tell you, they got some horses from Trinidad in this meet that's making ours look like they running backwards. Be-Jees, I wouldn't bet on a Bajan horse tomorrow if Christ heself was to give me the tip. Those bitches might look good but they's nothing 'pon a track" (11).

Comic relief is certainly welcome here, but the author seems to be pointing to the more important element of comic survival. In other words, Mr. Goodman's portrait illustrates his ability to face adversity with a smile—not because he is the frivolous, immodest, and wanton glutton Watford believes him to be; nor because he is insensitive to the misery and poverty that surround him. He has learned the indispensable lesson of deflecting the pain and unhappiness by appreciating the joys of comradeship and the pleasures of unpretentious fun. It is well considered that Marshall has Goodman, despite his former acquiescence to colonialization, explain in clear, straightforward terms, the meaning of the "new order":

> "Things is different to before. I mean to say, the young people nowadays is different to how we was. They just not sitting back and taking things no more. They not so frightened of the white people as we was. No man. Now take that said same boy, for an example. I don't say he don't like a spree, but he's serious, you see him there. He's a member of this new Barbados People's Party. He wants to see his own color running the government. He wants to be able to make a living right here in Barbados instead of going to any cold England. And he's right!" (13)

Goodman agrees that hard work is necessary, but he adds compassionately, "It's up to we that got little something to give them work." Goodman is diplomatically leading up to the central objective of his visit: to convince Watford to hire a servant girl.[16] Of course, he must extol the virtues of the girl—virtues which, if she were forced to work for whites, might be despoiled. "I gon send she," Goodman concludes as Watford dismisses him and his proposal with a laugh.

The girl appears the next day with valise and shoes in hand. Note the narrator's description:

> She was standing in his driveway, her bare feet like strong dark roots amid the jagged stones, her face tilted toward the sun—and *she might have been standing there always for him.* She seemed of the sun, of the earth. The folktale of creation might have been true with her: that along a riverbank a god had scooped up the earth—rich and black and warmed by the sun—and molded her poised head with the tufted braids and then with a whimsical touch crowned it with a sober brown felt hat which should have been worn by some stout English matron in a London suburb, had sculptured the passionless face and drawn a screen of gossamer across her eyes to hide the void behind. Beneath her bodice her small breasts were smooth at the crest. Below her waist, her hips branched wide, the place prepared for its load of life. (15, italics mine)

As we read the line italicized above, we suspect that the girl, who intentionally remains unnamed, also represents the unnamed fear Watford has been fleeing. Since she is described in terms of an African folktale of creation, her presence connotes not only the continuity of time but also its permanence and durability. The hat she wears, which is clearly incompatible with her natural grace and tender years, suggests the "whimsical" intrusion of colonial England—an intrusion that prompts her to wear a mask ("a screen of gossamer across her eyes"). Watford himself sees her as an "intrusion," an "evil visitation," and this is consistent with both the alien values he has accepted and his projection onto the girl of his own pain and shame. But the author is also unearthing the ambivalent feelings that Watford holds toward the girl. The narrator explains, "[I]t was the bold and sensual strength of her legs which completely unstrung Mr. Watford. He wanted to grab a hoe and drive her off" (15). The girl, we can see, is not merely a sexual symbol but, ultimately, a symbol of those African values which the old man denies within himself.

Despite Watford's sharpness and his intention to dismiss her immediately, "she became as fixed and familiar a part of the house as the stones—and as silent" (20). He consciously ignores her. Even during quiet evenings when relaxing in the alcove, he sits reading his newspapers with his back turned against her. Her utter loneliness is described as a "low cry" when on one evening she attempts to reach out to him. But Watford, fearing the closeness that will result, fends her off. "He would be forced then to acknowledge something about her which he refused to grant; above all, he would be called upon to share a little of himself" (20). Here Marshall skillfully adds another manifestation of self-hatred: a tendency to distance those who most remind us of our own oppression. But a major crisis must occur before this acknowledgment becomes apparent. For Watford, the crisis occurs on a holiday when the villagers board excursion buses for their annual outing. The sounds of the festivities evoke within him a disturbing memory of his mother: "the white head tie wound above her dark face and her head poised like a dancer's under the heavy outing basket of food. That set of her head had haunted his years, reappearing in the girl as she walked toward him the first day" (21). Marshall invokes the cycle of time and simultaneously reveals Watford's yearning for that love of an ancestry which, despite his efforts to destroy, remains a persistent mystique.

The girl comes to play a "vital part" in Watford's life, and though she is given the day off to join the excursion, he is unable to go about his usual routine. All day long, well into the evening, he anxiously anticipates her return. With dusk comes the seductive sounds of the steel band, and Watford imagines the villagers carousing with the girl. He conjures up images of "someone like Goodman clasping her lewdly or tumbling her in the cane-brake" (22). It seems to Watford an insulting betrayal when he sees the girl dancing in a nearby yard with the very boy who wore the political button on his shirt: "They were joined together in a tender battle: the boy in a sport shirt riotous with color was reaching for the girl as he leaped and spun, weightless, to the music, while she fended him off with a gesture which was lovely in its promise of surrender" (23). Even nature seems to applaud their performance as the trees sway to their rhythms and the moon rides the sky.

Hidden in the shadows, Watford senses "the familiar specter which hovered in the night reaching out to embrace him, just as the two in the yard were embracing" (23–24). Blinded by jealousy, he rushes into his house only to find "an accusing silence from the clock," which he had forgotten to wind. Marshall inserts this detail to show that Watford has forfeited precious time throughout his life. But the following passage makes clear his urgent need to recapture it:

> He lay in bed in the white uniform, waiting for sleep to rescue him, his hands seeking the comforting sound of the doves. But sleep eluded him and instead of the doves, their throats tremulous with sound, his scarred hands filled with the shape of a woman he had once kept: her skin, which had been almost bruising in its softness; the buttocks and breasts spread under his hands to inspire both cruelty and tenderness. His hands closed to softly crush those forms, and the searing thrust of passion, which he had not felt for years, stabbed his dry groin. (24)

Watford's own raging passion is projected onto the boy and the girl, and in a fit of self-righteous anger, he determines to interrupt their lovemaking. He stumbles toward the girl's room only to find her alone, "dreamily fingering" the political button which was now pinned to the bodice of her dress. Her mouth, Watford sees, was "shaped by a gentle, ironic smile and her eyes strangely acute and critical." The narrator continues: "What had transpired on the cot had not only, it seemed, twisted the dress around her, tumbled her hat and broken her sandal, but had also defined her and brought the blurred forms of life into focus for her. There was a woman's force in her aspect now, a tragic knowing and acceptance in her bent head, a hint about her of Cassandra watching the future wheel before her eyes" (25).

The allusion to Cassandra, the Greek prophetess whose tragic knowledge went unheeded by men, suggests not only the saving role the girl might have played in Watford's life, had he allowed her, but the role she is surely to play in the lives of others. Marshall's use of Greek mythology appropriately removes Watford from a specifically racial/cultural context to place him squarely in the position of Western man obsessed with materialism. The protagonist in hushed reverence, is suddenly confronted with the awful realization that it had been "love, terrible in its demand, which he had always fled. And love had been the reason for his return" (26).

Watford, however, cannot admit his love—a love that is disguised by his repugnance toward Mr. Goodman and his envy of the boy. Neither can he acknowledge his own responsibility for the emptiness that pervades his life. However, in this painful moment of subconscious awareness, he does recognize his desire to live, and he knows that "the girl held life within her as surely as she held the hat in her hands" (26). In his attempt "to wrestle from [the girl] the strength needed to sustain him," Watford confuses lust with love. The girl seems not intimidated but filled with pity when he reaches out to fling her back on the cot. Her "benign smile" changes into a scathing accusation: "But you best move and don't come holding on to me, you nasty pissy old man. That's all you is, despite yuh big house and fancy furnitures and yuh newspapers from America. You ain't people, Mr. Watford, you ain't people!" (27). With this bitter condemnation, the girl leaves and the dreaded presence that Watford had always feared captures him. Marshall concludes the tale where she began: "He moaned—and the anguished sound reached beyond the room to fill the house. It escaped to the yard and his doves swelled their throats, moaning with him" (28).

Having prepared us to understand Watford's predicament, the author ensures that the reader is sympathetic to Watford's plight. We are, nonetheless, in agreement with the girl's vitriolic words. Marshall's intent is to show the reader one process by which self-hatred can be subconsciously projected upon the very people who offer love and meaning to our otherwise fractured lives. She applauds the endurance and resistance of the islanders as well as their developing political awareness, but through the characterization of Watford, she reveals as well the social and psychological ills that are a part of West Indian society. The senseless pain he inflicts not just upon the girl but upon countless others, the derisive laughter and haughty condescension, depreciates the dignity granted to all people. Marshall provides us with a glimpse of how one man, by accepting values which ignore that dignity, pathetically excludes himself from participating in the sacred cycle of life itself.

"Brooklyn"

The story "Brooklyn" moves to the new immigrant home of Marshall's parents and to the more familiar sights and sounds of urban America. Despite the background of neon signs and clashing noises, the character foregrounded is reminiscent of Mr. Watford. Sixty-seven-year-old Max Berman sits alone in a room with the windows closed against the night air. B.A., 1919; M.A., 1921, New York; Docteur de l'Université, 1930, Paris—these are the credentials of academic respectability which distinguish Max Berman's public life. Beneath his professional dignity, however, lies an ugliness bred by consuming indifference. And that indifference, because it stems from self-loathing and socially imposed isolation, becomes even more heinous in its capacity to defile his own life as well as the lives of all who have acknowledged his existence. What is especially interesting about "Brooklyn" is the author's attempt to refract a young black woman's psychological conflict through a white male Jewish perspective.

Once again, the author draws upon her personal experience to create a story about sexual harassment. As a college student, she had been propositioned by one of her professors. In the fifties, though, no support systems existed to mitigate such acts of impropriety. "If propositioned, you either cooperated, and were sometimes rewarded with an 'A' whether your work deserved it or not; or you refused and ran the risk of getting a 'C' or worse; or you dropped the course."[17] Marshall rejected the many advances of her professor, all the while calling him "everything but a child of God" under her breath. But she stayed on in the course, which she needed to graduate. Afterwards, to rid herself of the anger she had held in check over the months, she took notes for the story which nine years later became "Brooklyn."

As the story opens, Berman seems engaged in some type of silent repentance. His roguishness and his need for physical stimulation reflect the

unventilated passion that suffocates his life. The way in which he manipulates his cigarette says as much: "For some time he fondled it, his fingers
shaping soft, voluptuous gestures, his warped old man's hands looking
strangely abandoned on the bare desk and limp as if the bones had been
crushed, and so white—except for the tobacco burns on the index and
third fingers—it seemed his blood no longer traveled that far" (31–32).
The disparity between his age and his passion is quickly established, as
are the details which provide the story's meaning and context. Passages
developed from seemingly casual references provide the necessary material for important flashbacks. A case in point is Berman's glance at his
shoes as he sits in a classroom awaiting the arrival of students enrolled
in the summer evening session of his modern French literature course.
"Somewhat foppishly pointed at the toes," his shoes, which he had cus-
tom-made in France, evoke the memory of his first wife, "a French Jewess
from Alsace Lorraine." Quite simply, he met her while studying in Paris
and married her to avoid returning home. Pausing for a moment to delve
into Berman's consciousness, the narrator reveals: "She had been gay,
mindless, and very excitable—but at night, she had also been capable of a
profound stillness as she lay in bed waiting for him to turn to her, and
this had always awed and delighted him. She had been a gift—and her
death in a car accident had been a judgment on him for never having loved
her, for never, indeed, having even allowed her to matter" (32).

When Berman welcomes the first student, he seems ready to begin
what he thought of as another phase of his life, which had been "divided into many small lives, each with its own beginning and end." His
thoughts continue: "Like a hired mute, he had been present at each dying
and kept the wake and wept professionally as the bier was lowered into
the ground. Because of this feeling, he told himself that his final death
would be anticlimactic" (35–36).

One lifetime began and ended with his childhood and early schooling.
He recalls the occasional taunts at his yarmulke and the conflict he felt
over his academic brilliance. It seems that "he could never believe that he
had come by it naturally or that it belonged to him alone. Rather, it was
like a heavy medal his father had hung around his neck—the chain bruising his flesh—and constantly exhorted him to wear proudly and use well"
(34).

Another lifetime revolved around the investigation of his political activities. The charge that he was a communist seemed so ludicrous then
that he had refused to answer his accusers. But the result of that error was
the dismissal from his thirty-year teaching post in a small community college in upstate New York. He had, in fact, joined the party in his middle
age, when his cynicism had blossomed modestly, but he had never taken

his membership seriously. In fact, his second wife, "a party member who was always shouting political heresy from some picket line . . . promptly divorced him upon discovering his irreverence" (37). The root of Berman's problem is the painful, gnawing awareness that he has never taken anyone or anything seriously.

A third lifetime is represented in the period of exile he served after his dismissal from the college. He seemed content to live alone in a small house he had built near it. An occasional visit from a colleague or the tutoring he sometimes provided for students gave him the human contact he needed. And he received an income from property his parents had left him in Brooklyn. However, as the visits became fewer and farther apart, "a silence had begun to choke the house, like weeds springing around a deserted place." His solitude was so profound that "he had even begun to think of his inquisitors with affection and to long for the sound of their voices. They, at least, had assured him of being alive" (36).

Condensed into five pages of Berman's musings is his history of the past several decades. The story at hand begins like that of the prodigal son, for Berman has returned to Brooklyn to the house of his father. Without mentioning his previous political indiscretion, he has obtained his current teaching post and is striking forth, one more time, upon another life. The only thing that has survived Berman's many lives—resurrected, as it were, from the ashes of his past—has been his total disinterest, which even now imbues the students who fill the classroom. Compatible with this disinterestedness are his waning blue eyes, which "never seem to focus on any one thing." As he scans the collected body of students, he is saddened by the thought that they, too, will lose the faith and innocence of childhood. One student reminds him uncomfortably of his first wife, but there is another student, somewhat older, who captures and holds his attention. She is a "slender young woman with crimped black hair who sat very still and apart from the others, her face turned toward the night sky as if to a friend" (37).

Berman's interest in this young woman is piqued because of the depth of her loneliness, a feeling with which he can easily identify. When he sees that she is a Negro of fair complexion, he supposes correctly that she is a school teacher from the South taking summer courses toward a graduate degree. The narrator moves directly to the heart of Berman's lifelong feeling of rejection and victimization, which supersedes his own complicity in racism:

> He felt a fleeting discomfort and irritation: discomfort at the thought that although he had been sinned against as a Jew he still shared in the sin against her and suffered from the same vague guilt, irritation that she recalled his own humiliations: the large ones: such as the fact that despite

his brilliance he had been unable to get into a medical school as a young
man because of the quota on Jews (not that he had wanted to be a doctor;
that had been his father's wish) and had changed his studies from medicine to French; the small ones which had worn him thin: an eye widening
imperceptibly as he gave his name, the savage glance which sought the
Jewishness in his nose, his chin, in the set of his shoulders, the jokes
snuffed into silence at his appearance. (38)

To stay his anger and fatigue, Berman yearns for the escape of sleep and
some "pleasantly erotic image" to induce it. "But this time," reveals the
narrator, "instead of the usual Rubens nude with thighs like twin portals
and a belly like a huge alabaster bowl into which he poured himself, he
chose Gauguin's Aita Parari, her languorous form in the straight-back
chair, her dark, sloping breasts, her eyes like the sun under shadow" (39).
The associations with the Negro girl are apparent as the professor imagines her slender, amber-colored body posed nude in a straightback chair.
Reminiscent of Watford, who had reached out to the servant girl to revive
the life he had kept at bay, here Berman determines that only this young
woman can be the bridge to the new life upon which he now embarks. He is
not so foolish as to think his challenge will be easy, "for she would surely
refuse him." And "even if she did not, what could he do—his performance
would be a mere scramble and twitch" (40). Yet there is a certain presumptu-
ousness—perhaps even arrogance—in his resolve to have her.
The story advances quickly to midterm when Berman receives a note
from the administration informing him that his past political activities
have been discovered and that he will be dismissed at the end of the session. With his new start at life now suddenly thwarted, he is reminded
that he has not yet even approached the Negro woman. Sensing his opportunity, he asks her to remain after class to discuss the paper she has
just submitted on Gide's *Immoralist.*
Marshall chooses to name the female figure in this novella and to ex-
pose, in depth, her personal dilemma. Although Miss Williams (perhaps
a common name to emphasize a common black female experience) says
very little initially, it is significant that the author later gives her dispro-
portionate and, in relation to the other novellas, inconsistent attention.
Though important to our understanding of this black woman, it nonetheless detracts from and perhaps minimizes Berman's full realization as a
Jew who is haunted by the horrors of the McCarthy era and its devastating effects. Yet Berman's reaction to Miss Williams is as a white male
whose cultural authority is gained from Europe. If we remember his earlier marriage to an Alsatian woman, his relationship to Europe is clearly
different than that of the young black woman.

Berman suspects that Miss Williams may have understood his intentions from the start, for "she was always late and disappeared as soon as
the closing bell rang, leaving him trapped in a clamorous circle of students around his desk" (41). Now, as she approaches Berman's desk, there
is obvious apprehension. She nears him "like a child who has been cau-
tioned not to talk to strangers, her fingers touching the backs of the chairs
as if for support, her gaze following the departing students as though she
longed to accompany them" (41). Berman interprets her reticence as a
form of submissiveness, a submissiveness which gives him control, certainty, dominance. The sexual overtones are clear, but Marshall seems just
as interested in revealing how he seeks empowerment through Euro-
American racial values and assumptions:

> Her hesitancy was somehow in keeping with the color of her skin. She
> seemed to bring not only herself but the host of black women whose bodies
> had been despoiled to make her. He would not only possess her but them
> also, he thought (not really thought, for he scarcely allowed these thoughts
> to form before he snuffed them out). Through their collective suffering,
> which she contained, his own personal suffering would be eased; he would
> be pardoned for whatever sin it was he had committed against life. (41–42)

Marshall shows here that the historical effects of racism may extend beyond a single individual to encompass nameless and faceless others, then
turn on itself to assuage the guilt.

Too desperate and too selfish to be deterred from his goal, Berman ush-
ers the young woman into the corridor, and calling forth all of the
manipulative tactics of an easy, professional tone, an urbane and courtly
manner, he works to gain the student's confidence. As they discuss the
reasons for her selection of *The Immoralist,* we note a double edge to Miss
Williams's responses: she seems to be cautious, bracing herself against ex-
posing the mounting fear so closely guarded within. Then again, her mild-
mannered smile belies the strength of a burgeoning conviction. Interpreting the significance of the book, she says: "You see, to me, the book seems
to say that the only way you begin to know what you are and how much
you are capable of is by daring to try something, by doing something
which tests you" (43).

As if to gain, in advance, her consent to his plan, Berman suggests that
that "something" might be a bold action or even a sinful one. He play-
fully quips, "The salutary effects of sin, you might say." Unwittingly, Miss
Williams scourges him for his previous actions when she continues: "And
another thing, in finding out what he is, he destroys his wife. It was as if
she had to die in order for him to live and know himself. Perhaps in order

for a person to live and know himself somebody else must die. Maybe there's always a balancing out." Marshall draws symbolic literary parallels and simultaneously creates a vehicle to underscore her thematic concern with rebirth. Certainly Berman is attempting to begin his life anew, but the young woman also seems to be struggling to make a new start. Here Marshall opens a discursive space for Miss Williams and forecasts the concern that will dominate her later fiction: women growing in consciousness of their own strengths and abilities.

In "Brooklyn" and in her other works of fiction, the author pays particular attention to the eyes of her characters. Berman's eyes are a "waning blue that never seemed to focus on anything." Miss Williams has eyes which, from a distance, appeared to be black, but they were actually "a strong, flecked brown with very small pupils which seemed to shrink now from the sight of him" (42). Later her eyes are compared to "dark, shattered glass that spared Mr. Berman his reflection" (51). But as they continue their conversation, Berman "edged back as he glimpsed something move within her abstracted gaze: It was like a strong and relentless seed that had taken root in the darkness there and was straining now toward the light. He had not expected so subtle and complex a force beneath her mild exterior and he found it disturbing and dangerous, but fascinating" (44).

Despite the many warnings, the professor proves persistent. Maneuvering very carefully, he learns that her interest in French stemmed from her Creole mother, who was born in New Orleans and spoke a French patois. This time, the Western influence is empowering. Miss Williams majored in French at Howard University and is teaching a beginner's course at a junior high school in Richmond. As Berman had suspected, she has come north to start taking courses toward a master's degree in order to move gradually into more exciting teaching. She is grateful and elated when he suggests that he would be willing to offer a few pointers for expanding her present essay on Gide to a master's thesis. This, for her, just might represent the something bold that she must undertake to get on with her life. But her disappointment is paralyzing when Berman invites her to discuss the matter during a weekend visit at his country place:

> It was as though she had never learned the forms and expressions of anger. The outrage of a lifetime, of her history, was trapped inside her. And she stared at Max Berman with this mute, paralyzing rage. Not really at him but to his side, as if she caught sight of others behind him. And remembering how he had imagined a column of dark women trailing her to her desk, he sensed that she glimpsed a legion of old men with sere flesh and lonely eyes flanking him: "old lechers with a love of every wind." (47–48)

Marshall again turns to Yeats, but she changes the context to point to a moment of illumination: Berman equates his prejudice toward the young black woman with her prejudice toward him. As if to acknowledge this fact, he apologizes, half welcoming the anger she feels.

The author insists that his crudity cannot be excused by what he correctly terms his "approaching senility"; a just resolution must be reached. Marshall therefore moves immediately to the night of the final examination. Miss Williams, we learn, has not attended classes since the conversation in the corridor, but there she sits prepared to take the final examination. Berman has nearly forgotten her, "for her face had been absorbed into the single, blurred, featureless face of all the women who had ever refused him" (49). He does, however, seem genuinely pleased that she has not completely forfeited the course. Though she is as before (absorbed in her loneliness), there is something different about her. We suspect, along with Berman, that "during her three week absence she had waged and won a decisive contest with herself and was ready now to act" (49). Marshall makes reference to the woman's demeanor to suggest that the limited circle of her former life, to be described later, is gradually expanding. For Berman, however, the configuration spirals in an unaltered groove. The final evening of class becomes not a triumph but a painful reminder of the despair that awaits him. With his head bowed in defeat, he thinks of the two options available to him: he can either return to his country place to die from the choking silence, or he can remain in Brooklyn to live in his father's house. The house is the place "where the memory of his father's face above the radiance of the Sabbath candles, haunted him from the shadows, reminding him of the certainty he had lost and never found again, where the mirrors of his father's room were still shrouded with sheets, as on the day he lay dying and moaning into his beard that his only son was a bad Jew" (50).

Roused from his morbid musings, Berman notices that the room is empty save for the Negro girl, "smiling across the room at him—a set, artificial smile that was both cold and threatening" (51). (The servant girl in "Barbados" has prepared us for what lies behind that smile.) With shame, he feels "utterly denuded . . . wildly angry suddenly that she had seen him give way to despair." And he articulates, at least to himself, what he could not express before: "He wanted to remind her (he could not stay the thought; it attacked him like an assailant from a dark turn in this mind) that she was only black after all" (51). We are suspicious when she tells him, "without passion or promise," that she would still like to spend a day at his country place. Berman seems hopeful that "her presence, even if it was only for a day, would make his return easier." And his passion does not lessen despite the sound of her receding heels tapping "like a warning finger on Max Berman's temple" (52).

The final segment of the story takes place at Berman's country cottage and the setting provides Marshall an opportunity to fuse the scenery with her two-pronged message: "The morning mist and pale sun, the green that was still somehow new, made it seem that the season was stirring into life even as it died, and this contradiction pained Max Berman at the same time it pleased him. For it was his own contradiction after all: his desires which remained those of a young man even as he was dying" (52). But now we are dealing with Miss Williams's story as well, and the end of the season presages a new beginning for her. She musters unusual control in comparison to Berman's mounting anxiety. Suspense builds through the old man's thoughts that her plan all along was to play a trick on him—to remain in New York or to return to Richmond, derisively laughing at his well-deserved disappointment.

Disappointment would certainly be a plausible alternative, but the resolution would remain unsatisfactory. If her reading of *The Immoralist* has had any real effect, Miss Williams is truly prepared to confront Max Berman face to face, without fear or apology. And that she does in a slow and deliberate fashion. Berman ceases to question her curious smile when she suddenly laughs aloud at the sight of her sneakers "wet and dark from the dew secreted in the grass." Like the servant girl in "Barbados," Miss Williams becomes nature itself: "The sound, coming so abruptly in the midst of her tense quiet, joined her, it seemed, to the wood and wide fields, to the hills; she shared their simplicity and held within her the same strong current of life. Max Berman had felt privileged suddenly, and humble." This passage parallels Watford's humility at the sight of the servant girl.

When Miss Williams changes into her bathing suit, she becomes a "pale-gold naiad, the spirit of the lake, her eyes reflecting its somber autumnal tone and her body as supple as the birches" whose branches bent over the water. Unaware, or perhaps uncaring of "the sudden passion of his gaze," the young woman leaves Berman standing ashore and walks slowly into the water, holding out her arms "in what seemed a gesture of invocation (and Max Berman remembered his father with the fringed shawl draped on his outstretched arms as he invoked their God each Sabbath with the same gesture); her head was bent as if she listened for a voice beneath the water's murmurous surface" (56). The baptismal imagery is clear, for when she emerges from the depths of the water, she seems born again, renewed in her determination to do something bold. Berman himself changes his views as he realizes "the profound cleavage between them and the absurdity of his hope": "The water between them became the years which separated them. Her white cap was the sign of her purity, while the silt darkening the lake was the flotsam of his failures. Above all, their color—her arms a pale, flashing gold in the sunlit water and his bled white and flaccid with the veins like angry blue pencilling—marked the final barrier" (56). A crow is heard in the late afternoon, an omen of the disaster yet to come.

In sadness and quiet remorse, Berman tells Miss Williams of the investigation, and through his confession we understand the absurdity of the proceedings. He correctly opines that had he made up names or admitted his association with people he had not known, his life would have been quite different: "Instead of my present ignominy," he jests with biting accuracy, "I would have been offered a chairmanship at Yale. . . . No? Well, Brandeis then" (57). To her question about his reasons for refusing to answer, Berman replies that "none of it really mattered that much." "What did matter?" she continues to probe. Though he realizes that this had been "the real accusation behind the charges of his inquisitors at the hearing," he cannot respond to the question satisfactorily. In his heart, however, he knows that, since childhood, there had been nothing "to which he had given himself or in which he had truly believed" (58). As to her question about what he would do now, he shrugs. This seems to be a thoughtless gesture on the surface, but Marshall intends for us to understand that "that motion, a slow, eloquent lifting of the shoulders, brought with it suddenly the weight and memory" of his past: "It was the familiar gesture of the women hawkers in Belmont Market, of the men standing outside the temple on Saturday mornings, each of them reflecting his image of God in their forbidding black coats and with the black, tumbling beards in which he always imagined he could hide as in a forest. All this had mattered, he called loudly to himself " (59). Marshall's familiarity with Jewish culture is apparent, and this passage anticipates the Brooklyn scene she later describes in "Reena" as well as the memories she gives to Saul in *The Chosen Place, the Timeless People.* Her central point, however, concerns the sense of alienation and displacement which minority peoples experience. She suggests here and in future pieces the need for reconciling cultural conflict through self-empowerment, which becomes possible with responsible involvement with others.

Unfortunately, Berman's life has been spent with a vague awareness of this lesson, but the disillusionment and despair which he has been unable to shake has made it impossible for him to recover. The young woman, in contrast, illustrates that recovery is possible, once she accepts responsibility for the direction of her life. Berman inadvertently provides a new and powerful impetus. Recognizing that she has found "something vital and purposeful," something "precious," he seems less interested in venting his physical passion than in grabbing whatever that something is. As he catches her arm and draws her close, however, he sees the disgust in her eyes and drops his hold. But with her new strength in control, her new self-assurance driving her forward, Miss Williams pulls him close again and quietly, without passion, explains her new bravery in confronting racism:

> "And do you know why, Dr. Berman, I feel almost brave today? Because ever since I can remember my parents were always telling me, 'Stay away from white folks. Just leave them alone. You mind your business and they'll mind theirs. Don't go near them.' And they made sure I didn't. My father, who was the principal of a colored grade school in Richmond, used to drive me to and from school every day. When I needed something from downtown my mother would take me and if the white saleslady asked me anything she would answer." (61)

Protecting her from whites, to be sure, was her parents' way of shielding her from the cruelty and insensitivity that they themselves had experienced. But Miss Williams, not very dissimilar from Berman, had no comfort or solace in associating even with her own: "And my parents were also always telling me, 'Stay away from niggers,' and that meant anybody darker than we were. . . . I was so confused I never really went near anybody" (61–62). The problems of race and identity in the United States have shaped her life, leading to ambivalence and self-loathing. She even refused to marry the man she loved because she knew her parents would disapprove of his darker color. Marshall makes clear that the confusion, fear, and shame would have continued to misdirect Miss Williams's life had it not been for Max Berman: "In a way, you did me a favor," states the young woman. "You let me know how you—and most of the people like you—see me" (62).

While it may tax our notion of reality to believe that a woman now well into her twenties could have led such a completely sheltered life, we need only recall the length of time Mr. Berman has sheltered himself against any real involvement with life. With a twist of irony, he has become, if not the source of Miss Williams's salvation, at least the stimulus for the anger that prompts her to find it. "I can do something now! I can begin," she says, with her head poised high.

> "Look how I came all the way up here to tell you this to your face. Because how could you harm me? You're so old you're like a cup I could break in my hand." And her hand tightened on his wrist, wrenching the last of his frail life from him, it seemed. Through the quick pain, he remembered her saying on the landing that night: "Maybe in order for a person to live someone else must die" and her quiet "I believe this" then. Now her sudden laugh, an infinitely cruel sound in the warm night, confirmed her belief. (63)

Again, Marshall has the female character inflict severe punishment, but the sin Berman has committed against her (and, by implication, against all black women) cannot be exorcised by a casual wrist slapping. Berman accepts "his responsibility for her rage, which went deeper than his, and for her anger, which would spur her finally to live" (64). And she will. The real tragedy is that Berman will spend his last days with the haunting memory of all those, including himself, "whom he had wronged through his indifference." We may feel joy for Miss Williams and indescribable sorrow for Berman, but Marshall has clearly illustrated the collision of race, gender, and ethnicity with personal responses to exclusion and discrimination. As the novella draws to a close, Berman's numbed eyes follow the rear lights of the train retreating into the darkness. In remorse and solitude, he will face his final and, indeed, anticlimactic life.

"British Guiana"

If Berman's indifference stems from a loss of faith in his cultural heritage, the indifference of the main character in "British Guiana" is a direct result of his never having established a cultural identity. Gerald Motley, whose name suggests the various strains which constitute his cultural background, seems a man of all peoples but a child claimed by none. Curiously enough, it is in a drunken stupor when he seems more aware of his multiple racial background. "B.S.W.C." is the title with which he knights himself: "Bastard Spawned of the World's Commingling." The narrator explains:

> He could have been white then (and he had often been taken for an Italian or Spaniard in England), for early in his long complex history a British officer sent out to B.G. had bequeathed him thin features, the fair skin and hair; or black, since the slave woman the officer had used once and forgotten had passed her dark hand lightly over his paleness and claimed him with a full expressive mouth; or East Indian, for some Hindu brought to the colony along with the Chinese when the slave trade was over had added a marked passion and tension to his thin nose and touched his eyes with an abstract and mystical fire. (69–70)

Marshall is more expressly political in this culturally expansive story. The text alludes to the miscegenation that occurred as a result of the trans-Atlantic slave trade in operation from the sixteenth through the nineteenth centuries. En route to the New World, which included the Indies and the Americas, Africans were transported to several Caribbean countries, which were alternately controlled by various European colonial powers. Each country established brutal, exploitative measures to enforce the production of plantation crops. The novella also establishes the context for the class and caste system which evolved in that region of the world after slavery was abolished. As a source of cheap labor intended to bolster the plantation labor force, Chinese and East Indians were encouraged to emigrate, and a distinct hierarchy of power and wealth emerged. "British Guiana" reveals that, centuries later, the same power structure remains intact.

While Marshall does not actually describe the wealthy English planter and businessman, his presence is ubiquitous, influencing the ambitions and desires of those who live under his rule. And those under his rule include the high coloreds or Creoles who, in terms of wealth, are followed by the occasional well-to-do East Indian or Chinese. Next in line of privilege are the black professionals and politicians. And at the bottom, we know, are the poor—poor blacks, poor Chinese, and poor Hindus. All seem to go about their daily tasks as if their various lives were preordained, but as the story unfolds we see a confusion of attitudes and values at odds with a deep-seated love for the land and its peoples. Motley, himself the personification of confusion, evaluates the situation as hopeless: "The only solution to what ails B.G. is a bomb at the heart of Georgetown. And *mirabile visu,* our problems are solved! An end to the P.P.P., the unholy triumvirate of poverty, politics (he bowed to a member of the House of Assembly) and prejudice which rules B.G. still. An end to a sun which burns our brains to an ash and a rain that drives us all to drink and delirium tremens. One bomb, gentlemen, and oblivion!" (98–99).

In allowing us to glimpse the natural physical setting, the author signals the major character's inward dilemma. A Hindu village, for instance, contributes to one portion of Motley's enigma. Driving through the countryside on the outskirts of Georgetown, he observes that "the land on both sides of the narrow road stretched like a vast empty stage waiting for the props to visit it with life." The props include "the sun-bleached wooden houses raised on stilts above the flooded ground, the frayed prayer flags on tall poles outside each house, the mosques angled toward Mecca and the swarms of Hindu children digging for shrimp in the mud of the drainage trenches which lined the road, while their mothers swathed in saris squatted under the gnarled, leafless forms of the saman trees" (71–72).

As Motley continues down the road watching other children ("mere sticks draped in dun-colored rags") play at cricket, he sees a small rice field that formed the border of the village. This rice field "yielded to an interminable wall of sugar cane, and, as he sped by, the black men cutting the cane paused and held their machetes at a quivering height for a moment, and he waved back" (71). In these "forms and rituals of the land," the protagonist sought meaning, something to give his life coherence, and his behavior is both a reflection and a deflection of the cultural maze surrounding him.

As if in search of all the answers to the contradictions in his life and in that surrounding him, Motley had studied at the prestigious schools in England: law at the Inns of Court, medicine at Edinburgh, economics at the London School, and the classics at Oxford. His "stay at each school had been brilliant but brief and at the age of thirty-four he had left England well educated but without a career" (70). He is well into his sixties now. As a member of the privileged high-colored class, various jobs were secured for Motley by influential family members and friends. He lived comfortably among his peers, "sharing their indifference to the colony's troubles," and he married at the appropriate time into an appropriate family. Again, when the time seemed appropriate, he fathered a child. Even then, when his life had no apparent difficulties, Motley seemed troubled by something inexplicable. Quite inconsistent with his social status, he frequented the sailors' bars and was said to have attempted to lead the stevedores in a strike against Orly Shipping Ltd. However, it was his bold affair with Sybil Jeffries, a part-black, part-Chinese woman from the village, no less, that broke up his marriage and sent his wife and child to America ("where they passed for white and forgot him"). Ironically, Motley's scandalous divorce led to his public success.

Numerous references are made to the subtle and direct signs of deference extended to the main character, and honors are bestowed not because Motley had done anything outstanding as the program director for British Guiana Broadcasting, but because he had been the first colored in the whole of the West Indies to hold such a position. Motley must have been in his early forties when Cyril Orly, the English entrepreneur who owned nearly all of Georgetown, had offered him his current position. Envisioning the face of the now deceased Orly, Motley remembers the veins which had "fingered the white parchment skin. The eyes had still been shrewd beneath their thick rheum." Consonant with the image are "the panelled walls and heavy maroon drapes in the office, the portrait of George V amid the shadows, which somehow denied that this was B.G and that there was a torpid sunshine outside" (73). Motley had been struggling long ago to find an identity that had not been imposed by a colonial power, an identity that reflected his own deep-seated values and experiences. Yet he seemed unable to identify them. We surmise that in his early manhood, Motley had sincere desires to change conditions in British Guiana. Cyril Orly, no doubt, had recognized Motley's potential leadership abilities and had had the good sense to try to "transfer those talents to [his] camp." During the week he was given to make up his mind, Motley, along with

Sybil and a guide, took a trip to Kaieteur Falls, a jungle area deep in the interior.

Wandering alone into the bush surrounding their camp, Motley was "curious to know what it would be like away from the marked trail they were following." We know that the "marked trail" Motley had been following had led him to no important discoveries about himself or his native land. The unmarked path, though fraught with danger and uncertainty, might help him shape the vision he needed to clarify his own position in preparation for social change. I quote here at length Marshall's description of the bush:

> Slowly, as he had moved over the thick underbrush, parting the tangled branches and looped vines which hung like a portiere before him, he had sensed it. The bush had reared around him like the landscape of a dream, grand and gloomy, profuse and impenetrable, hoarding, he knew, gold and fecund soils and yet, somehow, still ravenous. So that the branches clawed at him, the vines wound his arms, roots sprang like traps around his feet and the silence—dark from the vast shadows, brooding upon the centuries lost—wolfed down the sound of his breathing. He had felt a terror that had been the most exquisite of pleasures and at his awed cry the bush had closed around him, becoming another dimension of himself, the self he had long sought. For the first time, this self was in his grasp. If he pursued this dark way long enough, he would find it hanging like a jeweled pendant on the trees—and it would either shape his life by giving him the right answer to Orly's offer or destroy him. (74)

Beyond depicting the contours of land, Marshall suggests symbolically that Motley experiences his African heritage initially as threatening, as entrapment—perhaps because it is unknown, unrealized, unappreciated. That experience changes, though, to indicate the potential of his hidden heritage to lead him to knowledge and self-possession. Immersion into one's cultural heritage, no matter how difficult, is a necessary prerequisite to positive social change.

Motley is never to penetrate the bush, for at a fateful moment Sybil calls him back. "He had turned to drive her away but her expression had stopped his angry gesture and her eyes, which she had inherited from her part-Chinese father—swift, prescient, set at a slant in her dark face—gazed past him to the bush ahead" (75). Here again the female character is introduced, at a moment of crisis, to offer salvation. In this case, however, Sybil denies Motley his chance for salvation—not out of malice or vengeance, not even from the humiliation and pain she feels in his refusal to marry her. The real reason for her interference is that "she clearly saw what he had only glimpsed and understood better than he ever would its danger; . . . and with a protective cry she had rushed forward and placed herself between him and what could have been a vision of himself " (75). Marshall's allusion to Greek mythology is fitting, for Sibyls were prophetesses whose special function was to intercede with the gods on behalf of human supplicants. It is not yet clear what it is that Sybil Jeffries sees, and Marshall avoids telling us by temporarily removing Sybil from the story. Motley accepts the job with B.G. Broadcasting, and thus gives up a political career that could have affected the future of British Guiana. Shortly thereafter begins his gradual dissipation into "rum and inertia."

Despite the smiles that hide disapproval of his wanton lifestyle, Motley's outrageous behavior is excused by the people of Georgetown. After all, he is one of the few remaining members of the old, established families, and deference is granted that enviable status. He is not merely accepted but elevated to a position of public envy and respect. His public image, however, is not his real self, and the author introduces Sidney Parrish to both accentuate this point and reveal another aspect of Motley's character.

Parrish, a twenty-five-year-old black man who stands "tall and slim-hipped," serves as a contrast to the aging Motley. The latter dons a white linen suit, and a Panama hat tops his sagging frame. Sidney, on the other hand, wears a white shirt and a tie, but no jacket, and a watch, "a harsh, cheap gold against his black wrist. A part cleave[s] his rough hair down the middle like a narrow track through a jungle" (76). This image not only intentionally mirrors the tangled undergrowth of the bush, but it also suggests that Parrish may have clearer direction.

In many respects, Parrish, who works for Motley as a radio announcer, represents Motley's alter ego. His arrogance and contempt, his open disdain for Motley's indifference, merely reflect what the main character feels is his just due. Motley both welcomes and accepts Sidney's abuse as a type of penance and, as if to encourage it, he buys him drinks, treats him to lunch, and promotes him regularly. Of late, he has taken Parrish to and from work and, against all social prohibitions, Motley has invited the young man to accompany him to elite Georgetown parties. In short, Sidney Parrish has become what Motley's peers call his "aide de camp."

Initially, Parrish symbolizes Motley's lost youth, and the young man's bitterness stems from their mutual knowledge that the class and color structure of British Guiana will not permit his advancement. As the eldest son of a stevedore who was accidentally killed on the docks, Sidney had been compelled to forfeit a scholarship to study in England so that he could support his sizeable family. He clearly resents those who flaunt their good fortune, and Motley, despite his generosity, is a part of that oppressive social structure: "the boy became the part of him which refused to spare him the truth, which remained always critical and unforgiving" (77). But Sidney, whose shoulders "were drawn in slightly as if he disliked being touched," represents far more to Motley. To sustain suspense, however, the author postpones her revelation and, instead, dwells on an unnamed disturbance paralleled by the unseasonable rains that begin the story.

Taking advantage of an opportunity to explore time as an unending cycle, Marshall turns to other elderly characters. Singh, the old Hindu waiter who serves Motley his usual morning drink, resembles a fakir and represents "agelessness." Motley seems drawn to this "monument of time" as an abstract expression of what is now a fading hope of his own immortality. Medford, another aged figure, symbolizes the opposite end of this continuum. Motley's servant since childhood, Medford is described as "ageless as Singh," but in her "innocent, murky gaze . . . she had kept, and would always keep, the memory of his boyhood safe—and thus somehow alive" (108). From another perspective, time stands still when Sybil, after a nearly twenty-year absence in Jamaica, returns. She states: "B.G. is the only place on God's earth you could leave for a century and come back to find nothing's changed" (116). Finally, Marshall connects the past with the present toward the end of the story when Motley sees Sybil face to face: "Time was reversed suddenly. The years telescoped. The past, which had trailed and nettled him like a dog's tail, had been caught finally in the teeth of the present" (112–13).

To illustrate this static dimension of time, the author again refers to the bush: "Perhaps neither of them had moved beyond that time and place. They might have left their selves behind among the trees and wandered in ghost forms down the years" (115–16). It is clear that Sybil continues to love Gerald Motley. Her precipitous marriage in Jamaica led to divorce and her subsequent affairs lasted only as long as she maintained a passing interest. Motley's own amorphous existence contributes to his growing uncertainty about his present state. His habitual drinking has become a salve—a way to not only erase the pain of his aimlessness but also obliterate his consciousness of the movement of time.

Marshall is equally concerned in this novella with the effects of time when it spirals out of control. In both human and environmental terms, she paints a picture of the natural order of things gone berserk. Singh comments: "The paper says it's the bombs the Yankees are dropping in the sea for practice that's got things so turned around. Well, I guess we ought to be glad they ain't practising on us yet." Motley's response is telling: "You don't know it, but you're living in the safest place on God's earth. The Yankees won't be dropping any bombs here because they've never heard of a place called B.G. In fact, nobody is quite certain of our existence except a few chaps in the colonial office and they don't count." Marshall later makes a connection between the heat and the bomb with nuclear war:

Each noon it was as if Singh's fear was made flesh: the Yankees had dropped the bomb. For the heat then, searing white on the chalk-white buildings, must have been similar to that which comes at the moment of a massive explosion. The glare offered even the blind of Georgetown a vision of the apocalypse and the weighted stillness mushrooming over the city was the same which must follow a bombing, final and filled with the broken voices of the dying. Georgetown at noon was another Hiroshima at the moment of the bombing. (96)

The author's intention is to rouse the reader's consciousness of the possibilities of environmental holocaust, but she is also making a charged accusation. In controlling national territories from a distance and in fighting among themselves, Western powers destroy countries they deem worthless and insignificant. Further, they reduce the effectiveness of government and, in the process, dehumanize the people who are governed. The end result is the underdevelopment of potentially independent nations. This notion of political autonomy—of a people's right to govern themselves—is a theme to which Marshall alludes in "Barbados." She explores the same idea in greater depth in her next novel, *The Chosen Place, the Timeless People,* and later in *Daughters.* In "British Guiana," however, she outlines her approach. Motley clearly understands the imbalance of power in colonized countries, as do the major characters in *The Chosen Place* and *Daughters.* Sarcastically he proposes a solution for the problems of B.G.:

"an army, gentlemen. . . . That's another thing this colony needs. And some guns. And once we get the army and some guns, we must do one of three things. Either invade Surinam to the east, declare war on Venezuela to the west or provoke Brazil to the south. That's the only way the world will ever know there's a place called B.G. Or better yet, call on the Russians. And then watch, gentlemen. Overnight we will have arrived! Uncle Sam will toss a few million our way and the Queen herself will be hotfooting it down here with some pounds." (98)

Motley mocks the absurd stance of the use of coercive power by the West. Only military aggression, he suggests, will make the world notice B.G. Keenly aware of the disturbing social and moral implications, he knows a "domino effect" is perpetuated, creating a turbulence that moils about without any direction, form, or purpose.

Such turbulence is captured in Motley's portrait. To plumb the depths of his torment, Marshall turns to the manipulation of fictional time. Coinciding with Sybil's return is the death of a ninety-five-year-old woman, "the beloved mother of fifteen and the revered grandmother of sixty and

great-grandmother of well over a hundred" (88). Sidney Parrish dramati-
cally reads the obituaries, which, along with cricket and news from the
BBC three times a day, were a part of the daily programming. On the
Queen's birthday, listeners could look forward to the governor's speech.
Ordinarily, the obituaries prompted no reaction from Motley. In many
respects, he "was only certain of being alive in the midst of the dead." But
Motley is disturbed about this particular announcement, for he had passed
the old woman many times on the road through Kitty Village. His secre-
tary remarks, "Nobody interesting today, sir. . . . But at least Mr. Parrish
didn't forget the Tide again." Motley forgives this irreverence, the narrator tells us, "because he considered her no more than the part of himself
which had remained callous and mean-spirited and filled with an abstract
resentment" (88–89). He attempts to shrug off these thoughts through
paper work, but he is clearly dissatisfied with his unimaginative and, for
the most part, irrelevant work. Part of his problem stems from the fact
that he is powerless—and perhaps afraid—to change things as they exist.
Despair leads him back to the King George Bar, where he nods into a
troubled dream that reflects his unconscious thoughts.

Motley had been listening to the sound of a shrike in the palm trees
when

> the shrike's piercing sweet cry became a siren's call which urged him
> through the deserted streets of Georgetown at night, through a swirling
> yellow fog of heat to the empty house where his wife had once lived. He
> ran through rooms which no longer had walls between them, searching
> for her, until he came to the servant's quarters in the back yard. There he
> found, not his wife, but Sybil, her face covered with a whitish powder and
> a flamboyant blossom growing from her mouth. Beneath the shroud she
> wore, her body above the waist was that of an old woman with shriveled
> flesh and dry flapping dugs and, below, the lithe, pleasing form of a
> young boy. (89–90)

It is not coincidental that Sidney Parrish awakens Motley from his dream.
When he invites Sidney to the party being held in Sybil's honor, Sidney
reminds him that it was color and class that caused him to reject his
former lover in the first place, even when marriage was possible. Motley is
grateful for the truth, but the more important reasons for his rejection of
Sybil he keeps to himself:

> that whenever he had slept with Sybil, she had not only brought her body
> and laid that beside him, but her loneliness also, stretching it out like a
> pale ghost between them, and her intense, almost mystical suffering, ask-

ing him silently to assuage it. But she had asked too much. He would have had to offer up himself to do so, and he refused. Nor could he admit to Sidney the most important reason: that he had never forgiven her for having denied him that vision of himself that day in the bush. (94)

Later, Motley tries to conjure up the image of Sybil as a young woman. "But even this was distasteful and he had to admit what he had long denied: that he had always been secretly offended by the lack of purity in her woman's form, the slight fullness to her breasts and hips" (101). Here and elsewhere, Marshall presents sexuality as a subtext for ambivalence and confusion. Note in the following passage how Motley, mixing freely with the patrons of a sailors' club, feels sexual attraction mingled with revulsion:

> As he penetrated into the violent center of the crowd and felt the intimate press of their bodies against his and the hands clawing at his arm for the bottle, as the warm yeast smell of their sweated, unwashed bodies overwhelmed him and the noise roared like a rough sea in his ears, he felt rid of himself: of his old man's body, that sodden slow-moving hulk he hid in expensive linen suits, of his face which had come to remind him of a reflection seen in a trick mirror where all the features appear to thicken and dissolve, of his mind which had grown barren waiting for the seed. (104 -5)

Foreshadowings of Motley's death quickly follow each other, but the most effective is when he returns home to dress for the party and calls for his servant, Medford. Emerging from the dim passage dressed in white, she seems like an "apparition." Marshall illustrates that in the Caribbean and in many non-Western countries, white symbolizes death. Medford, we learn, had attended the funeral of Millicent Dembo, the woman whose death Sidney had announced earlier. And it is Sidney who makes reference to traditional African funeral rites when he comments to Motley: "Think of the funeral, man! The weeping and wailing of the fifteen head of children and the hundred and sixty-odd grands and great-grands. Think of the women at the funeral dressed up in white like Foolish Virgins. And the cars lined up from here to Kitty Village. The rum flowing" (90). Medford confirms this observation: "She had a hard life, but a sweet funeral. You never saw so many cars, Mr. Motts. And Millie made such a pretty dead" (108). Medford also comments that during the preparation of the body for burial, she noticed that the limbs were "still warm even though [Millie] had passed early the night before." An old African proverb is put to effective use when she adds, in ominous fashion: "And they say when you see a dead come like that, the limbs soft and limber so and warm, you can always look for somebody else to dead soon" (108).

Motley finally arrives at the party without Sidney and parks his car some distance away from the house. As thoughts of the festivities begin to depress him, he is about to leave when the now "resolute" and "assured" Sybil appears on the veranda and then joins him in his car. More the Sybil of his remembrance than the Sybil of his dream, Motley is relieved. That relief, however, turns into prolonged and agonized laughter when he understands that she has, indeed, come back with a plan. Radio Jamaica has a vacancy for someone to coordinate operations, and he is her choice. The narrator tells us that "the absurdity of her offer, its irony convulsed him; life offering itself when there was hardly any life left. It was a rare grotesque touch which appealed to his taste, the fitting coda to his long day, and he wished that Sidney was present to enjoy the moment with him" (121). In fact, he thinks of Sidney and Sybil as one. Motley's excuses about his age and his need for drink are valid, but they cover up the devastating secret that the author has carefully concealed: "That it was not hesitancy or lack of confidence on his part, but, simply, the terrifying awareness of his own deficiencies" (122). And his deficiencies include his uncertainty about his cultural and sexual identity.

Sybil has heard of Motley's attachment to Parrish, and as she waits for Motley's denial, the silence becomes an admission. She searches his face whose features had become a discolored and shapeless blur: "He could no longer be mistaken for white or black for that matter, or East Indian. Over the years, the various strains had cancelled out each other, it seemed, until he was a neuter" (125–26). Homosexuality becomes a figure for paralysis as Sybil concludes that "the confusion which had begun with his heritage, spread over the whole of his life and found its final expression in Sidney" (126). Assuming her former role as prophetess, Sybil further sees imminent death. His final request of her is to advance Sidney's career.

Concluding the story is Sybil's cry, "This damn place. This damn bloody place." We are reminded of Motley's outburst about the bomb. Someone had then added that Motley would come crawling out of the ashes, holding a bottle of Russian Bear. Motley's response: "You're damn right. . . . And do you know why I'll survive, gentlemen? Because I'm the only one out of the lot of you who really loves the place. I am B.G." (99). Marshall here makes clear that "what he had sought all along had been the reflection of himself in each feature of the land." And, as in the bush, "he had been there, although he had not been able to see himself" (99). The confusion which stems from Motley's multicultural and multiracial background combines with his confusion and uncertainty about his sexuality to build a stagnating form of psychological repr∽ssion. Symbolically, the repression is paradigmatic of British Guiana as well as all other countries affected by colonialism. By placing at least some of the blame for Motley's wasted life on history, on circumstances beyond his control, the author suggests, as in Greek tragedy, the inescapability of human destiny. Even as Marshall proceeds in her search for alternative systems of thought and action, she unequivocally repeats her dominant theme of the destructive influence of Western values. With the final selection in *Soul Clap Hands and Sing,* a fictionalized account of O Grande Othello, a real-life African-Brazilian entertainer,[18] she prepares us to appreciate the amount of strength and stamina required to resist the anonymity of difference. Caliban, the last of Marshall's aging figures, literally fights to reclaim his identity.

"Brazil"

Marshall begins "Brazil" with the "whinnying chord" of the trumpet and the "erotic beat of the samba," and we move to the glittering night life of Rio de Janeiro where colonization, under the Portuguese, takes on a different shape. We are in the Casa Samba watching *O Grande Caliban e a Pequena Miranda.* The act begins:

> There was a rap on the drums and Miranda clutched one of her buttocks as if she had been struck there; another rap, louder this time, and she clutched the other, feigning shock and outrage.
>
> "Hey, lemme in, stupid!" a rough male voice called in Portuguese behind her, and she whirled like a door that had been kicked open as a dark, diminutive figure burst around her thigh, wearing a scarlet shirt with billowing sleeves and a huge *C* embroidered on the breast like the device of a royal house, a pair of oversized fighter's trunks of the same scarlet which fell past his knees and a prize fighter's high laced shoes. (132–33)

In and of itself, this description may not strike the reader as particularly funny, but imagine the woman, unusually tall and long-limbed, to be taking mincing steps across the stage. Imagine her having white skin and blond hair piled high atop her head and wearing a "brief costume of sequins and tulle." Then try to picture this Amazon feigning fear and intimidation and singing with a timid, soprano voice. Against this image place a black man, a dwarf, bellowing out "an ominous bass." Finally, envision him as old and decrepit but moving with such agility as to astound. The author tells us that his boxing maneuvers were "so brilliantly timed, so visually lethal, that those in the audience who had never seen him before jerked their heads out of the way of that fist. 'Joe Louis, the champion,' he cried, and held up a triumphant right hand" (133–34). The contrast created could be hysterically funny, especially during the finale when the roles are reversed and Miranda scoops "Caliban up with one hand and [marches] triumphantly off stage with him kicking, his small arms flailing, high above her head" (136).

This contrast, suggests Marshall, could invite another form of hysteria. Consider the audience's reaction:

> The audience laughed, but for reasons other than his jokes: The Brazilians out of affection and loyalty, and the tourists, mostly Americans from a Moore-McCormack ship in the harbor, out of a sense of their own well-being and in relief—relief because in the beginning when Caliban's dark face had appeared around Miranda's white thigh they had tensed, momentarily outraged and alarmed until, with smiles that kept slipping out of place, they had reminded each other that this was Brazil after all, where white was never wholly white, no matter how pure it looked. They had begun laughing then in loud, self-conscious gusts, turning to each other for cues and reassurance, whispering, "I don't know why I'm laughing. I don't understand a word of Spanish. Or is this the place where they speak Portuguese?" (136)

No comment seems necessary on these senseless, paranoid fantasies about interracial sex and white supremacy. But Marshall's story is about an African-Brazilian searching for his own identity, not so much because of his color but because his real self has been nearly obliterated by some "vague elusive form outside him."

Heitor Baptiste Guimares, whose stage name is Caliban, has recently decided to retire from show business, and he is understandably ambivalent about leaving the world he has grown to know so intimately. After more than thirty-five years of performing burlesque and a number of slapstick routines, the prize-fighter's routine has really made him famous. In fact, the caricature is so well known that it has become his trademark, and people find it difficult to separate the real Guimares from O Grande Caliban.

The positing of opposites is particularly prominent in this tale. From the physical description of the characters to the contrast between the hillside and the city, contradictions and incongruities prevail. Indeed, at the heart of Caliban's comic act is a series of extended contradictions. The same might be said of Caliban, whose perceptions of his diminutive size contribute to his problem. He remembers the demeanor he assumed when he became famous:

> He had held himself like a military man, then, very erect, his small shoulders squared, all of him stretching it seemed toward the height which had been denied him—and this martial stance, so incongruous somehow, had won him the almost hysterical admiration of the crowds. Yet, in the midst of this admiration, he had always felt vaguely like a small animal who had been fitted out in an absurd costume and trained to amuse, some Lilliputian in a kingdom of giants who had to play the jester in order to survive. The world had been scaled without him in mind—and his rage and contempt for it and for those who belonged was always just behind his smile, in the vain, superior lift of his head, in his every gesture. (140)

It might seem odd that someone so preoccupied with his height would ally himself with someone who, by comparison, is a Titan, but Caliban understands what it is like to be different, and he included Miranda in his act, initially, for effect. She has no talent, he explains to his valet, Henriques, but she does have imagination. As a matter of fact, it was she who thought up the prize-fighter routine. Over the years, however, she has become more demanding of a larger role and more demanding of Caliban's energies. "Perhaps I would have another five, ten years left if not for her. She has become a bane. She has used me till I'm dry, the pig!" Although they now openly hate each other, Caliban admits that Miranda has been something of a "weakness" with him. He has continued to indulge and pamper her even after his arranged marriage to young Clara, the daughter of a distant cousin.

Caliban's age is affecting both his attitude and his professional performance, and though the acrobatics he executes look "effortless," his "outraged muscles rebel" and his "joints stiffen angrily." Marshall describes his face as "lined with wrinkles which like fine incisions had drawn his features into an indistinct knot." This lack of distinction is significant to the dilemma at hand. Marshall provides a closer look:

> Without the make-up [his face] reminded him of a piece of old fruit so shriveled and spotted with decay that there was no certainty as to what it had been originally. Above all, once he removed the make-up, his face was without expression, bland, as though only on stage made up as Caliban in the scarlet shirt and baggy trunks was he at all certain of who he was. Caliban might have become his reality. (139–40)

And this is the crucial concern of the main character, for when asked his real name, he has to stop and think. Now that he is retiring and the advertisements announcing his last performance will be in place tomorrow, he wants to resume his real identity. A series of subsequent events, however, make him rebel against accepting the bitter knowledge that the real Heitor Baptiste Guimares has been all but effaced.

As in the previous novellas, the author augments her theme by integrating aspects of the physical surroundings with her characters' psychological condition. In this instance, Caliban notices the details of the distant mountain and subconsciously parallels them with his lost identity. "What had been for years just another detail in the familiar frieze that was Rio," adds the narrator, "was suddenly separate and distinct, restored." Caliban's ambivalence and apprehension are apparent. What little pleasure he derives from the thought of the wind tearing down the signs that announce his retirement is quickly dispelled when American tourists recognize him as Caliban. In a voice "loud and severe, addressed not only to them but to the mountain and the night," Caliban cries, "Heitor Baptiste Guimares." His insistence that he be granted his true identity is just beginning to surface, and as the unfamiliar name continues to echo in his mind, he feels suddenly alone.

This episode is quickly followed by another seemingly harmless encounter with his wife, Clara. Given the preceding novellas, we may be tempted to speculate that Caliban's twenty-five-year-old bride represents his yearning for lost youth. But Clara becomes a symbol for something else which, while connected with his youth, is more directly aligned with his present dilemma. As Caliban watches her sleep in mildness and repose (an attitude so discordant with his troubled state of mind), he recalls their first meeting in the small town of Minas Gerais where he had been born. In explaining his adoration for the girl, the author tells us that "he had almost instinctively crossed himself."

> She had looked like a Madonna painted black. He had wanted to confess to her as to a priest, seeing her that first time. He would have confessed now if he could have named his fear—whispering to her while she slept. And she would have, blindly in her sleep, curved her body to receive him, nesting him within the warm hollow of her back as if he were the child she bore. He hesitated though feeling, oddly, that he was no longer entitled to her comfort, just as he was no longer entitled to use the name Caliban. (152–53)

Exhausted, Caliban falls asleep quickly to dreams of being "caught in a mine shaft without a lantern to light his way." Clara, it is inferred, might be his source of light.

When Caliban awakens, still fully clothed, Clara has already attended mass and is standing "like a petitioner in the doorway, holding a cup of coffee as though it were an offering" (153). "Is there a wind, today?"

Caliban asks, and the narrator reminds us that the old man's thoughts have been of the signs announcing his retirement. He is driven by a deep-seated need to reestablish his identity, and this need compels him to delve into his past. Time takes on special significance when he asks Clara what her mother and grandmother had said of him as a young man before his fame. However, Clara cannot recall, and Caliban's disappointment is wrenching. He seems especially annoyed when Clara attempts to adjust to the new name by repeating as if mesmerized, "Heitor Guimares . . . Senhora Guimares." She explains, "[I]t's just that until I get used to it I will keep looking for someone else when I say it. I'm so used to you being Caliban" (156).

Memories of his former life seem unable to shape themselves in his mind until Caliban vaguely remembers the restaurant where he used to wait tables. A concrete link to his past, this memory pushes him toward the Rua Gloria, where he spent his boyhood. His hopeful anticipation becomes a descent into time:

> Parking his car, he started down, eagerly suddenly. Instinctively, as if the years had not passed, his legs made the slight adjustment to the sloping street and his feet sought out the old holes in the pavement; halfway down he passed the boys' school and his head turned automatically, expecting the boys in the yard to wave and shout, "Ohla, Senhor Heitor, when are you going to stop growing?" (159)

Instead, he is greeted by a retinue of school boys, one of whom simulates the famous "fighter's crouch" while shouting, "O Grande Caliban." As the others join in a chorus of praise, Caliban stiffens each time they sound his stage name. But the children become a buffer of sorts, "a solid wall between him and the apprehensiveness which trailed him. Because of them he was certain that he would find the restaurant intact, like the setting of a play which had not been dismantled" (160).

The theatrical imagery is certainly appropriate to the make-believe existence that Caliban has led and to add a fanciful touch, a huge sign reads "BEBE COCA-COLA" has miraculously replaced what used to be an expansive awning. As if transported to another time period, Caliban sees the "modern glass front" that proclaims the new name of the restaurant, O RESTAURANTE GRANDE CALIBAN. Caliban's fantasy becomes a monstrous nightmare as he notices the changes that obliterate his past:

> . . . the tile floor whose every imperfection he could have traced in the dark had been covered in bright linoleum; chrome chairs and tables had replaced the marble tables and wire-back chairs, while booths covered in

> simulated leather lined one wall. The air smelled of stale coffee and . . .
> Caliban, jarred by the sight of faded newspaper photographs of himself
> crowding the walls and a garish oil painting of him in the scarlet shirt
> hanging over the bar, placed his hand on a table to steady himself. (160)

He is greeted warmly by the current owner of the restaurant, a Sarara,
who proudly presents what is a veritable shrine. A Sarara, we deduce, is a
Brazilian of mixed African blood who has very light, often freckled skin,
agate eyes (sometimes bluish-green), and reddish, kinky or curly hair. But
this color distinction seems only a point of information to increase the reader's
knowledge of the extensive dispersal of blacks throughout the Western
hemisphere. The restaurant owner's fictional purpose is to lead Caliban to
Nacimento, whose name, significantly, means "birth." He is the old man
who not only hired Heitor so long ago to wait tables but who also encouraged him to enter the amateur contest at *Teatro Municipal.* It was Nacimento
who had accompanied Heitor that night when his identity became another's.

Although Caliban cannot summon up the image of Nacimento's face,
he feels that if he can find the old man, who now lives in one of the *favelas*
above Copacabana, his lost identity might be restored. The author presents here the contrast between the city and the hillside and, at the same
time, reveals the devastating effects of Western colonization:

> He could see just above him the beginning of the slums—a vast, squalid
> rookery for the poor of Rio clinging to the hill above Copacabana, a nest
> of shacks built with refuse of the city: the discarded crates and boxes, bits
> of galvanized iron and tin, old worm-eaten boards and shingles—and all
> of this piled in confused, listing tiers along the hillside, the wood bleached
> gray by the sun. The *favela* was another city above Rio which boldly
> tapped its electricity from below—so that at night the hills were strewn
> with lights—and repulsed the government's efforts to remove it. It was an
> affront—for that squalor rising above Rio implied that Rio herself was
> only a pretense; it was a threat—for it seemed that at any moment the
> *favela* would collapse and hurtle down, burying the city below. (163)

The imagery of the fantastic is sustained as we are told that Caliban had
long ceased to see the ugliness there. Since his stardom, it might have
been for him a mirage—a sight too painfully familiar to acknowledge.
Now, however, the *favelas* are real. He recalls "the stories of strangers who
had ventured into the *favelas* and had either disappeared or been found
garotted the next day at the foot of the hill" (164). Such thoughts conjure
up visions of his own death, and Caliban sees "the thronged cathedrals,
the crowds standing a thousand deep outside, the city hung in crepe; he

heard the priest intoning his name—and at the thought that perhaps no one would recognize the name Heitor Guimares, he stumbled and nearly fell" (164). His fear of total oblivion becomes more conceivable.

We see something of an African cultural survival in Marshall's description of the children of the *favela*, "some of them balancing gallon tins of water on their heads or smaller children on their hips." And we also see something that has been suggested in this collection as a whole: an unending cycle of defeat when values alien to the indigenous population begin to destroy the lives of the young. The children "seemed born of the dust which covered them, like small, tough plants sprung from the worn soil, and their flat, incurious eyes seemed to mirror the defeated lives they had yet to live" (164).

The youngsters guard their terrain with the caution of their elders, and it is not until they are convinced that Caliban is a friend that they point out Nacimento's house, situated "beside the tree without a head." The dead palm, without its "headdress of fronds," symbolizes an existence bereft of an identity and, significantly, it resembles a "derisive finger," pointing the way to darkness and doom. Even the makeshift house beside it becomes a darkened tomb, for inside is a lonely and feeble man who, in his blindness, prefers the shadows to the light. Caliban remembers how the old man used to send him "to roll down the restaurant awning against the sun each afternoon."

Although Caliban is persistent in his efforts to help Nacimento recall the former days, the old man repeats, "I know no Heitor." But it is with pride and admiration that he does remember O Grande Caliban. Caliban's defeat seems nearly complete as he realizes that the old man "had retained only a few things: his fear of the sun, the name O Grande Caliban, a moment of success in a crowded theater in which he had shared. That was all. The rest had been stripped away in preparation for his death which, in a way, had already begun" (168). Groping toward the door, Caliban jars a table, causing a cup to fall and break, and we recall the cup he had broken earlier. The day has come full circle, and finding no satisfaction, Caliban returns to the city.

Marshall creates Miranda to reflect the city. "In her need to dominate, Miranda is the W.A.S.P. woman who is the microcosm of a self-destructive world."[19] Indeed, Miranda replaces Shakespeare's Prospero as the dominant figure, forecasting Marshall's later depiction in *The Chosen Place* of the white woman as the power behind Western imperialism. In "Brazil" Miranda's might is given special attention:

> She filled the night club with a powerful animal presence with a decisive, passionless air that was somehow Germanic. And she was part-German,

one of those Brazilians from Rio Grande do Sul who are mixed German, Portuguese, native Indian and sometimes African. With her the German had triumphed. She was a Brunhilda without her helmet and girdle of mail, without her spear. (132)

Wagnerian imagery is mixed with revisions of Shakespeare's *The Tempest,* but we prepare ourselves for the storm that has been brewing. Marshall turns to the physical environment once again as she describes Miranda's apartment as emblematic of Rio:

The great squares of black and white tile in the foyer suggested not only the stark white buildings reared against the dark hills and the sidewalks of Copacabana—a painstaking mosaic of small black and white stones, but the faces of the *Cariocas* themselves—endless combinations of black and white. The green rug in the living room would have been a swatch cut from one of the hills, while the other furnishings there—elaborate period pieces of an ivory finish, marble tables cluttered with figurines, sofas of pale silk and down, white drapes and gilt-edged mirrors—repeated the opulence, self-indulgence, the lavish whiteness of the city. (170)

Caliban is aware of his own inconsequence to the city and, by extension, to Miranda, when he sees himself reflected in one of the mirrors: "He was like a house pet, a tiny dog, who lent the room an amusing touch but had no real place there. The pale walls and ivory furniture, the abundance of white throughout stripped him of importance, denied him all significance" (171). We recall his earlier comparison to a small animal trained to amuse, but as in Shakespeare's dramatic rendition, Caliban's trainers had not anticipated ingratitude. The author builds suspense through her continued play upon opposites. Miranda has already dressed her hair and applied her make-up in preparation for the evening show. In a sheer pink dressing gown, she sits "enthroned in splendor" while "her maid massage[s] her feet in a basin of scented water—the girl's black hands wavering out of shape under the water" (171). Caliban glimpses her breasts and feels alternately "repelled, weary and then angry again." Another realization becomes conscious: "He understood suddenly that her refusal ever to leave him and marry, to have children and use those ample breasts, was, simply, her desire to remain the child herself—willful, dependent, indulged—and that she had used him to this end, just as she would use someone else now that she had exhausted him." (171).

As in the calm before the storm, Caliban quietly dismisses the maid and "deliberately [places] his trouser leg with the red dust and clay from the *favela* against the pink coverlet." This symbolic juxtaposition denoting Caliban's origins creates a mounting tension that crescendos with Miranda's shrill cries. The tension is increased as Caliban, still calm, says, "Tell me, do you know a Heitor Guimares?" Miranda is clearly frightened by Caliban's puzzling behavior, but his refusal to answer her questions about Heitor Guimares goads her on to an extended tirade in which she attacks everything in his life from his peasant background to his child bride and his senile hallucinations. When Caliban finally responds, again with calmness, "I am Heitor Guimares," Miranda can only reenact the stunt she had made famous for him.

Without warning, the tempest hits, and within moments, the bedroom with its shattered chandeliers, smashed mirrors, slashed sofas, and overturned furniture is embroiled in a swirl of down feathers. To connect his outward behavior with his inner turmoil, the narrator explains: "It was as if the illusion of strength he had created on stage for so long had been finally given to him. With each blow he felt the confusion and despair congested within him fall away, leaving the emptiness which, he knew, would remain with him until he died" (176).

The tale moves toward its resolution not with the "sound of the trumpet the night before" but with Miranda's piercing shriek. As she rushes toward Caliban, now standing atop a marble table and wielding a curtain rod, "he leaned down and struck her with his small fist on her head and the hair cascaded down like a curtain over her stunned face" (177). No theatrics come into play when she speaks the words of the finale: "What did I do? Was it me, Caliban, *meu,* was it me" (177).

The implications of the final lines suggest that Miranda's view (and therefore Rio's view) of Caliban is predicated upon color. Certainly, as we have seen, Marshall is concerned with describing the various combinations of black and white. But Marshall's much greater concern is to examine the human problem of discovering one's identity in a complex cultural and social foundation. It is not a casual observation when she writes that Miranda had created Caliban's image for him. This is not to exonerate Caliban, for he has become so caught up in catering to the worthless values of a world which refuses to see him as an individual in his own right that even he has lost all sight of who he is. He has become, by the story's end, a monster violently groping for some tangible means of making his life of pretense real. His final outburst proves that he, like his Shakespearean counterpart, has learned to curse those who have taught him their language. A spark of hope flickers at the resolution, however; instead of accepting old age and loneliness, Caliban is fighting back.

If we view *Soul Clap Hands and Sing* as a single piece, the author strikes an optimistic note in what may otherwise seem a dreary pronouncement about aging. By ordering the stories as she does, Marshall shows a progression toward wholeness. Though her several characters respond differently to the contours of colonialism, they point toward the road of possibility. Certainly this is the case for Caliban in the last novella. Instead of the lonely final moments experienced by the other characters in this collection, he has vitality enough at least to begin composing a new song (and perhaps in a new tongue). Paule Marshall "sails the seas" to create in *Soul Clap Hands and Sing* her own "artifice of eternity." By describing the lives of lonely old men facing real-life dilemmas and obsessions, she helps us to appreciate more fully the process by which the contemporary New World exacts opposing values and allegiances, especially among men. Remaining in the background, however, is Marshall's persistent concern for the female who is sexually harassed or exploited. In her later fiction, this concern will dominate her work. In *Soul Clap Hands and Sing,* however, she loudly sings of what is past or passing or to come. And as if to insure that her song becomes a "monument of unaging intellect," she dedicates the book to her son, who may represent the next cautionary generation—a generation attuned and attentive to gender inequities within the Western patriarchal system of practices and beliefs.

Chapter Four

Maturation and Multiplicity in Consciousness

The Short Stories

The fiction I consider in this chapter reflects Marshall's increasing mastery of the short story form and her experimentation with plot construction and character delineation. I use the word *experimentation* to suggest that many of the patterns and images the author describes in these short selections are later augmented and perfected to give her longer fiction full verisimilitude within artistically contrived structures. Experimentation also refers to the author's multiple cultural identity, which ultimately does not allow one to obscure the other. In the short stories, Marshall begins to draw more consciously from her knowledge of African cultural survivals as they function in contemporary African-American, West Indian–American, and African-Caribbean societies. In them she sketches more consciously the lines of the African-centered epistemology that informs her opus as a whole.

"Reena," "Some Get Wasted" and "To Da-duh: In Memoriam"—all written during the sixties—are direct reflections of the cultural fervor of that period. Black nationalism, as a political and aesthetic ideology, swept the country and provided for African Americans the inspiration for the bold, defiant, and jubilant voice that was soon to change the tone and content of both American politics and American letters. Indeed, in many if not most instances, politics and art were deliberately brought together to create a decidedly new and exhilarating social consciousness. A case in point was Marshall's membership in the Association of Artists for Freedom, an organization created shortly after the 1963 church bombing in Birmingham, Alabama, where four little black girls were killed by racist whites. The association, which included such notable artists as Ossie Davis, Ruby Dee, and the late John O. Killens, resolved "to impress upon other Blacks the necessity to be actively involved in the independence of their own people." To that end, they even proposed a national economic boycott the following Christmas. Without the support of the NAACP, however, their efforts were unsuccessful.[1]

But other political and social upheavals across the country inspired a dramatic transformation in African-American literature, especially in poetry and theater. The first was readily accessible to the black population through private printings of small collections or through small black presses; the second was accessible through amateur or professional performances supported by repertory theaters, which began to flourish in major cities. It was also significant that various African nations gained independence during the 1960s, and expressions of black pride were evident in open identification with things African: fashion, hairstyles, languages, etc. Among people of color, then, it might be said that assimilation of a different order (a reverse direction) was taking place. As Roy Bryce LaPorte wrote: "The more minute (not necessarily minor) differences [were] apparently . . . sublimated; terms such as "Black," "Afro-American," and "African" [acquired] symbolically generic properties—representing a rising consciousness of kind which [transcended] formerly accepted (or imposed) distinctions of tribes, statuses, shades, colonial states, religions, and language groups."[2]

"Black is beautiful" was the popular slogan resurrected from the 1920s and 30s, and all elements of black culture began to be interpreted with new insight and pride. And in their search to uncover their unique cultural heritage—to celebrate the positive values inherent in black cultural traditions—black artists turned more decisively to the folk heritage. No longer writing to appeal to white society, they began to focus exclusively upon audiences of color, using black settings, black themes, black language and customs. Further, the "Black arts writers insisted that their works be evaluated only by critics sympathetic to the Black Arts Movement."[3] Marshall, though not specifically identified with this movement, was sensitive to the transformations in African-American life and drew upon themes compatible with the tenets of the Black Arts Movement. Divorced in 1963, she also experienced a personal transformation as she struggled to write her next novel, which, significantly, centers her artistic imagination not in America but in the Caribbean.

Through the range of settings in her short fiction, Marshall illustrates the differences within the amalgam of experience loosely referred to as "black." Black cultural diversity is evident not only in the story lines but also in the imagery used in each short story. In "Reena" the images reflect American subcultures: traditional Jewish, African-American, West Indian–American. In "Some Get Wasted" and in "To Da-duh: In Memoriam" the images are African-American and African-Caribbean, respectively, but especially in the latter story, the African world looms large to suggest the author's continuing movement toward a symbolic ancestral homeland. In all these short stories, the author presents a panoramic view of a multicultural society with which she is personally familiar. The strains of each seem to pull her in several directions, for she embodies all these cultural variants. She, of course, sees distinctions in her role as a black woman which, on the one hand, makes her a member (albeit secondary) of a male-dominated society and, on the other hand, excludes her (albeit racially) as a social outcast.

Although Marshall's experience as a first-generation African American closely parallels that of her African-Caribbean kin, the careful reader can detect differences that mark the separate cultures. An obvious distinction is in the language. Through characters like Aunt Vi and Da-duh, we once again are treated to the flavor and rhythmic lilt of the West Indian dialect already transcribed for us in *Brown Girl, Brownstones.* Another distinction can be readily deduced: West Indian immigrants traveled to America of their own volition in pursuit of the American Dream. African Americans, we know, did not have this option. Thus, as I have already discussed in chapter 2, the two groups hold very different perceptions of "the land of opportunity." Finally, these short stories examine lower-class black American life and middle-class black immigrant life. Such classifications become artificial when viewed by the dominant society, for both groups are black and therefore relegated to second-class citizenship. What is of primary importance to Marshall, however, is the journey toward her own reconciliation with her immediate society and the larger world. In all the short stories discussed below, she documents her own search for a single unambiguous cultural source with which to identify. She also suggests that black societies, in spite of varying histories, reflect elements of a core African value system.[4]

"Reena"

Her first and only commissioned piece, "Reena," first appeared in *Harper's* October 1962 special supplement on the "American Female." "Reena" deals with the conflicting attitudes of creative women who struggle with the questions of their responsibilities as women, as wives, as mothers. This time, however, the questions are entertained by women with whom Marshall is most familiar: urban, middle-class, West Indian–American black women—those educated women of her own generation who understand the historical and social dimensions that shaped their own particularized responses to racism, sexism, and classism.

Choosing to write in the first person, the author immediately draws us into her private world of memories. Our suspicion that what we are about to read is autobiographical is confirmed when we learn that the narrator is a writer named Paulie. Further, we read that the story takes place in Brooklyn, the place of Marshall's birth. Briefly we see the world of a traditional Jewish community where "Sunday became Saturday, with all the stores open and pushcarts piled with vegetables and yard goods lined up along the curb, a crowded place where people hawked and spat freely in the streaming gutters and the men looked as if they had just stepped from the pages of the Old Testament with their profuse beards and long, black, satin coats."[5] Marshall's description of Brooklyn, however, is targeted upon a small West Indian community where the brownstones of old have been replaced by city housing projects. A tone of sad nostalgia is evoked as she writes of the bittersweet period in which she "served out her girlhood."

But Marshall is careful to make a distinction between the people and the places of her past. The former represent a community whose faces are but "myriad reflections" of her own. She continues: "'Whenever I encounter them at a funeral or a wake, the wedding or christening—those ceremonies by which the past reaffirms its hold—my guard drops and memories banished to the rear of my mind rush forward to rout the present'" (156). It is during one such ceremony, a funeral and a wake, that Paulie, after a twenty-year separation, is reunited with her friend Reena.

The story proper covers a period of only one long night, but compressed in that brief period is the history of generations of black men and women. The author's manipulation of time may be seen as a "symbolic victory" over the chaos and dispossession that mar the lives of black people in general.[6] Her major concern, however, is the black woman. In the words of the narrator, Reena's story explores "'the most critical fact of my existence—that definition of me, of her [Reena] and millions like us, formulated by others to serve out their fantasies, a definition we have to combat at an unconscionable cost to the self and even use, at times, in order to survive; the cause of so much shame and rage as well as, oddly enough, a source of pride: simply, what it has meant, what it means, to be a black woman in America.'" (155)

Marshall writes a story within a story, and it is so densely packed with historical and cultural information, so intense in its portrayal of ambiva-

lent attitudes and emotions, that it is difficult to offer a coherent inter-
pretation. "Reena" has no conventional plot line clearly delineating action that rises to a central conflict, reaches the point of climax, and ends
with a standard resolution. Rather, there seems to be a series of plots in
which conflict is assumed as part of the daily facts of black life. Resolution becomes not only a desirable end to perpetual conflict but, importantly, an essential impetus to continued existence. Only two active characters (the narrator and Reena) are foregrounded, and they become almost
archetypal in nature, representing the millions of black women who have
shared the experiences described. Furthermore, the story often reads like
an essay, for scattered throughout are passages that clarify the ideas presented.[7] Curiously enough, this authorial intrusion does not take away
from the tale because, in many respects, we need a guiding hand to comprehend a pattern of life that is "foreign" to some and not yet articulated
for others. Marshall has already suggested in the passage quoted above
that the lives of black women have been all too frequently misinterpreted—most often to the detriment of black women. Reena's story seems
to offer a perspective that emphasizes the positive values of the black female experience. Perhaps this explains the titular character's name, which
in Hebrew means "joy." In a sense, the story documents Marshall's own
life as a black woman growing in maturity during the 50s and 60s. As we
begin to understand her purpose to show in microcosm the pain, the
beauty, and the strength of a minority group experience, authorial intrusion becomes authorial inclusion instead. The result is a picture that is
totally unified in its theme of collecting from one's heritage the strength
and vision to live with purpose and dignity.

The secondary story, which really takes prominence, extends over a period of several years and is a synopsis of Reena's life. However, it is framed
within the setting of an evening wake typical of African-American and
African-Caribbean cultures. The two major characters remove themselves
from the immediate scene and become engaged in a conversation which,
on the surface, seems totally irrelevant to—perhaps even irreverent toward—the solemn occasion that has brought them together. As the others conduct their own private ritual, Reena is given full sway to describe
the people and the events that have most influenced the direction of her
life. To repeat the episodes of the main character's life would entail too
lengthy a discussion. For the black female reader who nods assent to nearly
every detail, the episodes might even appear redundant. Perhaps it is in
recognition of this that Marshall chooses an unusual approach.

Early in the story, we learn that Reena has long possessed the sense of
purpose that marks her character. From the moment she enters the church
where the funeral service for Aunt Vi is being held, her presence seems to

command attention. The narrator explains, "It was as though she, not the minister, were coming to officiate" (155). Through flashback we are told that even as a child, "she seemed defined . . . all of a piece, the raw edges of her adolescence smoothed over" (156). Paulie remembers Reena as precocious, socially responsible, and politically conscious of the larger world around her. Her college years were filled with the crusading efforts of a young woman seriously committed to social equality and justice. She picketed, boycotted, handed out leaflets, solicited signatures for petitions—all of which eventually led to her temporary suspension from college.

As Reena talks of occasional romances, we realize how perceptions of color affect the black woman who is constantly bombarded with white society's standards of beauty: it is an experience of painful rejection that often leads to a negative self-image. Reena is not alone as she describes the psychic wounds inflicted because of the imprint of color. "'Like nearly every little black girl, I had my share of dreams waking up to find myself with long, blonde curls, blue eyes, and skin like milk'" (158).[8] Rejection by one's own, however, carries the more devastating effect, and Reena is subjected to the humiliation and shame of being denied an innocent romance simply because the boy's parents see her as too dark: "'We live surrounded by white images, and white in this world is synonymous with the good, light, beauty, success, so that despite ourselves sometimes, we run after that whiteness and deny our darkness, which has been made into a symbol of all that is evil and inferior. I wasn't a person to that boy's parents, but a symbol of the darkness they were in flight from'" (158).

Color, as a symbol and as a reality, impinges upon Reena's sense of self when she is involved with a white student: "'Bob was always, for some odd reason, talking about how much the Negro suffered, and although I would agree with him, I would also try to get across that, you know, like all people we also had fun once in a while, loved our children, liked making love—that we were human beings for God's sake. But he only wanted to hear about the suffering.'" (159) The relationship ends when Bob insists that she meet his father, who is visiting New York. The author's allusion to Conrad's "Heart of Darkness" is poignant: "'I'll never forget or forgive the look on that old man's face when he opened his hotel-room door and saw me. The horror. I might have been the personification of every evil in the world'" (159).

Bob's reaction is a laughter filled with vengeance—not against Reena, but against himself, against his own uncertainty, against his father with whom he shared a painful relationship. Reena, however, cannot be completely exonerated and confesses that she had used Bob "to get at that white world which had not only denied [her], but had turned [her] own against [her]" (159). Somewhat like Conrad's Kurtz, who loses his past in order for his true self to emerge, so also the truth of Reena's life emerges. Significantly different, however, is that her past cannot be lost; it is inextricably woven into her present life. Both the then and the now must be confronted and ordered before the confusion that prevails can be dispelled.

At times, Reena is able to use her color to advantage. Speaking at a college debate on McCarthyism, she seems intimidating not only because of her radical position but also because of "the sheer impact of her blackness in their white midst." Paulie recalls the following:

> Her color might have been a weapon she used to dazzle and disarm her opponents. And she had highlighted it with the clothes she was wearing: a white dress patterned with large blocks of primary colors I remember (it looked Mexican) and a pair of intricately wrought silver earrings—long and with many little parts which clashed like muted cymbals over the microphone each time she moved her head. She wore her hair cropped short like a boy's and it was not straightened like mine and the other Negro girls' in the audience, but left in its coarse natural state: a small forest under which her face emerged in its intense and startling handsomeness. (158)[9]

Her hair and her colorful, conspicuous presence contribute to Reena's self-acceptance. In embracing her African ancestry, she develops the strength to combat all that the white world refuses her.

That strength is built upon the foundation of the extended family, which may be defined as a "philosophical orientation" toward a group identity. The priority afforded the community in traditional African society is widely documented. Marshall seems to acknowledge contemporary kinship patterns as but a variant of that family system. Reena's graduation from college, for instance, represents not just a personal accomplishment but a triumph for both her mother and father and their parents before them. "'It was as if I had made up for the generations his people had picked cotton in Georgia and my mother's family had cut cane in the West Indies'" (160). The extended ties are also connected through the relationship of the major characters' mothers. They had known each other since childhood in Barbados and, further, it was they who initiated—more accurately "forced"—the relationship between Reena and Paulie. Aunt Vi provides another example. While she is blood related to Reena, she is godmother to the narrator, who also refers to the woman as aunt. Both women know that because of her sleep-in job, Aunt Vi seldom enjoyed her bed of roses ("the pink satin bedspread with roses of the same material strewn over its surface"). Now seated on that bed, another generation connects once again with the now deceased family member. Over and over again,

Marshall shows us both obvious and subtle connections between individuals who have shared a similar space in time and who have gained from that sharing a special insight about conquering its exigencies to keep their past, present, and future communities intact. In both fact and symbol, the community thrives beyond temporal measurement to embrace perpetual duration.[10]

While this perpetuity is affirmed in the reunion between Paulie and Reena, it is also celebrated in the wake itself. With the juxtaposition of specific cultural rituals that mark the actual beginnings and endings of life, the author seems to be moving toward an exploration of the cyclical nature of time as perceived by traditional African societies. Contrary to the notion of death as the termination of life, it becomes for this small West Indian community a celebration of the continuity of life. Again we see a clear example of an African cultural survival. John S. Mbiti explains that in traditional African society, the departed one, while physically dead, is categorized as the "living-dead." That is, as long as the deceased is "alive in the memory of those who knew him in his life as well as being alive in the world of spirits, . . . he is in a state of personal immortality."[11] Marshall seems to be illustrating this concept.

The author's description of the wake is also reflective of traditional African rituals for the dead. Foods and drink, gaiety and laughter attend the present ceremony in which friends and relatives gather at the home of Aunt Vi to commemorate her special inclusion. Appropriate to the festivities is a bit of comic relief, which is provided by a brief reference to the time Aunt Vi "had missed the excursion boat to Atlantic City and had held her own private picnic—complete with pigeon peas and rice and fricassee chicken—on the pier at 42nd Street" (156–57). Such memories distinguish the woman's personality and are retained as a part of the present celebration, the recollection of which will ensure her imprint upon the future.

Time recedes to the past as Reena recalls her earlier, promising marriage to Dave, a talented and ambitious photographer. They were so compatible and happy together that Reena confesses to being "frightened at times." "Not that anything would change between us," she explains, "but that someone or something in the world outside us would invade our private place and destroy us out of envy" (162). That something is reflected in Dave's "diffidence"; his need for success seems second only to his fear of it. This is a problem with which Reena cannot cope, and "for her own sanity" she returns to work.

It is not difficult to hear reverberating in Reena's tale echoes from "The Valley Between." Like Abe, Dave is threatened by Reena's interests in things outside the home. He interprets them as "a way of pointing up his deficiencies." Additionally, he must take on new family responsibilities, which he resents. Note the similarities between Cassie's predicament and Reena's: "After a time we both got caught up in this thing, an ugliness came between us, and I began to answer his anger with anger and to trade insult for insult" (162). But there is a significant difference between the husbands' predicaments. We are never told what Abe does for a living, though he seems satisfied with his work. Dave, on the other hand, is dissatisfied. Despite the professional recognition he has gained through various awards and photographic exhibits, he "also wanted the big, gaudy commercial success that would dazzle and confound the white world downtown and force it to *see* him" (162). His reluctance to try leads to a defensive posture. The effects of racism combined with sexism and low self-esteem bring about the inevitable divorce.

Reena also differs from Cassie in that she refuses to capitulate to the bitterness of a relationship that provides no mutual fulfillment. It is only in retrospect, however, that she can posit at least a tentative answer to the question first raised in "The Valley Between": On whose terms must individual value be determined? Referring to black men, she states: "'We have got to understand them and save them for ourselves. . . . By being, on the one hand, persons in our own right and, on the other, fully the woman and the wife'" (161). This is indeed a tall order for the woman who suffers under the double constraints of racism and sexism. In fact, it calls for devotion and strength that seem nearly impossible to achieve. But Marshall, through the story, firmly believes that the history of the black woman confirms her ability to survive. She seems to resolve that the black woman must take charge of her life and accept the responsibility for her decisions. There is, of course, a sacrifice to be made, and both Paulie and Reena can identify that sacrifice as being alone and lonely. Consider, for a moment, the difficulties involved in finding a suitable mate. Reena tells us that the black woman who has sought to improve her lot by getting an education and a decent job is really at a disadvantage. Her "intellectual or professional peers," if they marry at all, tend to choose the younger woman without a degree or they marry white women. This is an ire-provoking subject for many black women, and the author minces no words in presenting their long-standing grievances.

In a call-and-response fashion, Reena and Paulie recite the reasons some black men offer for preferring white women to black. The familiar accusations range from black women's sexual inhibition ("and the old myth of excessive sexuality goes out the window") to castrating independence. On an intellectual level, the two women can understand a black man's right to choose a white mate. "In fact," quips Reena, "some of my best friends are white women" (161). Emotionally, however, the resentment runs deep.

The pain, the anger, the understanding, and the compassion are evident as Reena summarizes: "'They condemn us . . . without taking history into account. We are still, most of us, the black woman who had to be almost frighteningly strong in order for us all to survive. For, after all, she was the one whom they left (and I don't hold this against them; I understand) with the children to raise, who had to make it somehow or other. And we are still, many of us, living that history.'" (161) In this brief passage, Marshall hones in on the myth of the matriarchy, a theme which had already been addressed in her first major novel, *Brown Girl, Brownstones.* In many respects, Reena may be seen as an heiress of that indomitable spirit reflected in the characterization of Silla Boyce. But an indomitable spirit is not to be equated with power—strength, perhaps, but not power.

Reena considers the historical circumstances of powerlessness for both the black male and the black female when she speaks of her resolve to spend an indefinite period of time in Africa with her children: "'It is important that they see black people who have truly a place and history of their own and who are building for a new and, hopefully, more sensible world. And I must see it, get close to it because I can never lose the sense of being a displaced person here in America because of my color'" (163). Reena's sense of displacement leads her to question the very essence of American life "with its complacency and materialism, its soullessness" (16). Although she realizes she should stay and fight for change, Reena is determined to travel to Africa.

This journey to Africa, though actual in intent, is equally symbolic. It signals Marshall's abiding concern for the need to establish cultural roots—not just to locate one's ancestral source, but to glean from one's historical past the values that have proven viable and sustaining. As Mary Helen Washington observes: "Reena and Paulie, as representatives of the next generation, review Aunt Vi's past and their own, not for nostalgia, but to collect the strength and vision in that life: They must go back before they can go forward."[12]

Reena's story draws to a close as the dawn breaks, and once again we are reminded of the cyclical nature of time. Reena affirms the continuity of time on another level in her devotion to her children: "'I will feel that I have done well by them if I give them, if nothing more, a sense of themselves and their worth and importance as black people. Everything I do with them, for them, is to this end. I don't want them ever to be confused about this. They must have their identifications straight from the beginning. No white dolls for them!'" (163). The story comes full circle as our attention is brought back to Aunt Vi and the wake. "Our lives have got to make more sense if only for her," remarks Reena. Thus, we can see that the rituals attending physical death become an affirmation for the living. Accordingly, as the two friends separate at the end, the spiritual ties remain taut.

The force, the conviction, and the unsparing honesty that mark this short story strengthen the voice that Marshall sought in *Brown Girl, Brownstones*. They indicate as well the cultural and ideological direction that is to distinguish her subsequent fiction. Africa remains, to a large extent, symbolic, but it is accepted without question as the central referent. It becomes, in short, the common denominator of the collective black experience. As for the black woman, who carries the additional burden of learning to be comfortable with her strength, Marshall presents not a dismissal of the male but an affirmation of the female in a female-supported community. "Their [black women's] common celebration," as Bonnie Barthold states, "is large enough to accommodate the ambiguities they carry within themselves, and their complexity reduces neither their strength nor their capacity to celebrate their common heritage."[13]

"Some Get Wasted"

In "Some Get Wasted" (1964), Marshall examines the learned responses of African-American teenage boys who inhabit an "underground" but highly visible world. It is a world of bravado, of tough-minded, tough-skinned youngsters who refuse to succumb to the hopelessness surrounding them. But Marshall seems no longer preoccupied with clarifying meanings beyond the narrative description and dialogue. She moves away from the fictional essay style so freely used in "Reena" to allow the story to speak for itself.

> A shout hurled after him down the rise: "Run, baby. Run, fool!" and Hezzy knew the terror snapping the tendons which strung together his muscles, that he had been caught in a sneak, was separated from his People, alone, running with his heart jarring inside his narrow chest, his stomach a stone weight and his life riding on each rise and plunge of his legs. While far behind, advancing like pieces of the night broken off, were the Crowns. He couldn't dare turn to look, couldn't place their voices because of the wind in his ears, but he knew they were Crowns. They had to be.[14]

So begins the story, and the reader, along with Hezzy, is breathless with the pace, the tension, the mystery, and the violence of the world of teenage gangs. An omniscient point of view informs the story to help us understand the loneliness and desperation of black boys who, needing both recognition and a sense of belonging, defy the value system that refuses to acknowledge and include them. They invent, instead, their own values, their own symbols, their own rituals and conventions and, in doing so, gain for themselves some semblance of individual worth and communal involvement. "In this club," states the leader, "when we go down, everybody goes together. When we split, everybody splits together" (136).

As we observe the last half of a Memorial Day parade, symbolic in its commemoration of soldiers and veterans of foreign wars, we soon learn that there is another type of soldier in training. He is the young recruit learning offensive maneuvers for nothing less than survival in a brutal and long-standing domestic war. The "Big People" are the ranking officers. They include Sizzle, who "lived only to fight," and Turner, distinguished by and promoted within the ranks because of the bullet crease on his forehead. There is Big Moose—"the baleful Moose who had done in a Crown when he was Hezzy's age (thirteen) and gotten busted, rehabilitated, paroled and was back bopping with the cats" (142). And then there are the recruits, the "Little People," for whom Hezzy, the main character, serves as "sergeant." The role models are fierce and dreadful, demanding—without uttering a word—allegiance, respect, submission. Hezzy describes Turner as follows:

> It was like the cat's skin was so tough the bullet had only been able to graze it. It was like nothing or nobody could waste the cat. You could tell from his eyes. The iris fixed dead-center in the whites and full of dark swirls of colors like marble and cold, baby. When Turner looked sideways he never shifted his eyes, but turned his head, slow, like time had to wait on him. Man, how them simple chicks goofed behind that look. The stud didn't even have to talk to 'em. Just looked and they was ready to give him some. (138)

Such are the heroes of Hezzy's world, and they seem to mirror the environment which he has no choice but to claim:

> And all around him the familiar overflow of life streamed out of the sagging houses, the rank hallways, the corner bars, bearing him along like a dark tide. The voices loud against the night sky became his voice. The violence brooding over the crap games and racing with the cars became the vertigo inside his head. It was his world, his way—and that other world beyond suddenly no longer mattered. (139)

But that other world really does matter if only because it is in opposition to the deep-seated yearnings of poor black children and the dreams they will never be able to realize. That other world has made inaccessible to them not only material possessions but the possession of time and its continuity. A tinge of scornful envy belies Hezzy's remark that he feels sorry for the "squares" who are marching with holiday cheer. "They just don't know what's happening. I mean, all they got is this little old jive parade while tonight here we are gonna be locking with the Crowns up on the hill" (140).

We learn that the Crowns have been violating the turf of the Noble Knights, and as honor would have it, there must be a "showdown." Memorial Day, Prospect Park in Brooklyn, Massacre Hill, dusk—these are the particulars of the scheduled skirmish, and Hezzy listens intently, "his stomach dropping as it did on the cyclone in Coney Island." Note the juxtaposition of childlike adventure against the violent episode that is to come. Marshall uses this technique repeatedly to highlight the contradictions and paradoxes of a life ruled by circumstances of poverty that force young children to become seasoned delinquents. Having gotten separated from Turner and the "Big People," Hezzy and the boys visit the amusement section of the park, clamber aboard the merry-go-round, and grab for the rings. In an almost defensive yet playful way, Hezzy pokes fun at this unmanly activity, even though he has thoroughly enjoyed his own participation. Then they sneak through the zoo, teasing and taunting the animals and playing "the dozens."[15] "And all the while," comments the narrator, "they ate, downing frankfurters and Pepsis, and when their money was gone, they jostled the Boy Scouts around the stands and stole candy" (141). To culminate their small festivities, they share a pint bottle of wine, "folding their small mouths around the mouth of the bottle and taking a long loud suck and then passing it on with a sigh" (141).

Grown-up male activities seem to be pitted against childlike play to emphasize that there is an overriding need to be granted recognition. For one of the boys, recognition can be gained through ownership of things. When he dreams of getting a new Buick, which he can neither afford nor drive, he concedes: "I just want that number sitting outside my house looking all pretty" (141). In sad and gentle reproof, Hezzy rejoins:

> "That's what I mean about you studs. Always talking about stealing cars and robbing stores like that's something. Man, that slop ain't nothing. Any jive stud out here can steal him a car or rob a store. That don't take no heart. You can't build you no rep behind that weak slop. You got to be out here busting heads and wasting cats, Jim. That's the only way you build you a rep and move up in the club." (141)

In capturing the esoteric nature of African-American speech, the author shows how language can be a direct manifestation of resistance to that other world. In effect, it becomes what John Edgar Wideman calls "a language of immediate, sensual, intimate reciprocity, of communal and self-definition."[16] Marshall duplicates words and phrases to reflect the rhythms and tones that give the vernacular vitality; she also makes clear the "poetic meaning" to provide the story with its forceful impact.

Tension mounts with Hezzy's climb in the club, but disaster is foreshadowed in several ways. First of all, the Noble Knights have decided not to wear their labeled jackets, "cause there ain't no need to let the Man know who we is. And another thing," adds Turner, "It's gonna be dark out there so watch whose head you busting" (138). The reader feels apprehension when the little "man-child" wets his bed the night before the event and has a dream that he cannot recall. On the morning of that tragic day, his mother, in her tired and lifeless voice, admonishes: "But you watch, you gonna get yourself all messed up one of these days" (139). Hezzy "fled that voice, he had to," the narrator adds, "since something in him always threatened to give in to it. Even more so this morning, for her voice recalled something in his dream. It seemed to reach out in place of her arms to hold him there, to take him as she had sometimes done when he was small, into her bed" (143). Such is the wavering response of a young boy who is determined to deny any type of female (maternal) dependence that might question the virility and strength of his masculine code of behavior.

The actual confrontation lasts only two or three minutes, but "time accelerates out of control" as knives, pipes, and guns clash fiercely against human targets. With the shrill sound of a policeman's whistle piercing the night, "their bodies froze in the violent attitudes of fight—and it was as if they were playing 'statues.' Knights and Crowns were one suddenly, a stunned, silent, violently cohered mass. Comrades. For the whisper passed among them without regard to friend or foe: 'The Man, baby! The Man'" (144).

"The Man" as a symbol of ultimate power is the unmistakable enemy; and every member, despite his club affiliation, recognizes The Man's final authority. Not only is he able to demolish the boundaries they have erected for themselves, but he can also disband the closely knit community they have worked so hard to build. What the boys seem to suppress and sometimes deny is that the process of gaining and maintaining control causes them to act out a role which is, at bottom, contrary to their normal behavior. This is evident in Hezzy's reaction to those gang members who had not shown up: "At the thought of them out on the corner drinking and jiving with chicks, having a good time, safe, the wine curdled in his stomach. For a dangerous second, he wanted to be with them" (141).

Hezzy overcomes that fleeting desire through sheer force of will, but for another dangerous second—another untimely pause—his fear becomes the felt sensation of paralysis:

> His fear suddenly was a cramp which spread swiftly to all his muscles. His arms tightened. His shoulders. The paralysis reached his legs so that his stride was broken and his feet caught in the ruts of the path. Fear was a phlegm in his throat choking off his air and a film over his eyes which made the black wall of trees ahead of him waver and recede. He stumbled and as he almost went down, their cry crashed in his ears: *The Noble Knights, punk!* The Knights are down! (144–45)

Before he can identify himself, a bullet sears his body, and unrecognized by his comrades, Hezzy dies. Even in death, however, Hezzy smiles allegiance: "Even when they were gone and he was dead, a spoor of blood trailed after them." It seems almost unnecessary to continue: "As if, despite what they had done, they were still his people. As if, no matter what, he would always follow them" (145).

Marshall grants the reader a specifically male vantage point from which to view Hezzy's ultimate victimization. The destructive maze that defines his environment is a result of the larger white society's refusal to grant him and the other boys any fulfillment. It is from an intense feeling of alienation and dispossession that the boys create their own anti-community; only there can they gain a sense of belonging and, ironically, a sense of their human worth. In grief we participate in the Memorial Day commemoration, and we more fully understand the double meaning of the story's title. Marshall concludes the story symbolically: "Overhead the black dome of the sky cleared and a few stars glinted. Cold tears in the warm May night" (145).

"To Da-Duh: In Memoriam"

"To Da-duh: In Memoriam," the most autobiographical of Marshall's short stories, originally appeared in the West Indian magazine *New World* (1967). It has since been reprinted in several anthologies as well as in Marshall's collection, *Reena and Other Stories* (1983). Similarities between Da-duh and other matriarchal figures in Marshall's previous fiction are striking. Da-duh is a part of Aunt Vi in "Reena" and Medford in "British Guiana." She also embodies features of Aunt Leesy, the prophetess in *The Chosen Place, the Timeless People,* and the unforgettable Aunt Cuney in *Praisesong for the Widow.* As Marshall puts it, "Da-duh turns up everywhere. She's an ancestor figure, symbolic for me of the long line of black women and men—African and New World—who made my being possible, and whose spirit I believe continues to animate my life and work. I wish to acknowledge and celebrate them. I am, in a word, an unabashed ancestor worshipper."[17]

Certainly this celebration of her ancestry is evident in *Brown Girl, Brownstones,* and specific characters from that novel can be identified in "To Da-duh." For instance, Adry, the narrator's mother in the story, is briefly sketched as a "formidable figure." We immediately picture Silla Boyce. The first-person narrator refers to her own obstinate character when she outstares the scrutinizing look of her grandmother's first appraisal: "Da-duh had recognized my small strength—and this was all I ever asked of the adults in my life then."[18] This is surely Selina Boyce. And the pretty, mild-tempered sister is none other than Ina, Selina's sibling rival. Marshall puts all of these characters together to create a fictional reminiscence of her childhood visit to Barbados. Of course, she relates her impressions after many years. That distance, however, provides the perspective the author needs to return to the scene with a new vision. In some respects, nevertheless, Marshall writes as if the Caribbean must be seen from the eyes of a child to help us fully appreciate the ramifications of her experience.

Marshall returns to the use of the epigram to introduce the story:

> ". . . Oh Nana! All of you is not in
> this evil business Death,
> Nor all of us in Life."
>
> "At Grandmother's Grave"
by Lebert Bethune

Capsulated here is the theme of the story, which is technically advanced again through Marshall's masterful skill with juxtaposition. In this case, the asphalt jungle of New York City is fixed against the dense vegetation of a Caribbean isle. Characteristic of Marshall's artistry, however, we see not only how the configurations of the landscapes differ but also how those landscapes affect the configuration of thought.

Traveling with her mother and her sister, the child meets for the first time her maternal grandmother (nicknamed Da-duh) at the port of disembarkation. The old woman rushes toward them "so swiftly it seemed that she did not intend stopping when she reached them but would sweep past them out the doorway which opened onto the sea and *like Christ walk upon the water!*" (206, emphasis mine). The biblical image summoned up by Marshall may very well forecast the continuing influence that the grandmother will hold over her. At the time of this writing, though, the author seems to have subconsciously attributed something sacred—almost saintly—to her progenitor. The following excerpt describing Da-duh's face suggests that, back in 1967, Marshall was more consciously integrating into her thinking and writing the African-based metaphysics that makes a harmonious whole of coexisting polarities:

> It was as stark and fleshless as a death mask, that face. The maggots might
> have already done their work, leaving only the framework of bone beneath
> the ruined skin and deep wells at the temple and jaw. But her eyes were
> alive, unnervingly so for one so old, with a sharp light that flicked out of
> the dim, clouded depths like a lizard's tongue to snap up all in her view.
> Those eyes betrayed a child's curiosity about the world, and I wondered
> vaguely seeing them, and seeing the way the bodice of her ancient dress
> had collapsed in on her flat chest (what had happened to her breasts?),
> whether she might not be some kind of child at the same time that she
> was a woman, darkness and light, past and present, life and death—all the
> opposites contained and reconciled in her. (206)

Da-duh seems a bit disarmed as she gazes at this youngster with the "fierce
look," but she takes a decided liking to the song-singing, toe-tapping,
truculent little creature who seemed something of "an emissary from some
world she did not know but which intrigued her and whose power she
both felt and feared" (211).

We already know from "Reena" that white or near-white has privileged
status in the United States, and it seems to be no different in the Caribbean. The narrator states that she and her sister were presented "apolo-
getically because not only did Da-duh prefer boys but she also liked her
grandchildren to be 'white,' that is, fair-skinned; and we had, I was to
discover, a number of cousins, the outside children of white estate manag-
ers and the like who qualified. We, though, were as black as she" (206–7).
Color distinctions have now touched two shores and appear ubiquitous in
their pejorative valuations. While the author here underscores one of the
negative effects of African displacement, the stronger concern, at least for
Da-duh, is the increasing presence of Western technology, which will
stifle and suffocate her peaceful world.

Da-duh owns a fairly large plot of land, which was purchased with
"Panama money sent her by her eldest son . . . who had died working on
the canal" (209).[19] And it is with considerable reverence and pride that
the old woman shows the child the wonders of her tropical paradise. There
were breadfruit, papaw, guava, mango, sugar apples, limes, bananas, and
the endless procession of cane stalks. "I bet you don't know that these
canes here and the sugar you eat is one and the same thing," boasted Da-
duh. "That they does throw the canes into some damn machine at the
factory and squeeze out all the little life in them to make sugar for you all
so in New York to eat. I bet you don't know that" (209–10).

While a sense of pride is apparent in Da-duh's words, we detect that
same dread of the mechanical that the narrator described earlier as they
rode toward Bridgetown. It was not just the lorry "with its asthmatic mo-

tor" but a fear and distrust of all machines. This dread of the mechanical restates Marshall's concern with the destructive power of Western values earlier described in *Soul Clap Hands and Sing* and the symbolic rise of the humanitarian values associated with black cultures. In this short story the author explores mechanization as a symbol of the "civilized monster" encroaching upon colonized countries.[20] At the time of the narrator's visit, however, the full effects of Western "progress" and its accompanying materialistic values have not spoiled Da-duh's Eden. It is a place for now that can contain contradictions and yet remain whole. Later, in the novella "Merle," it becomes a place that has been socially and economically ruined by the intrusion of the West. Da-duh, however, is unimpressed with things Western and takes every opportunity to point out the advantages of her homeland. She has heard, for instance, that one can walk for miles in New York and never see a tree. When the little one says there is a chestnut tree in front of her house, Da-duh inquires, "Does it bear?" "Not anymore," is the reluctant response. "You see," retorts Da-duh, "nothing can bear there" (210).

Within the grandmother, nonetheless, is a threatening tension, which the narrator captures in the following description:

> Her face was drowned in the shadow of an ugly rolled-brim felt hat, but the details of her slight body and of the struggle taking place within it were clear enough—an intense, unrelenting struggle between her back which was beginning to bend ever so slightly under the weight of her eighty odd years and the rest of her which sought to deny those years and hold that back straight, keep it in line. (205–6)

Nature, too, struggles to reconcile "warring tendencies," and it becomes a paradigm for human conflict. Note the atavistic quality of a tropical wood:

> [It was] a place dense and damp and gloomy and tremulous with the fitful play of light and shadow as the leaves high above moved against the sun that was almost hidden from view. It was a violent place, the tangled foliage fighting each other for a chance at the sunlight, the branches of the trees locked in what seemed an immemorial struggle, one both necessary and inevitable. But despite the violence, it was pleasant, almost peaceful in the gully, and beneath the thick undergrowth, the earth smelled like spring. (210)

The implied contrast with the urban scene in America carries subtle, moral overtones, and the baffled child becomes hard-pressed to argue a superior urban lifestyle.

Yet Da-duh is fascinated with the people and the goings-on of New York, and in answer to her queries, the child imaginatively re-creates the things, places, and events with which she is most familiar. Over the weeks, the woman learns about everything from household appliances to subways. Electricity is described as similar to "turning on the sun at night." What seems most incredible to Da-duh, however, is the fact that her granddaughter has had the audacity to beat up a white girl in her class. "She called me a name," explains the child in justification. "Beating up white people now!" Da-duh repeats in a "hushed, shocked voice." "Oh, the lord, the world's changing up so I can scarce recognize it anymore" (212).

The episode that marks the grandmother's slow decline is a visit to a gully that the child had not seen before.

> There in a small clearing amid the dense bush, she stopped before an incredibly tall royal palm which rose cleanly out of the ground, and drawing the eye up with it, soared high above the trees around it into the sky. It appeared to be touching the blue dome of the sky, to be flaunting its dark crown of fronds right in the blinding white face of the late morning sun. (212)

Surely there was nothing as tall as that in New York, thought Da-duh. The narrator comments: "I almost wished, seeing her face, that I could have said no." The child's description of the Empire State Building seems too much for Da-duh to comprehend, let alone accept.

> All the fight went out of her at that. The hand poised to strike me went limp to her side, and as she stared at me, seeing not me but the building that was taller than the highest hill she knew, the small stubborn light in her eyes (it was the same amber as the kerosene lamp she lit at dusk) began to fail. Finally, with a vague gesture that even in the midst of defeat still tried to dismiss me and my world, she turned and started back through the gully, walking slowly, her steps groping and uncertain, as if she were suddenly no longer sure of the way, while I followed triumphantly yet strangely saddened behind. (213)

Da-duh's spirit begins to languish, and their daily walks become quiet and shortened. "Some huge, monolithic shape had imposed itself, it seemed, between her and the land, obstructing her vision" (213). Before departing for the United States, the child is to hear the grandmother's last words: "Girl, you're not to forget now to send me a picture of that building, you hear" (214).

Da-duh was never to see the picture postcard of the Empire State Building, for shortly after her daughter and granddaughters had left, she died, literally of fear. England, then the colonial power over Barbados, engaged in the "Strike of 1937" and, in a show of force, flew airplanes low over the tropical terrain. Although everyone else fled to the cane fields for cover, Da-duh

> remained in the house at the window . . . watching as the planes came swooping and screaming like monstrous birds down over the village, over her house, rattling her trees, and flattening the young canes in her field. It must have seemed to her lying there that they did not intend pulling out of their dive, but like the hardbacked beetles which hurled themselves with suicidal force against the walls of the house at night, those menacing silver shapes would hurl themselves in an ecstasy of self-immolation into the land, destroying it utterly. (214)

The story ends where it began with a direct allusion to the epigram: "She died and I lived but always, to this day even, within the shadow of her death" (214). The past, it can be seen, remains a part of the narrator's present, and it is to be a part of Marshall's future. This point could be no better emphasized than in the closing passage:

> For a brief period after I was grown, I went to live alone, like one doing penance, in a loft above a noisy factory in New York and there painted seas of sugar cane and huge swirling Van Gogh suns and palm trees striding like brightly plumed Watussi across a tropical landscape while the thunderous tread of the machines downstairs jarred the floor beneath my easel, mocking my efforts. (214)

We can see that the narrator's sorrow stems not from innovation and change but from the loss of values that seem unable to coexist in the "mechanistic milieu of America itself."[21] The author's deliberate reference to Watussi warriors is African, as is her description of her grandmother's face. When she thinks back on it, it is "like a Benin mask, the features drawn and almost distorted by an ancient, abstract sorrow" (213). By evoking African images and the values they connote, the author makes symbolic associations between the Caribbean and the continent that lies adjacent in the distance.

There is no question that Marshall's West Indian background is a major component of her cultural identity. Yet there is an obvious and unavoidable identification with things Western. As she struggles to place these opposites in a comfortable balance, we see an inner struggle to retain the values of her Caribbean heritage. By describing the tensions within her grandmother, within herself, and within nature, she creates a nostalgia—idyllic and idealistic—that triggers a sense of loss and dislocation. The loss, however, is one of innocence, a necessary step that leads the author, in her later fiction, to a more realistic assessment of the extremes that must be considered in her search for a personal identity. The Caribbean isles, Marshall seems to say, are but a temporary weigh station on the journey still to be undertaken.

Chapter Five

Changing the Present Order

Personal and Political Liberation in *The Chosen Place, the Timeless People*

[I]t is only when the society, or elements of the society rise up in rebellion against its external authors and manipulators that our prolonged fiction becomes temporary fact.

Sylvia Wynter

In *The Chosen Place, the Timeless People* (1969), Marshall combines and expands the themes developed in previous fiction to create a kaleidoscopic novel intricate in design and resonant with meaning. We see direct comparisons with male characters from *Soul Clap Hands and Sing,* and suspect the author's continuing concern with Western civilization and its materialistic values. Through the black female characters in the novel, we get yet another penetrating view of the West Indian women so lovingly described in *Brown Girl, Brownstones.* Now that they are placed in the environment of a fictionalized, quasi-independent homeland, we appreciate more fully the strength they gain from their African heritage. With the numerous references to and images of Africa, we recall Marshall's early short story, "Reena," and some passages of the novel evoke the grandmother in "To Da-duh: In Memoriam." In short, *The Chosen Place, the*

Timeless People seems to be a recapitulation, an artistic reconstruction, of Marshall's literary canon published to date.

This is not to suggest that Marshall merely repeats what she has already written. Rather, she brings together in one novel a global consideration of the two themes that have been central to all of her fiction: "the importance of truly confronting the past, both in personal and historical terms, and the necessity of reversing the present order."[1] What is particularly striking about this novel, initially entitled *Ceremonies of the Guest House,* is Marshall's new approach to these ideas. History is made to come alive as we read the separate stories of the African-Caribbean, the Jew, and the White Anglo-Saxon Protestant. While they have a clear, symbolic function in the novel, they are also presented to us as distinct individuals—real people with human strengths and human failings. In fact, we become so deeply involved in the lives of each that our sympathies move from one to the other with equal intensity. It is important to note, however, that the artist's emphasis is not upon the individual. As Barbara Christian correctly observes, in *The Chosen Place, the Timeless People* Marshall "moves away from the way the world affects an individual psyche to how our many psyches create a world."[2] Thus, each character is carefully developed and placed within a particularized social and historical context to reveal his or her relationships to others. Individual portraits then merge into a collage to help us see, in microcosm, images of separate peoples and cultures interacting in a global environment.

Although *The Chosen Place, the Timeless People* received fine critical reviews in the United States, it did not immediately become well known. Barbara Christian speculates that because the novel was published at a time when "much of Afro-American literature was focused on the urban ghettos, when the popular genres of the black movement were poetry and drama, and when so much of the major literary works focused on male conquest and on exclusively black characters, Marshall's complex and convoluted novel did not suit the tenor of the times."[3] Curiously, though, in its political stance the novel does reflect the momentum of the American women's movement in the 1970s. Perhaps Marshall's portrayal of white women as indirect agents of destructive power disenchanted any number of white female readers. And because the artist develops in the novel an exploitative lesbian relationship between a black and a white woman, the reading public may have labeled it homophobic.[4] However, with the reissue of the novel by the Feminist Press in 1983, many are taking a second look at the text. Indeed, Christian refers to it as "integral to the development of a black female novel tradition in the United States."[5] In the Caribbean as well, *The Chosen Place* has been acclaimed, and it was translated into French under the title *L'île de l'éternal Retourne* (Paris: Ballard Press, 1986).

For her epic consideration of the development of colonialism and the process of political and psychological liberation, Marshall turns to a symbolic Caribbean setting. Since the plot revolves around the infiltration of an American team of researchers who plan to assist an "underdeveloped" country, implications for contemporary world politics are apparent. The plot, however, translates into a structured series of metonymies that include, first, the seasonal world and, second, the cultural constructs developed to reflect that world. While a third symbolic action concerns the colonial relationship between black and white women, it also represents the lifting of the veil to liberate the self. Finally the trope of cleansing, imaged through the sea and through Judeo-Christian analogues, marks the creation of a new self and the advance out of colonialism. These multiple levels of plot and theme help to form what becomes a metaphorical or mythical experience.

To signal her increasing commitment to the aesthetic and ideological embrace of traditional African culture, Marshall selects as an epigraph to *The Chosen Place* a quotation from the Tiv of West Africa: "Once a great wrong has been done, it never dies. People speak the words of peace, but their hearts do not forgive. Generations perform ceremonies of reconciliation, but there is no end."[6] Immediately evoked is the immutability of memory—the African memory of violation, exploitation, and injustice. But just as strong in the novel is the African memory of freedom, dignity, and self-respect. It is not surprising that Marshall constructs the novel to reflect artistically the traditional view of African time. In fact, concentric patterns inform the work to become a part of its organically conceived meaning. But the author goes one step farther by cleverly organizing the novel to simulate psychologically the major divisions of the African agricultural year. In such a year, the calendar is not calculated in mathematical terms but according to seasonal activities.[7] The Western calendar is, of course, operative in the Caribbean, and this confluence is appropriate and necessary to her concern with cultural collusion and conflict. But the general populace she describes in the novel responds to a system that reckons two major divisions in the year: the "in-crop" season, which runs from January through June, and the "out-of-crop" season, which extends through December. Within these two major divisions are holidays. During "in-crop" the people first celebrate Carnival, then Easter, and finally Whitsuntide in May. During "out-of-crop" comes the August First Holiday, commemorating Emancipation, and in November, All Souls' Day, a time set aside to attend the burial sites of the dead. Christmas follows All Saints' Day to close out the year.

Although Marshall does not present the Carnival celebration until Book Three in the novel, I begin my discussion with this holiday for three reasons. First, Carnival serves as a reference point to review the stories of the several characters introduced in the novel. Second, the pageant enacted at Carnival presents, in synopsis form, the author's uncompromising statement about the powerful and the weak, about colonialism and subjugation, about confrontation and change. Third, Carnival represents the central climactic episode of the novel when secrets are revealed and resolutions come about.

For two full days all work ceases on Bourne Island. Race and class distinctions become irrelevant as the entire population (visitors as well as residents) joins in a "unanimity of conduct and underlying value." Colorful floats, billowing banners, new costumes, holiday foods, and rum aplenty—all represent "Bacchanal! Big Fete!" On Monday evening a big dance is held in the several districts of the island, and on Tuesday there is the magnificent parade that traditionally takes place in the main town of New Bristol. The people of the Bournehills district prepare as the others, but, instead of new costumes, they air out the ones they have worn for years: a replica of the dress worn during the time of the slave insurrection in Bournehills. The Guinea-blue banner has "Pyre Hill Revolt" emblazoned in white across it, and beneath the title is printed "Best Local Historical," which, the narrator explains, was the name of the award given them "the year, long ago, when they had first performed the masque, and which they still stubbornly laid claim to" (281). Marshall emphasizes the notion of timelessness when she describes the marchers in the first line raising their right hands in the "classic Bournehills greeting." It is similar to the gesture of "someone about to give evidence in court," but suggests "a meaning beyond the ordinary," something encompassing "both hail and farewell, time past and present" (103). The reader may recall a similar greeting in Marshall's novella, "British Guiana." Her purpose here, however, is twofold: to prepare the reader to acknowledge a painful past and to establish a forgotten kinship within the territorial boundaries of the mythical and mystical Bourne Island.

From the eldest to the youngest, the entire population of Bournehills is represented. First come the women and children, then the "towering replica" of Pyre Hill. Next, we see "an endless coffle of men and boys dressed in the Osnaburg overblouses and, finally, toward the rear, a small group dressed in the "red-coated uniform of the British soldier at the time." They march with a "restrained, rhythmic two-step that scarcely [brings] the foot up off the ground," but it is more than a way of conserving energy for the long parade. It is a deliberately "pronounced" movement, accentuated with the metronomelike clash of the heavy bracelets that the women wear. The narrator describes it as an "awesome sound":

It conjured up in the bright afternoon sunshine dark alien images of legions marching bound together over a vast tract, iron fitted into dank stone walls, chains—like those to an anchor—rattling in the deep holds of ships, and exile in an unknown inhospitable land—an exile bitter and irreversible in which all memory of the former life and of the self as it had once been had been destroyed. (282)

As time moves backward to the beginning of African enslavement and the horrors of the "Middle Passage," Marshall invokes a past that is still curiously present. This overlap of historical and present time becomes a central motif in the novel: an insistence that the crowd (and we as "viewers") "not only acknowledge them, but love them and above all act in some bold, retributive way that would both rescue their memory and indemnify their suffering" (283). With a sound from a conch shell, the marchers halt, and the silence in its loud abruptness seems to pervade even distant parts of the island. The Cuffee Ned Slave Revolt is in progress.

The pageant that the narrator goes on to describe seems to draw parallels from the Berbice Rebellion led in 1765 by Cofee (Kofi-Akan), now a national hero of Guyana. The author may have borrowed facts from this historic event to create something of a subtale within the larger novel. Yet, as Hortense Spillers states, "Cuffee Ned perfectly embodies Bournehill's idea of subversion that is rehearsed in various New World historical narratives—Haiti's Touissant L'Ouverture and Nat Turner and Denmark Vesey of the southern United States share the same heroic constellation."[8] Small but significant details of Cuffee's attire are duplicated and include an "obeah man's wallet . . . stocked with the farrago of his calling: the rusty nails and broken bits of glass, the bright-hued parrot feathers and small clay figures of his enemies, among them the planter Percy Bryam" (284). So real is the drama of Cuffee Ned capturing the sleeping Bryam, "who had owned all of Bournehills and everyone in it," that a little boy standing on the sidelines cries, "Look sharp, Mr. Bryam, Cuffee coming!" The Bournehills band then breaks rank to act out the revolt. Artificial fire sets aflame the house and the hill upon which it stands, and a mock battle between slave and soldier ensues. With Bryam captured, the band joins in a triumphant dance that is followed by a "long recitative." The African oral tradition remains alive, indeed, as the women weave the story from its beginnings to celebrate the deeds and exploits of their hero.

Marshall builds with dramatic intensity the story of Cuffee Ned to suggest that it is "the experience which *any* people who find themselves ill-used, dispossessed, at the mercy of the powerful, must pass. No more, no less. Differing in time, in the forms it takes, in the degree of its success or failure, but the same. A struggle both necessary and inevitable, given man" (286–87, italics mine). The author is not satisfied merely to make an imperative statement; she reveals in the pageant the process of change. *"They had worked together!"* sing the voices of the people in unison. "If we had lived selfish, we couldn't have lived at all. . . . Under Cuffee . . . a man had not lived for himself alone, but for his neighbor also. They had trusted one another, had set aside their differences and stood as one against the common enemy. *They had been a People!"* (287) Notice the sense of continuity provided through the shift in pronoun usage from "they" to "we."

In reviewing their history, the Bournehills people present a complete account—one that acknowledges their success as well as their defeat. Accordingly, the recitative goes on to tell that Cuffee's example spread throughout the island, and the people "lived for almost three years like the maroons of Jamaica and the bush Negroes of Guiana—free, at peace, dependent only on themselves, a nation apart" (280). The government, however, eventually responded by sending out a full regiment of soldiers. Following a bloody suppression, Cuffee's head was severed and, as a warning to the people, placed on a pike along Westminster Low Road.

But Cuffee did not die. "Obeah man that he was, a true believer, he believed that death was not an end but a return, so that in dying he would be restored to the homeland and there be a young warrior and hunter" (288). Symbolically, the cycle of time has not been disrupted; the legendary figure is very much alive in the minds and hearts of the Bournehills people. However, the silence returns. Momentarily, we hear the gradual buildup of the same "awesome sound" that began the pageant, that "dull tramp and the intermittent tolling of the women's bracelets" (288). As the band continues to march past Barclay's Bank and the air-conditioned offices of Kingsley and Sons, the powerful English entrepreneurs, Marshall underscores her point about the past continuing in a different form.

Importantly, however, the current residents of Bournehills do not change. Merle Kinbona,[9] the pivotal character in the novel, explains: "Sometimes strangers to Bournehills wonder why we go on about Cuffee and Pyre Hill when all that happened donkey's years ago and should have long been done with and forgotten. But we're an odd, half-mad people, I guess. We don't forget anything, and yesterday comes like today to us" (102). These are the "timeless people" of the novel's title. They await a new Cuffee Ned. And the "chosen place" is Bourne Island, which Marshall earlier described as one of many small islands following "each other in an orderly procession down the watery track of the Caribbean." As its name suggests, though, Bourne Island "had broken rank and stood off by itself to the right, almost out in the Atlantic . . . [marking] the eastern boundary of the entire continent. And ever mindful of the responsibility placed upon it from the beginning, it remained—alone amid an immensity of sea and sky, becalmed now that its turbulent history was past, facing east, the open sea, and across the sea, hidden beyond the horizon, the colossus of Africa" (13).

The sea, of course, plays an important function in the novel not only to emphasize its importance to world trade but also to return us to the historical reality of the slave trade. With this in mind, Marshall describes the sea in anthropomorphic terms. From the Atlantic side of the island, it is

> a wild-eyed, marauding sea the color of slate, deep, full of dangerous currents, lined with row upon row of barrier reefs, and with a sound like that of the combined voices of the drowned raised in a loud unceasing lament—all those, the nine million and more it is said, who in their enforced exile, their Diaspora, had gone down between this point and the homeland lying out of sight to the east. This sea mourned them. Aggrieved, outraged, unappeased, it hurled itself upon each of the reefs in turn and then upon the shingle beach, sending up the spume in an angry froth which the wind took and drove in like smoke over the land. Great boulders that had roared down from Westminster centuries ago stood scattered in the surf; these, sculpted into fantastical shapes by the wind and water, might have been gravestones placed there to commemorate those millions of the drowned. (106)

But some survived and the effect of history and myth upon the human consciousness becomes unforgettable as we follow the lives of the several characters who are brought together in this remote place.

Like *Brown Girl, Brownstones, The Chosen Place* is divided into books. Book One, appropriately entitled "Heirs and Descendants," introduces us to the major characters: Merle Kinbona, the West Indian woman who serves as host and landlady to the American research team; Saul Amron, the Jewish anthropologist who directs the "up-lift" project; his second wife, Harriet, a mainline Philadelphian WASP; and Allen Fuso, the part-Irish, part-Italian research assistant and statistician. We also meet Vereson Walkes, who incidentally is the subject of Marshall's "Return of the Native," published as a work-in-progress in *Freedomways* (1964). Adopting one of the techniques employed in traditional African oral narrative, Marshall incorporates Vere's story as another tale within the larger novel to reinforce her message about the destructive nature of Western values. Book One also introduces us to the elite of Bourne Island, primarily Lyle Hutson, a leading colored barrister, and a few white expatriate businessmen and government officials.

Marshall sketches briefly, but with bold and telling lines, a portrait of

the bourgeoisie that has separated itself psychologically and geographically from the indigenous population. Their speech, their dress, their
drinks, their politics suggest their identification with all that is Western.
When Saul implies that a large, though unspecified, amount of money will
be spent on the project in Bournehills, one character responds: "Bournehills!
Man . . . you don't know the place. There's no changing or improving it.
You people could set up a hundred development schemes at a hundred
million each and down there would remain the same" (56). In much the
same manner as their former white oppressors, the black elite rail against
their fellow islanders as lazy, shiftless, ignorant, backward. "Those people?
They're a disgrace!" The narrator explains what we begin to understand as
an expression of self-hatred. Importantly, the thought is given to Saul:

> They might have been speaking about a people completely alien to them-
> selves, who did not even inhabit the same island. . . . But then who, he
> reminded himself, can speak calmly of the brother who shames him? Be-
> cause listening to them he had suddenly remembered, to his own shame,
> how, as a boy, he had fled his brothers, those with the sallow, long-nose
> look, sloping shoulders and side curls, whose bodies always appeared to be
> cowering out of the way of an impending blow. The Ashkenazi look he
> had called it as an arrogant young man who had taken pride in his large,
> straight-shouldered build—the look of the long-persecuted; and while
> maintaining his allegiance (for they were his people after all) he had still,
> at the same time, often been impatient, even angry, with them. (58–59)

Marshall's examination of oppression broadens to include the Jew and,
by extension, oppressed peoples everywhere. But clearly she is also building the character of Saul Amron, whose thoughts and impressions are frequently expressed in Judaic images and motifs. For example, when he first
meets Merle, he notes that she has the gestures of a Jew, and the shawl she
wears to protect her arms and shoulders against the night air reminds him
of a "prayer shawl." Later when he observes the cane workers, memories of
his mother invade his consciousness. She had been a "Sephardi, a rarity in
the almost exclusively Ashkenazic world of New York Jewry," and she
always spoke of that "special heritage" as though it were "the one outstanding example of suffering known to man." As a child, Saul had won-
dered "what difference did it make being an aristocrat among Jews if one
were still a Jew . . . thus committing his first heresy and beginning his
life-long apostasy" (164). However, his mother's story of "flight, priva-
tion, and wandering. . . , became the means by which he understood the
suffering of others" (164). Because of Saul's prominence in the story and
his own particular heritage as a Jew, the reader associates the title of the

novel with another, earlier "chosen people" of another "timeless place." By shifting these terms in the title, Marshall plays upon the biblical concept of "the chosen people" to suggest, first of all, cyclical repetitions of oppression and resistance and, secondly, the common cause uniting Saul with the Bournehills people. In both cases, she suggests that there is something marvelous—perhaps even sacred—about the resilience and faith of a people who, though oppressed, yet endure with dignity and purpose and keep alive hope for restitution and freedom.

Such are the people of Bournehills whom we meet in Book Two, entitled "Bournehills." When Saul views the actual site of the project, the connection between character and context merges: "Bournehills, this place he had never seen before, was suddenly the wind-scoured Peruvian Andes. The highlands of Guatemala. Chile. Bolivia, where he had once worked briefly among the tin miners. Honduras, which had proved so fatal. Southern Mexico. And the spent cotton lands of the Southern United States through which he had traveled many times as a young graduate student on his way to do field work among the Indians in Chiapas. It was suddenly, to his mind, every place that had been wantonly used, its substance stripped away, and then abandoned" (100).

Clearly, Bournehills is a paradigm for all economically impoverished countries. While one of Marshall's objectives in the novel is to describe the struggle for human survival, she is concerned as well with extolling the people's resistance to continued exploitation. She champions the "Little Fella"—those who are without economic and political power but who nonetheless bolster themselves with a profound wisdom gained from the past. These are the people who best reflect the African memory of independence and communal respect. And these are the people who revere African tribal customs that have sustained them through centuries of physical and psychological oppression. Some are named, others remain nameless; but assured of their self-worth, all resist their oppressors and live daily with the hope of their reunification as a people.

Unaffected by the many stop-gap measures offered to them in the name of progress, the Bournehills residents know the lessons of history and social revolution. Most work on small cane plots that they own, thanks to Merle's generosity, or rent from Kingsley and Sons. Some cultivate small private lots adjoining their houses. In describing these people, Marshall makes use of several African images or derivatives thereof. We meet Delbert, the local shopkeeper, who is described as "the chief presiding over the nightly palaver in the men's house [rum shop]." Consistent with this African imagery is an earlier passage in which Delbert substitutes white rum for "the palm wine with which he kept the palaver and made libation to the ancestral gods. . . . Each time he filled the glasses arranged before him on the counter, he made a point of first pouring a drop or two of the rum on the floor" (123). We note, too, Delbert's smile, which rearranged "the wrinkles that were scored like tribal markings into his flesh" (138). Then we meet Ferguson, the vociferous, Bible-quoting orator of the district and an avid supporter of Cuffee Ned. He is a tall, lean, old man whose every feature, like his mannerisms, is "overstated, exaggerated": "His face, his neck, his clean-shaven skull, had the elongated, intentionally distorted look to them of a Benin mask or a sculpted thirteenth century Ife head. With his long, stretched limbs he could have been a Haitian Hougon man. Or Damballa" (121).

In the first pages of the novel we meet Leesy Walkes, also a member of the Bournehills community. She sits uneasily in Merle's battered Bentley (a remnant of the old colonial powers) en route to the airport to greet her nephew, Vere. Leesy is so reminiscent of the grandmother in "To Da-duh: In Memoriam" that she seems a veritable reincarnation. First we notice their similar fear of machines. (Leesy's fear, in part, stems from the accidental death of her husband at Cane Vale, the major sugar factory in the district.) More than that, however, Leesy, like Da-duh, thinks of all things mechanical as inherently evil. Also like Da-duh, she is dressed in her Sunday best, wearing the proverbial brown felt hat and layers of petticoats to weigh down her "dry husk of a body." To her underskirt is pinned a bit of camphor, which she carries both as a protection against a variety of ills and as a "phylactery against imagined evils" (28). Iris Hurley of *Brown Girl, Brownstones* comes to mind as we recall that she also shielded herself against Obeah in a similar manner.

In characterizing Leesy, Marshall makes several references to the African traditions that remain a part of Caribbean life. Once a week, for instance, Leesy faithfully polishes "the silverplated plaques inscribed with the names and dates of the family dead" (28). Ancestor worship is further demonstrated when, before retiring for the night, she drapes "a dark cloth over the mirror so that the ghosts of the family dead would not come to look at themselves when she slept" (142). In many respects, Leesy seems like an African priestess, honoring tribal customs in the face of modern change. Later in the novel when Vereson Walkes is killed in the Whitmonday car race, Marshall extends her examination of African cultural survivals to include the preparation of the dead and the subsequent funeral proceedings. Ostensibly to ward off evil spirits, Leesy sprinkles "water and a few drops of rum at the foot of the bed, her bed, upon which he lay" (369–70). The entire district attends the funeral and we see a cortege of men dressed in dark suits and women wearing "bare white." We know from "British Guiana" that white in Caribbean countries symbolizes death and mourning. We also hear echoes from the same novella when the mourners cry, "Ah, Vere, he had a short life but a sweet funeral." Following the "pace set by Leesy, who had refused to ride in any of the cars," they arrive at the cemetery. Leesy will walk away with a silver plaque in her hand. She will also join the other villagers as they commemorate All Saints' Day, the rituals of which are similar to African ancestry worship:

> Gathered around the graves, their faces sculpted into abstract masks by the candlelight, they sang to the dead, throwing their voices against the surrounding hills and the black tent of a sky. And those voices welling up strongly into the night transformed the bleak joyless Protestant hymns of mourning into songs of celebration and remembrance, joyous songs. They made them their own. They sang loudly, as though hoping to rouse the dead at their feet. And it always seemed they succeeded. Because toward dawn when the sky began to clear, the gray shreds of morning mist that could be seen rising from the graves could have well been the ghostly forms of the ancestral dead who, in answer to their summons, had emerged from their resting place to stand at their sides. (268)

Other important African ancestral connections are presented in the novel. A house-raising, for instance, is described as "hard work but fun and very beautiful in a way." Cane cutter Cox has spent several years accumulating the money for the lumber, and, following custom, several men join in a work party to construct a one-room structure that, though "scarcely bigger than a closet," is nonetheless a house. We read that the cane cutter now plans to marry the woman who has had his children. "In Bournehills," Saul explains "a man doesn't believe in making it legal until he can at least offer his wife a house of her own no matter how small. It's their way, and as valid, in the final analysis, as any other" (182).

The Sunday morning "pig sticking," which takes place at dawn, is of major ritualistic importance. Marshall describes the process of slaughtering the pig in detail and, to involve the reader more fully, gives the animal human qualities. Initially, the men respond sympathetically to the sacrificial sow, but as they perform the process of dehairing and dismembering, they seem to Saul cold, methodical, ruthless, suggesting violent forces he had not suspected within them. The ritual, though, is a constructive act that acknowledges selfhood, brotherhood, and nationhood. Upon reflection, Saul seems to understand that "beneath the violence of the act" is "an affirmation of something age-old, a sense of renewal" (259). Such renewal is mirrored in the men and in his own "exhilarated mood." It is also mirrored in the changing moon, "still high but wafer thin now, a substanceless eucharist host, and its pallid light had been absorbed and supplanted by that of the sun which had risen unseen behind the sandhills" (256–57).

Expanding traditional religious dogma, Marshall augments this Christian imagery by including the rite of "communion." The men pass around a bottle of rum "along with the roasted tail from which everyone took a token bite." Importantly, Saul takes part in this communal activity and experiences a purging: "The rum not only, it seemed, neutralized the queasy bit of pork he had eaten, but had burned away, like a powerful acid, all that was impure in him, leaving him empty but clean inside" (259). Saul, as he does on other occasions, thinks of the old man of his youth who, wearing a soiled tallith, atoned for the world's sins by beating his chest. The old man would have cried "at the fall of yet another son of Israel" (257–58).

The reader may pardon Saul his act of Jewish cultural heresy, but when we view with him the one sugar factory in the Bournehills district, we join the old man of Saul's memory to scream loud execrations at a much more heinous sin. Significantly, Saul is reminded of the "deep hold of a ship":

> There was the noise, for one—the loud unrelieved drumming and pounding of the machines that powered the rollers which crushed the juice from the canes, and the shrill, almost human wail of the rollers themselves as they turned in their deep pit. There was the heat, for another, which came pouring up through the metal floor from the furnaces below to join the heat and steam flaring off the large open vats and boilers in which the cane juice was boiled till it turned to sugar. And the light in the place was dim and murky as in the hold of a ship, the color of molasses bubbling away in the boilers. Moreover, because of the dimness and the cane chaff which came flying up from the roller pit to whirl like a sandstorm through the air, the men working there appeared almost disembodied forms: ghosts they might have been from some long sea voyage taken centuries ago. (154)

And, as centuries ago, Sir John Stokes, head of the London office of Kingsley and Sons, makes his annual inspection of Cane Vale. Dressed as if for a safari, he wears "a belted khaki bush jacket with epaulets, shorts, olive drab knee socks and brown oxfords." As he emerges from his stately Rolls, which resembles a "hearse," he dons a pith helmet and in his hand he carries a swaggerstick. Despite his shortness, he gives "the impression of height and size because of the stiff-shouldered, military bearing [he affects] and a certain impatient imperious air" (220). The old order is still very much intact.

Marshall presents a scene of the devastating effects of exploitation and suffering as we watch Ferguson, who had vowed to tell Sir John that the rollers were worn and about to break down, waiting to speak. This otherwise vociferous black man cannot utter a syllable in the presence of the great white "plantation owner," and with the inspection quickly over, Sir John comments to Saul: "It's always a bit of a shock, don't you know, to realize that the thing that sweetens your tea comes from all this muck" (222). "Muck," we understand, carries multiple meanings. For Ferguson, it might refer to the condition of the island. For Saul as well as many of the other characters, it might refer to the mess they have made of their personal lives. For Sir John, it might refer to the islanders themselves.

In terms of the novel's broader message, "muck" might be a reference to the importance of sugar to the livelihood of the Bournehills people. In this connection, Marshall presents a rare view of the process of "caning" and "heading." A small work crew of men perform the cutting while the women gather the felled canes into bundles (well over two hundred pounds), which they bear on their heads down a hill to the lorries. Once loaded by another group of men, the lorries then transport the cane to Cane Vale. Stinger, the front man who sets the pace for cutting, concentrates on the canes "ranked like an opposing army before him up the slope, their long pointed leaves bristling like spears in the wind. . . . [E]ach time he brought one of them down, he would give a little triumphant grunt (the only sound he was ever heard to utter while working), and toss it contemptuously aside" (161).

Gwen, Stinger's pregnant common-law wife, executes her task also with strength and with a special grace:

> Behind him Gwen kept pace, gathering together the canes he flung her way into great sheaves which, with an assist from the other women, she then placed on her head and "headed" down to the truck below. And it was a precarious descent, for the ground would be slick underfoot from the "trash": the excess leaves the men hacked off the stalks before cutting them, and treacherous with the severed stumps hidden beneath. One bad slip and the neck would snap. But Gwen moved confidently down, as did the other women, her head weaving almost imperceptibly from side to side under its load (the motion was reminiscent of those child dancers from Bali, but more subtle, more controlled), her swollen stomach thrust high and her face partly hidden beneath the thick overhang. (161)

I have quoted at length the above passages both to highlight the dignity of human expression through "unskilled labor" and to emphasize its abuse. In such passages, Marshall clearly draws parallels between the plantation work of slavery and the plantation work under colonialism. In fact, time stands still when the white estate manager makes his rounds "dressed in jodhpurs, polished boots, a cork hat and riding a piebald horse." Marshall pointedly adds: "Seeing him ride past in the distance with his large black sun umbrella raised called to mind some ghost who refused to keep to his grave even during the daytime" (161).

But our attention is drawn to the horrendous misuse of the workers. It is important that Saul observes the transformation in Stinger, who is likened to "a winded wrestler being slowly borne down in defeat by an opponent who had proved his superior" (162). As for Gwen, her eyes have "the same slightly turned up, fixed, flat stare that you find upon drawing back the lids of someone asleep or dead" (163). Marshall, however, is intent on demonstrating that Gwen and the other people of Bournehills are neither asleep nor dead. They understand clearly that their economic condition has undergone no fundamental change since the days of enslavement, and they resist all efforts to keep entrenched the inequities of the present system.

Such inequities are so clearly depicted in the novel that they need no further comment. But Marshall includes in *The Chosen Place* a consideration of inequity from another perspective: the historic socioeconomic relationship between black and white women. At the same time, she explores the female psyche as it responds to cultural mandates and traditions. Through the interaction between Merle and Harriet and through Merle's relationship with a wealthy Englishwoman who, significantly, remains anonymous, the author reveals the continuation of patterns shaped by social constructions of race. She reveals as well what anthropologist Constance Sutton suggests is a "more authentic" representation of the development of colonialism: the real power behind continued oppression and exploitation is the white woman.[10]

Merle is a garrulous, neurotic, forty-year-old black woman whose ceaseless talk is only partially interrupted by her constant puffing of cigarettes. When we first meet her, she wears open-back shoes with "raised heels to give her height" and a flared print dress of a "vivid abstract tribal motif." Adorning her ears are silver pendant earrings that are a replica of the saints to be found outside Westminster Abbey. They are a gift from an Englishwoman who had been Merle's benefactress during her student days in London. And on her wrists, of course, are numerous heavy silver bracelets. "Like monk beads or a captive's chains," writes Marshall, "the clashing sounds announced her presence" (3).

We know that the author generally creates symbolic comparisons between the outward appearances of her characters and their inner emotional states. Of Merle, Marshall writes:

> She had donned this somewhat bizarre outfit, each item of which stood opposed to, at war even, with the other, to express rather a diversity and disunity within herself, and her attempt, unconscious probably, to recon-

cile those opposing parts, to make of them a whole. Moreover, in dressing in this manner, she appeared to be trying (and this was suggested by those unabashedly feminine shoes) to recover something in herself as a woman perhaps. There was no telling. But her face . . . attested to some profound and frightening loss. (5)

While that loss is suggestive of the Bournehills people in general, it is also a direct reference to Merle's personal loss, which is revealed at Carnival. However, she feels no loss of her cultural identity.

Merle embraces the people of Bournehills, and she unashamedly proclaims the "little fella" as her own. Her social commitment and political activism clearly reflect the ideas of black nationalism. Yet as we watch her move comfortably from one social context to another, she seems to be something of a "cultural broker," especially in her relationship to Saul. As the novel develops, they become close friends, unraveling their painful and complex histories to each other and finding a source of strength in their mutual understanding. Without always consciously realizing it, Saul actually seeks out Merle as on the day he wanders to the almshouse, where she can be found from time to time reading to children who have been orphaned or abandoned.

Marshall takes advantage of this scene at the almshouse to mention the popular Anancy tales, which originate from the African oral tradition. We read that throughout the islands are told these tales of a wily spider who, though small and weak, manages to "outwit the larger and stronger creatures in his world, including man, by his wit and cunning" (224). While the author alludes to the strength of the "Little Fella," she also refers to the unused strength that Merle possesses. Though Saul himself cannot see a similar pattern in Harriet, he recognizes that Merle needs a job that will fully utilize her talents. He has heard that she had recently been dismissed from her teaching post for telling the story of Cuffee Ned, but he is unaware of her larger problem. Merle explains in terms of Obeah: "I am like someone bewitched, turned foolish. It's like my very will's gone. And nothing short of a miracle will bring it back I know. Something has to happen—I don't know what, but something—and apart from me (because it's out of my hands I'm convinced) to bring me back to myself" (230). These words forecast an important confrontation with Merle's past and, significantly, Saul is a part of that experience. As Hortense Spillers contends, the two are, in some respects, reflections of each other: "Saul speaks the language of intellectual culture and the gestures of alienation. He eventually perceives himself not only estranged from those around him, but also cut off from the crucial emotional resources of his own past. Albeit for quite different reasons Merle, whose culture retains intimate contact with elements of its originary African source, shares with Saul some of the same symptoms of self-alienation."[11]

Merle's particular symptoms are conflated in the novel with a larger concern with historical social patterns. She is distantly related to Duncan Vaughn, the old English planter who had owned one of the largest sugar estates on the island. Apparently, the old man was "something of a legend": "People talked about how he had sired the last of the forty children he had had from the black women who worked on his estate at the age of seventy-five and then died six months before it was born sprawled in the planter's easy chair he slept in at night, his gout-swollen legs cradled in the chair's canvas sling" (69). Merle's father followed this example. Even as an adult, Merle continues to suffer extreme psychological damage because as a small child, she had witnessed her mother's murder but could not identify the murderer. Reportedly, her father's "legitimate" white wife arranged it all.

As Lizabeth Paravisini-Gebert correctly states, Merle's family history parallels the history of the "plantation patriarchy": miscegenation, violence, and, as we later see, neglect of "illegitimate" children. But Marshall also unveils the frequently overlooked relationship between the plantation mistress and the black woman.[12] Documented in any number of slave narratives is the displaced rage of white women over their husbands' lechery. This frequently led to white women's violence against black or mulatto women. In *The Chosen Place,* that historical pattern repeats and redoubles upon itself to take on new but familiar forms of exploitative female behavior.

Merle reveals to Saul at Carnival that she had studied in England. Her father, who had earlier refused to recognize her as his daughter, provided financial support until she became disenchanted with school and stopped attending classes. A wealthy white woman offered accommodations at her home, and Merle became involved in an apparent lesbian relationship with her. Despite the gifts (the silver earrings were but one of many) and despite the hospitality, Merle gradually realized that the woman was "draining [her] very substance." She then struck out on her own and, believing that her past was behind her, eventually met and married the African student of economics, Ketu Kinbona. Like Saul, Ketu believed that "the main job in . . . poor agricultural countries [had] to be finding ways of improving the lot of the Little Fella out on the land" (331). Ketu had not been taken in by the "glamour of the West," Merle tells Saul. "He had come for certain specific technical information and he wasn't interested in anything else they had to offer . . . their gods, their ways, or their women" (331). Against her better judgment, Merle secretly continued to accept money from the Englishwoman, for with the birth of their daughter, the couple's already poor financial situation worsened. Sexual jealously, economic stability, and malicious control prompted the woman to reveal to Ketu his wife's earlier relationship with her, and a short time thereafter Ketu and child returned to Africa.

With Merle's abandonment came severe depression, and she experienced the first of her prolonged comatose states. To the possible allegation that the author may be homophobic in her portrayal of the relationship between Merle and the Englishwoman, I agree with Spillers, who notes that Merle, in the scheme of the novel, must end the liaison "because she feels exploited by the dynamics of power." Spillers goes on to say: "There are grounds here for an 'inequality'—Merle is younger, poorer, and not only black-skinned and colonized, but also, primarily *not* English *culturally*."[13] The Englishwoman carries an assumption of cultural superiority and, perhaps in her adoration of the woman, Merle herself believes that assumption for a time. But inequality in political or personal relationships spells oppression.

Marshall uncovers the dynamics of oppression on several levels (race, class, gender, and culture) and proceeds to illustrate how these forces may overlap. But the richness of the text derives from her treatment of process. As a prerequisite to change, Merle must acknowledge and confront her past, as painful though it may be. So must it be with Harriet, whose inclusion in the novel is critical. Not only is Harriet emblematic of the peculiar historical relationship between white women and black, but she also personifies the origins of oppression—origins which she refuses to acknowledge because she denies her complicity in it. Upon first meeting Harriet, Merle makes the seemingly casual remark, "Why if you don't put me in mind of someone I knew in England years ago" (71).

Revealing her deep understanding of upper-class Anglo-American culture, Marshall paints a sensitive and compassionate portrait of Harriet. We read that she had divorced her former husband of twelve years and is filled with the excitement of building a new life with Saul in Bournehills. Curiously, her initial view of the island is not of a place but of "some mysterious and obscure region of the mind which ordinary consciousness did not dare admit to light: Suddenly, for a single, unnerving moment, she had the sensation of being borne backward in time rather than forward in space. The plane by some perverse plan might have been taking her away from the present which included Saul and the new life she was to begin with him, back to the past which she had always sought to avoid" (21). Marshall's skillful management of time takes on multiple, reflexive meanings as we discover that Harriet, much like other characters in the novel, seems reluctant or unable to disclose innermost feelings. She harbors a submerged guilt over her family's "questionable legacy"; ironically, they made their early fortune from speculating in the slave trade and by exporting edible commodities from the very islands she now plans to assist. Stronger than her guilt, however, is her fear that she will end up like her mother—a totally ineffective latter-day Southern belle.

Here Marshall intones Harriet's direct relationship to slavery and the plantation. However, on quite a different level, Marshall also begins her exploration of the female psyche. Mrs. Amron comes to represent the woman whose fulfillment is achieved only through her usefulness to others. Though she is not ill-intentioned and sincerely believes that her actions generally promote positive ends, she manipulates and controls—rarely stopping to question her behavior. Her fashionable education "prepared her to be little more than another attractive appointment, like an expensive Waterford chandelier, all cold-faceted crystal, in some well-to-do man's house" (41). Without any work of her own, without a career, she feels an emptiness that can only be filled through her importance or value to someone else. So it had been with her first husband, Andrew Westerman, a nuclear physicist. With his increasing success, Harriet found herself "longing for the years when he had been the poor but brilliant graduate student, whose career she had helped shape and secure with the little money left her and her family connections, with her love and support." Marshall helps us to understand that she had loved him, "since love for Harriet was intimately bound up with the need to *do* for the beloved, to be more than just a wife, and this, in turn, was part of an even larger need, present in her from a child—and innocent enough then—to wield some small power" (39).

Despite appearances to the contrary, Harriet continues to control the lives of others—never in any blatant manner, but with the quiet restraint reflected in her appearance and manner. Indirectly, through Harriet's influence with her family friend, Chester Heald, the Center persuades her present husband, Saul, to leave his teaching post in order to head the project in Bournehills. Harriet had carefully assessed Saul's abilities and his needs and had even patiently endured an intermittent long-distance affair, which lasted some three years before they were finally married. But time, Marshall tells us, was of little concern to Harriet. "She had come after all from a family that had always measured time not in years but in generations" (44). Strangely, Harriet recalls that her "great-uncle Ambrose Shippen, who had been affectionately dubbed the robber baron of the family, used to speak of the widow Susan Harbin [her forebear] in the present tense, as if she were still alive" (45). Past time is more symbolically contained in the present as Marshall describes the widow's picture hanging over the "stained, faded ledger still to be seen in a glass display-case at the Historical Society." The ledger kept careful accounts of the "salted cod, cornmeal" and other edibles imported to the West Indies. It also recorded the number of slaves taken on in Guinea.

Harriet feels strongly that she cannot be held responsible for what her family had done, but in many ways (not all of them conscious), her thoughts and actions manifest her assumption of privilege and power. In contrast to Saul, who involves himself with the people on a primary level, Harriet only *appears* to be involved. In fact, she assumes the role of a spectator in a theater—"close up on the action, almost part of it, . . . nonetheless, by virtue of her seat on the sidelines near the wings, remained apart, immune" (144–45). Though motivated by the best of intentions, she is reminiscent of the charitable plantation mistress as she dispenses to the Bournehills children gallons of fruit juice to help alleviate the vitamin C deficiency in their diets. Interestingly enough, the children remind Harriet of the many nieces and nephews of her mother's personal maid, who now, significantly, lives off a liberal pension that Harriet has arranged. Harriet recalls that every year, she and her brothers sent used clothing and discarded toys to these children whom they never met. One year, however, she refused to send one of her toys. "And it wasn't because the toy had been a favorite of hers," the narrator explains. "It was just that she had felt she was being asked to give too much and had balked" (169). The very same feeling is to recur in the latter part of the novel to reinforce the author's concentration on historical patterns.

Marshall makes yet another historical connection between white colonial powers and their subjects when she describes Harriet's amusement with the Bournehills people, who talk endlessly of past and present events on the island. Harriet notes with some discomfort that they treat "the events of the past as though they had only just occurred and [treat] her, almost from the beginning, as if she somehow knew about them, and was thus no stranger, but part of the place, bound to it and to them in some way" (171). The author adds, significantly: "She might have been annoyed with the manner they assumed toward her, had it not been for the feeling that had remained with her . . . , that sense of being a spectator" (171).

It is precisely that spectator role which prevents Harriet from understanding or appreciating the economic system under which her neighbor, Gwen, functions. We learn in an important scene that Gwen kept a "long-standing agreement with the postmaster to sell him all of her eggs. This money was then used toward purchasing the family's weekly supply of staples." Marshall suggests here the bread-winning capacity of the West Indian woman, a derivative of traditional African culture. Further, she makes reference to the bargaining power that is a part of the West Indian woman's separate autonomy. Harriet means well when, in Gwen's absence, she prepares an omelet to feed the woman's hungry children, but without stopping to question why a half dozen eggs had been set aside, she presumes she knows best. Even when she learns of her error, she responds: "Besides, it doesn't make any sense to sell perfectly good, nourishing eggs to buy that awful rice they all eat" (181). "It might not make sense to you," Saul admonishes, "but it obviously does to Gwen. She's probably discovered she can feed more mouths doing it her way. I don't know. What I do know is that you can't go around ordering other people's lives and trying to make them change long-standing habits overnight—especially food habits which are always the hardest to give. Everybody doesn't live by your standards. Your values aren't necessarily the world's. Why, the kids didn't even eat the goddamn omelet" (181). The author emphatically illustrates the Western tendency to dominate and to impose values that may be inappropriate in another cultural setting.

Harriet's need to dominate, her unquestioned sense of superiority, is dramatically disclosed at Carnival. The Bournehills women persuade her to participate in their pageant, and though she finds it all very interesting, she maintains her usual apartness. After two hours of marching, she feels that she has "proved herself" and begins to move out of the boisterous crowd toward the Cockerel Club where, as prearranged, she is to meet Saul. Before she can turn the corner, however, the "raucous green-clad guerilla band" from Harlem Heights, a shanty town, has swept her along in their midst. The mob seems to be heading directly for the bay at the foot of the street and she tries to divert them, ironically onto Queen Street. But they ignore her shouting voice and raised hand: "They hadn't heard her. Nor, she suddenly realized, her shock reflected in her eyes, had they really *seen* her. But how could this be? She was unmistakably among them with her hair (it was almost blonde now . . . from the long months of sun) and her face, which despite her tan was still nonetheless white. But even those closest to her, the ones bumping into and pummeling her as they rushed past, appeared totally unaware of her presence" (294–95).

Importantly, Marshall reverses the notion of "invisibility" as she has described it in previous fiction. Until this novel, whites have generally refused to recognize the personhood of blacks. In this passage, however, the black masqueraders completely disregard Harriet. They are infused with a collective power likened to "one of those powerful Bournehill breakers which give the impression they have been gathering speed and force across the entire sea" (293). If we remember Marshall's earlier description of the sea as having human qualities, it is apparent that the author makes reference to nascent black nationalism.

When Harriet is thrown against a black-bearded youth, the following occurs: "The youth's gaze, fixed on the invisible goal, shifted briefly and he saw her: her white annoyed face, the imperious hand pointing. And he remained strangely unimpressed. He heard and understood her order, but paid no heed. Instead, planting himself in front of her, his arm holding off the crowd moiling and tumbling around them moved his body from the waist down in a slow lewd grind" (295).

Harriet is shocked and terrified, but the narrator also tells us that she is "seized . . . by a revulsion and rage that was almost sexual in nature." Harriet loses control and lashes out, "slapping savagely at those closest to her," swatting, "the way one would a swarm of flies." The crowd, however, remains indifferent. Finally, as the guerilla band turns the corner away from the bay, merging so as not to fall into the water, Harriet is thrown against a door. As John Cooke observes, this entire episode represents a "ritualistic transformation of power: the unmasking of the West . . . through the islanders' new mask, one representing their Pan-African heritage."[14] Marshall reveals the true nature of Harriet's need to control. Symbolically, Harriet represents colonial and neocolonial powers attempting to assert authority and domination over the lives of others.

Harriet's need to control is enacted on a second level that connects her to the black-white female paradigm discussed above. Paradoxically, her connection is related to her lack of self-identity. She and Merle are very much alike in this respect. Marshall shows, though, that their separate histories mandate their separate behaviors. Harriet continually avoids the past; Merle eventually confronts it. As perhaps most poignantly illustrated through her marriage to a Jew, Harriet wishes to sever her ancestral ties. Through her marriage to an African and through the birth of her child, Merle connects with her ancestry. Yet they both share an intimate relationship with Saul, who inadvertently becomes for each an agent of liberation.

It is with Merle, though, that Saul reveals his undisguised guilt and anguish over the loss of his first wife, Sosha, who died during childbirth while on a field expedition in Honduras with Saul. She had accused him of being "a latter-day Moses come to deliver the poor and suffering of the world, including her, only to fail them" (326). Out of a sympathetic and mutual need for acceptance and confirmation, Merle and Saul spend the night together. (Merle, incidentally, counters her negative feelings about whites by thinking of Saul as a "Backra," a mixed people of the Canterbury district. Note the similarity between "Backra" and "Buckra," the latter word commonly used by African-American slaves to denote a person of Caucasian descent.) Their relationship continues until Lyle Hutson— perhaps goaded by Harriet's coolness, her calm, unruffled exterior—discloses the affair.

Harriet reacts to the messenger as well as the message. Throughout the novel she harbors a strong dislike of the barrister. His casual touch to her arm brings a "dark splotch like an ugly bruise or one of those Rorschach inkblots that would reveal her, surging to the surface" (48). We know that she is appalled, in part, by this black man's open extramarital relationship with a white woman and, in part, she is put off by his presumptuous, sometimes affected behavior. Just as importantly, Lyle vaguely reminds Harriet of her former husband:

> It was that both men conveyed the unmistakable impression of having accomplished all they had set out to do with their lives, of being complete and therefore no longer in need of anyone's help. There would be nothing, in other words, a woman could do for them. It would all have been done. If a wife, she would simply be part of the established constellation of their life—and not particularly central to it either; a peripheral star, rather. A mistress would merely be the spoils of their success. . . . Men like that, whose lives had achieved a finished form, held absolutely no interest for Harriet. She could feel nothing for them. (196)

We see from this and other passages Harriet's need to be needed, which is ultimately related to her need to control.

But in this multilayered novel, Marshall also probes the psychosexual effects of control when it is exercised between women within a racist, colonial social structure. Importantly, Harriet prefers to think of Saul and Merle's intimacy as "a minor indiscretion brought on by the holiday." As Paravisini-Gebert indicates, Harriet makes of the affair "the contemporary equivalent [of] a harmless tryst in the slave quarters—a response that implicitly confirms [her] superiority as massa's white wife as it dismisses Merle in her uncompromising blackness as incapable of inspiring a 'grand affair of the heart.'"[15] Saul, however, refuses to have Harriet accept this distortion. To her disbelief that he could even touch a black woman, he angrily responds:

> "Well, for your information that particular aspect of it presented no difficulty, perhaps because I've always been somewhat eclectic in my tastes as far as women go. The first woman I ever loved was Peruvian, a Mestizo—part Indian, part Spanish in case you don't know what that means. My first wife looked exactly like a Russian muzhik, broad slavic cheekbones and all; and here you are purebred Anglo-Saxon which, frankly, I find equally exotic. So for a man like me, someone with such wide tastes, Merle's color presented no problem. She was the one. She couldn't bear the thought of my being white and insisted on pretending that I was really one of the red people from up Canterbury.
> "And just think, someone could ask you the same question. They could

ask how it is that you, a Philadelphian blue-blood, could bear to have me,
a long-nosed Jew, touch you. They might not be able to understand that
either." (430)

Harriet does, nonetheless, understand Merle's threat as the unthinkable
sexual rival and immediately resorts to manipulative and controlling measures to be rid of her.

Merle, in addition to her guilt, understands the "love, desperation, and
need" that drive Harriet to visit her the next day. In fact, Marshall makes
it clear in the ensuing confrontation that despite their differences, Merle
and Harriet hold something in common: They are "two women who had
long been assailed by the sense of their uselessness, who had never found
anything truly their own to do, no work that could have defined them,
and so had always had to look outside themselves to the person of the
lover for definition, a sense of self, and for the chance in their relationship
with him, in helping to shape his life, to exercise some small measure of
power" (437). In a forceful, emotional scene, the two women exchange a
look of understanding, but Harriet's internal reaction is telling. Momentarily, she becomes "afraid the woman would do something truly foolish,
such as reach across and place a hand on hers to seal what she saw as a
bond between them; and offended beyond words, she felt her body brace
to spring out of the way of that touch" (437). Merle, on the other hand, is
"subdued, compliant, [and] sympathetic" as she tells Harriet of her plan
to go away to Trinidad. Feeling that Trinidad is not far enough away and
knowing that Merle cannot afford to travel elsewhere, Harriet offers to
pay her fare to Canada or Europe or Africa, where she could live near her
husband and child. Harriet even offers enough money to tide Merle over
wherever she goes until she finds a job.

Harriet clearly holds the far greater economic power that, when combined with racial contempt and sexual jealousy, re-create the old pattern
marking the relationship between black and white women. Harriet and
the Englishwoman become one. Merle, however, is now strong enough to
assert her autonomy, to liberate herself from the destructive power of the
white woman. The following passage reveals Merle's personal break from
domination:

> "Money! Always money! But that's the way they are, you know," she
> cried, informing the *sea,* the long, wearily sloping veranda, the house with
> its *ancient ghosts,* of the fact. "They feel they can buy the world and its wife
> with a few raw-mouth dollars. But lemme tell you something, m'lady . . .
> I can't be bought. Or bribed. . . . And I don't accept handouts. Not any-
> more at least. I used to. You might not have heard about that, but I did.

> And for the longest time. And because of it lost the two people who
> meant life itself to me. But not anymore. I've grown wise in my old age.
> And proud. Poor as the devil, but proud." (441, italics mine)

Merle, now for certain, will stay on in Bournehills until she can make a
move on her own.

That evening, Harriet writes to Chester Heald and, shortly thereafter, Saul
receives a cable announcing his transfer to the United States where he is to
head the program and development division. Harriet's need to control clearly
extends beyond Saul to include the suffering people of Bournehills. Here she
becomes the personification of colonial power.[16] *"What is it with you and your
kind, anyway?"* Saul questions. "If you can't have things your way, if you
can't run the show, there's to be no show, is that it? . . . You'd prefer to see
everything, including yourselves, come down in ruins rather than 'take
down,' rather than not have everything your way, is that it?" (454) Time
returns to its historical pattern as the narrator reminds us of Harriet's
childhood when she "had always refused, even when it would have saved
her from being punished, to admit either innocence or guilt" (454). Had
she been able to speak now, matters would have been no different.

As images from Harriet's past moil about in shadowy form, Marshall
uncovers Harriet's deeply entrenched racism and her cavalier assumption
of superiority. However, the author is careful to show that Harriet herself
is a victim. She is what Sharon Welch terms a "creation of oppression, a
person whose very concept of morality is poisoned by the legacy of oppression, unable to see the oppression that has been the work of whites
and unable to accept the seriousness of its damage."[17] In her moral certainty, Harriet cannot even fathom an alternative approach to life. *"What
is it they wanted?"* she queried about the islanders' lack of response to her.

> She could not have said. But it was too much, of that she was certain. She
> could not give it, whatever it was, without being herself deprived, dimin-
> ished; and worse, without undergoing a profound transformation in which
> she would be called upon to relinquish some high place she had always
> occupied and to become other than she had always been.
>
> She would never agree to do this; and so, in the face of what she felt to
> be their unreasonable demand, for the sake of her own preservation, her
> sanity, she had turned from Bournehills, slipping into an indifference
> which made everything going on around her . . . seem remote, unimpor-
> tant, having nothing to do with her. (408)

As Welch points out, Harriet equates change with loss: "She exemplifies
the upper-class person so identified with privilege that it has become his

or her sole identity. Without privilege, she fears that she would cease to exist."[18] Her fears, we know, are not recent. She had sought to flee the guilt and horror of her experience with Andrew Westerman only to repeat the pattern with Saul. Rather than confronting her past and creating a new identity, Harriet stubbornly remains the same. Her lack of respect for those around her is itself a "correlate of oppression." A minor white character muses aloud: "It's sad to say but I'm afraid we shall be done-in, the great white race, by our niggardliness and bad faith, our refusal to really take down and make room for the other fellow" (200). Because she cannot or will not change or because she comes to recognize her own destructiveness, Harriet chooses suicide. However, Marshall portrays her predicament in such a fashion as to indict not so much the woman as the Western ideology that has shaped her.

Since Harriet's body is never recovered from the Bournehills sea, we might interpret this as symbolic retribution. However, with Gwen's conviction that Harriet "had been borne back to America," Marshall invokes the traditional African belief that one's soul returns to its native homeland. The author may also be suggesting the continuation of willful destruction from the land of Harriet's birth. But the cycle of life goes on with all of its contradictions and unanswered questions.

The final book of the novel, entitled "Whitsun," makes reference to the Christian celebration of Pentecost. It also notifies the reader of the seasonal change to "end of crop" (dead season). Importantly, the sea undergoes its annual change:

> Every year at this time the water darkened, the tide rose to the point
> where it was difficult to withstand the undertow even in Horseshoe Pool,
> and the cry of the swollen breakers as they moved in over the reefs, that
> loud unremitting sob of outrage and grief, was taken to a new high.
> Moreover, each time the giant waves hurled themselves against the land
> now they left behind great masses of seaweed dredged up from the bottom, dumping it like mounds of rotting refuse along the length of the
> beach. The sea, Bournehills people said, was cleaning itself, and they
> stayed away from it. (414)

Here the imaging of the sea signals the ongoing natural cycle of the seasonal world as it cleanses and renews itself. It also symbolizes the movement away from domination and control, the advance out of colonialism.

To amplify the theme of resurrection, renewal, and change, Marshall describes the Cassia tree, which has stood leafless and barren before the guesthouse since the beginning of the novel but now has suddenly burst forth in bloom. The tree suggests symbolically the African notion of duality and contradiction, that in the midst of death there is life. Perhaps more particularly, the tree represents Merle, who, though "devastated both historically and personally, has within her the wherewithal to flower once again."[19] That flowering, however, is postponed until the end of the novel to allow us to learn more about Merle.

As Merle lies in a comatose state, brought on by the long-anticipated closing of Cane Vale, Marshall makes use of architectural imagery to present a still-life picture of Merle's past. The room holds items ranging from the massive antique bed (no doubt once used by Duncan Vaughn to sire his forty children) to books on West Indian history from Merle's student days in England. There are also prints of slave ships, plantation life, and more. The narrator summarizes: "It appeared she had brought the memorabilia of a life-time—and dumped it in a confused heap in the room." But there are also indications that she had tried to impose order as we see several books neatly arranged on a shelf and a small, uncluttered sitting area near the door: "It expressed her: the struggle for coherence, the hope and desire for reconciliation of her conflicting parts, the longing to truly know and accept herself—all the things . . . which not only brought on her rages but frightening calms as well" (401–2). The room is also like Bournehills:

> perhaps a kind of museum, a place in which had been stored the relics and remains of the era recorded in the faded prints on the walls, where one not only felt that other time existing intact, still alive, a palpable presence beneath the everyday reality, but saw it as well at every turn, often without realizing it. Bournehills, its shabby woebegone hills and spent land, its odd people who at times seemed other than themselves, might have been selected as the repository of the history which reached beyond it to include the hemisphere north and south.

In this passage, Marshall's vision extends beyond territorial boundaries to encompass a worldview in which colonialism continues to exist. Bournehills and its people represent an historical reality that remains. The feeling of stasis belies the "palpable presence beneath," for the author has repeated her message in multiple images: until the great evil of slavery is acknowledged and appeased, no fundamental change will occur. Despite the words of peace and reconciliation, people will continue to act and re-enact patterns of oppression and exploitation that began with the original sin.

We see another example of the duplication of that original sin as the narrator describes the closing of Cane Vale. When the machinery completely breaks down, the rural population breaks down as well. And with the so-called authorities either vacationing or in hiding, nothing can be done. We understand with sharp awareness the ineffectiveness of development schemes that do not take into account agricultural programs sorely needed by the general populace to feed itself. During the course of the project, however, Saul has had the foresight to form a Village Council, members of which are community leaders such as Delbert, the local rum shopkeeper. The only alternative, the council agrees, is to haul the local sugar cane to the factory in the district of Brighton, which was scheduled to close soon. The spirit of Cuffee Ned returns to the island, for over the next few weeks, cooperative efforts lead to the borrowing of every type of vehicle imaginable. In addition to their individual contributions, monies on hand from Saul's project help fund the effort. As the novel draws to a close, we see the people once again experiencing their unity as a people. Saul and Merle, however, are left to resolve the confusion of their separate lives.

The complexity of Saul's grief, guilt, and desires is staggering as he tries to unravel the questions and demands of love. We are reminded of Max Berman in "Brooklyn," when the narrator explains: "Part of him might have also drowned, part of him died with Harriet. And in a way, this was how he had come to see his death, as a series of small ones taking place over the course of his life and leading finally to the main event, which would be so anticlimactic, so undramatic (a sudden violent seizure in his long-abused heart, a quick massive flooding of the brain) it would go unnoticed. It was the small deaths occurring over an entire lifetime that took the greater toll" (465).

But Saul has not failed everyone. He returns to Bournehills only to bid Merle farewell, for he has heard that she is leaving the island. Sitting on the veranda of the familiar, old guesthouse, Saul and Merle appear "close, intimate, of a mind." However, we understand that "their separate thoughts—his of Harriet, hers of the journey ahead—had already taken them far from each other" (466). Merle has found the courage to travel to Uganda in search of her child. She has sold everything, including her earrings and the old Bentley car and, with ticket in hand, she seems able to begin anew.

The author returns to the sea a final time to suggest renewal, for it becomes a clear, deep-toned blue, filtered of all impurities, and less furious in its roar. With this "yearly cleansing" comes the marked change in Merle. She wears her hair in its natural, unstraightened state and omits the "talcum powder she was forever dabbing on her face as if to mute her darkness." The reader imagines a more mature Reena when Merle explains of Africa: "I have the feeling that just being there and seeing the place will be a big help to me, that in some way it will give me the strength I need to get going again. Not that I'm going expecting to find perfection. I know they have more than their share of problems, or to find myself or any nonsense like that. It's more what you once said: that sometimes a person has to go back, really back—to have a sense, an understanding of all that's gone to make them—before they can go forward. I believe that, too" (468). And like Reena, Merle understands that any real change has to be affected at home. "But I'll be coming back to Bournehills," she states. "This is home. Whatever little I can do that will matter for something must be done here. A person can run for years but sooner or later he has to take a stand in the place which, for better or worse, he calls home, to do what he can do to change things there" (468).

Saul also understands that change must stem from within one's own country as he considers his return to the States. He knows that if he is to live in America permanently, he will have to "take a stand, do something toward shaking up the system. . . . Despair . . . is too easy an out." Although he seems indifferent about returning to teaching, he expresses some interest in the possibility of "setting up a program to recruit and train young social scientists from overseas . . . to work in their own countries." To Merle he sighs, "Outsiders just complicate the picture—as you and I know only too well" (467). It is clear, however, that no matter what Saul decides to do, he will never again return to field work, and his reasons have nothing to do with "giving up" or "hiding out" as he has done before. The author need not clarify for us what he means when he states, "After Bournehills, there aren't any places left for me to go."

Merle, on the other hand, has a definite place in mind, and it is significant that she plans not to take "the usual route to Africa, first flying north to London via New York and then down."

> Instead, she was going south to Trinidad then on to Recife in Brazil, and from Recife, that city where the great arm of the hemisphere reaches out toward the massive shoulder of Africa as though yearning to be joined to it as it had surely been in the beginning, she would fly across to Dakar and, from there, begin the long cross-continent journey to Kampala. (471)

The reverse route serves to illustrate Marshall's artistic tracing of the black experience from the New World toward Africa, and the reader anticipates that a future novel will perhaps have as its setting an African community. Be that as it may, *The Chosen Place, the Timeless People* reflects the author's celebration of human resistance to and eventual triumph over oppression. She describes in the novel not the "politics of parliaments nor even of parties," but as John Reilly correctly qualifies, "the politics that grows from the knowledge that configurations of character and the complex relation-ships of love or resentment gain their shapes from historical cultures."[20]

Unequivocally, Marshall defines her personal cultural identity as Afri-can in its source, and it is in that naming (claiming) that she posits both a self and a community. Yet, as we have already seen, each self and each community is a part of a larger world. By creating *The Chosen Place, the Timeless People* to represent that larger world, she immerses herself within a sensibility that values cultural differences while celebrating a common humanity. She provides in this novel a vision of hope as she transforms suffering into creative, responsive, and responsible action. To readers the world over she offers the lessons of accountability and the possibilities of change for a new world configuration.

Chapter Six

Recognition and Recovery

Diasporan Connections in *Praisesong for the Widow*

Whereas Marshall traces historical patterns in *The Chosen Place, the Timeless People,* she traces cultural patterns in *Praisesong for the Widow* (1983). In the earlier novel, she uses a single symbolic setting; in *Praisesong* she moves the locale from North America to the Caribbean, which, symbolically, points eastward toward Africa. The title itself suggests the author's incorporation of cultural practice. "Praisesong" refers to a traditional heroic poem recited or sung at various celebrations in Africa. It refers as well to a religious song commonly used by African-American congregations. Before we even begin the novel, then, we prepare ourselves to listen to the musical composition Marshall composes. That composition, polyphonal in nature, is unified with a persistent drumbeat to reflect the African cultural influence throughout the Diaspora.

Praisesong takes on surreal, ethereal qualities emanating from dreams and memories that dramatically overlap opposing time frames or conflicting modes of temporality. For no apparent reason, the long-forgotten past of Avey Williams Johnson tumbles forth in bits and pieces to startle and sometimes paralyze the sixty-two-year-old widow of the novel's title. Associations, impressions, people, and events seem to evoke bizarre connections within her, and the reader is caught up in the whirlwind that is Avey's disoriented mind. As she sorts and rearranges thoughts and impressions, we see that Avey (short for Avatara) is really involved in a subconscious search to regain her lost identity. I deliberately refer to Avey's

search as subconscious rather than unconscious, for Marshall creates a subterranean current that flows throughout the novel.[1] That current keeps
the heroine afloat in her literal and symbolic travels over water. Ultimately, she arrives at the point of departure to acknowledge the indelible
imprint of her collective African heritage and to reclaim her preordained
role as a chronicler of history.

This is the first work in which Marshall focuses her attention at novel
length on a middle-class African-American woman. To be sure, that
choice indicates her continuing exploration of African cultural vestiges
that exist within the continental shores of North America. It indicates as
well her readiness to take on directly "the overwhelming complexity of
America"—something she was unwilling to tackle earlier. Perhaps she
tackles some of this complexity in *Praisesong* because of the changes in her
personal life. In 1970, she married her second husband, Nourry Ménard, a
Haitian businessman. Theirs was what Marshall termed "an open and in-
novative marriage" in which they visited back and forth from Haiti to the
United States.[2] Because they both remained professionally and financially
independent, Marshall began teaching in order to support herself and her
son. This, of course, was a difficult transition, for it necessarily limited
the time for her writing. It is not surprising, then, that *Praisesong* appears
so many years after *The Chosen Place.* Neither is it surprising that we see a
good amount of Haitian material in the novel.

Although Haitian and other Caribbean materials are woven throughout *Praisesong,* the artist is concerned with American materialism and how
upwardly mobile black people can fend off its spiritually debilitating effects. At no point does Marshall slip into the facile admonition that economic advancement signals the destruction of the soul. Rather, she cautions, as she has from the beginning of her career, that peoples of African
descent avoid false values that supplant and/or obviate spiritual needs. She
states in unequivocal terms that they must respect and revere the "nurturing ground" from which they sprang and instill that lesson in generations
to come. The novel itself is written in honor of one of her ancestors as it is
dedicated to her grandmother, Alberta Jane Clement (Da-duh).

What is perhaps Marshall's greatest achievement in *Praisesong* is her
ability to draw the reader into Avey's personal odyssey so that we respond
differently to each of the diverse cultural icons and codes within the text.
Abena P. A. Busia comments that "an African-American reader, for example, who recognizes lines from the songs of Nina Simone, but for whom
the Carriacou Tramp has no meaning or resonance, will experience the
journey differently from a West African such as myself, for whom the opposite is true; the ceremonies for the dead of Carriacou may resonate with
meaning while references to specific blues songs go unremarked."[3] Yet,

with Marshall's skillful artistry, all readers can detect cultural parallels between the Gullah people of South Carolina and the people of Haiti, Martinique, Grenada, and Carriacou.

Marshall employs the stream-of-consciousness technique and interweaves spontaneous associations of the moment with a past reality to create the mood and feel of vertigo. And like the main character, the reader's mind becomes a *tabula rasa,* open to new thought processes that lead to the surfacing of subconscious impressions and the reevaluation of old beliefs. The artist continues her stylistic interest in cyclical time, for in the space of four days (the actual period of the story), she covers the lifetime of an African-American woman and the ongoing history of another timeless people, the Ibos. Since this history forms the central myth around which the novel revolves, it is important to present it in some detail. Appropriately, it embodies both African folklore and ritual, and it is presented to us through the mediums of dream and memory.

The Ibos, the child Avey had been told by her Great-Aunt Cuney, were "pure-born" Africans, noted for their ability to see not only into the past but also into the future. When they were brought as slaves to the Landing in Tatem, South Carolina, they quickly assessed what was to befall them and, without bothering to get back on the ships, they simply walked out on the water. In a voice that seemed to *possess* her, Cuney would recall the exact words her grandmother had recited:

> "When they [the Ibos] realized there wasn't nothing between them and home but some water and that wasn't giving 'em no trouble, they got so tickled they started in to singing. You could hear 'em clear across Tatem 'cording to her. They sounded like they was having such a good time my gran' declared she just picked herself up and took off after 'em. In her mind. Her body she always usta say might be in Tatem but her mind, her mind was long gone with the Ibos."[4]

To the young child's question about why the Ibos had not drowned, Aunt Cuney had answered: "Did it say Jesus drowned when he went walking on water?" (40)

By making reference to biblical scripture and by using the oral storytelling form, Marshall allows us to overhear the sacred, unwritten history of the Ibo people. She also deftly establishes the central myth of the novel as well as its dominant motif: the human capacity to be physically in one place and mentally (spiritually) in another. Avey, in one sense, enacts this very concept, for as the novel begins she is aboard a luxury cruise liner significantly named *The Bianca* (white) *Pride* en route to the Caribbean. Her mind, however, is elsewhere. Only a few days into the cruise, she has a recurring and disturbing dream of her great-aunt beckoning her to come along on a walk to Ibo Landing.

In having Avey travel south each summer to visit her Great-Aunt Cuney, Marshall alludes to the common practice of African-American families, who, having migrated to different regions of the country, regularly returned themselves or sent their children to reunite with relatives and friends. Avey had long forgotten her many childhood treks across the mysterious, almost primeval woods, the denuded cotton fields, and the abandoned rice fields to reach Ibo Landing. There she would listen enraptured to the proud old woman retelling the Ibos' story of resistance, of self-determination, of empowerment. "Moreover," the narrator states, "in instilling the story of the Ibos in her child's mind, the old woman had entrusted her with a mission she couldn't even name yet had felt duty-bound to fulfill. It had taken years to rid herself of the notion" (42). Now invading Avey's waking and sleeping thoughts are memories of the old woman (long deceased) and her insistent plea: "Come. Won't you come . . . ?"

We are told that the walks had started when Avey was seven. This seems a credible enough statement, but the narrator adds, "Before she had been born even!" Cuney "had sent word months before [Avey's] birth that it would be a girl and she was to be called after her grandmother who had come to her in a dream with the news: 'It's my gran' done sent her. She's her little girl'" (42). This mysterious happening—a type of premonition announcing Avey's birth and making a claim of ownership—moves the reader into another realm of experience and time. It reflects a temporal dimension that John S. Mbiti refers to as the Sasa period: "Sasa is the time region in which people are conscious of their existence, and within which they project themselves both into the short future and mainly into the past (Zamani). Sasa is in itself a complete or full time dimension, with its own short future, a dynamic present, and an experienced past. We might call it the Micro-Time (Little Time). The Micro-Time is meaningful to the individual or the community only through their participating in it or experiencing it."[5]

What Marshall creates here and throughout the novel is a very complex and vacillating modality with at least two identifiable dimensions. Obviously Avey, when we first meet her, is a woman of the present necessarily functioning within a Western time frame, but simultaneously she is a child of the past. And beyond that, as the novel moves on, we see that she is an embodiment (or incarnation) of Cuney's grandmother, who represents a still more distant past. Her life then, if we understand time as "recurring," had not begun at the point of birth. It had been preordained through the conscious willing of an invisible ancestor. The following observation, also from Mbiti, might prove helpful here in our understanding of Marshall's application of time: "Sasa generally binds individuals and their immediate environment together. It is the period of conscious living. On the other hand, Zamani is the period of myth, giving a sense of foundation or "security" to the Sasa period; and binding together all created things, so that all things are embraced within the Macro-Time."[6]

Keith A. Sandiford applies this concept to the Ibos, whose actions were tantamount to "repossessing themselves of the time the white slave merchants had snatched from them. It validates the Ibos' free moral agency over their own time and over the veritable issues of autonomy and survival for a whole community of men and women."[7] In other words, the Ibos sanctioned and verified their own cosmology. Deliberately, they chose to continue participation in traditional African cyclic time as differentiated from the threat of imposed Western linear time. As for Cuney, the Ibo myth became a "bulwark of resistance" against her physical life in South Carolina and a "medium of spiritual transport" to her ancestral home in Africa.[8] Furthermore, in repeating the story, Cuney "initiate[s] her grand-niece properly into the mystery of the past and into the truth of her own particular racial reality."[9] The truth of Avey's racial reality has been so long submerged and disconnected that it is virtually severed from all ancestral ties. Inexplicably, however, thoughts of the past and the recurrent dream of Aunt Cuney disrupt her complacent life.

The details and the movement of the dream are particularly significant. Avey vividly recalls that her great-aunt, in the same ritualistic fashion, "would take the field hat down from its nail on the door and solemnly place it over her headtie and braids. With equal ceremony, she would then draw around her the two belts she and the other women her age in Tatem always put on when going out: one belt at the waist of their plain, long-skirted dresses, and the other (this one worn in the belief that it gave them extra strength) strapped low around their hips like the belt for a sword or a gun holster" (32). Importantly, Aunt Cuney would also wear her "dead husband's old brogans, which on her feet turned into seven-league boots." Cuney's attire suggests a type of androgyny, a fusing together of male and female, past and present, into one martial spirit in order to accomplish her mission. The entire ritual underscores the fact that "the life of an Ibo-American was a warfare on earth."[10]

The reader may be confused with this juxtaposition of time modes, but the end result is to make us *feel* Avey's dizziness spiraling out of control. She, in effect, is a combatant in her own personal war. Her mind seems to play tricks, racing back and forth from her childhood summers in Tatem, South Carolina, to her adult life in North White Plains, New York. Suddenly she remembers being fashionably dressed in a new spring suit with a fur stole draped over her arm. Resisting her aunt's persistent beckoning to "Come, won't you come," she dug her patent leather heels into the dirt and, with the neighbors looking on (including the few remaining whites), a tug of war between the two escalated into a "bruising fist fight":

> Brawling like fishwives! Like proverbial niggers on a Saturday night! With the fur stole like her hard-won life of the past thirty years being trampled into the dirt underfoot. And the clothes being torn from her body. The wood of cedar and oak rang with her inflamed cry. And the sound went on endlessly, ranging over Tatem and up and down her quiet streets at home. (45)

The deliberate overlap of time and place is critical to Marshall's theme, for it illustrates her continuing focus on the need to remember the past, to maintain spiritual connections in the present—especially in the face of economic and so-called social advancement. Avey has spent close to thirty years living in a suburb of *White* Plains, New York, but her humble beginnings in Harlem have all but been erased. She now has a secure civil service job and all three of her children (Sis, Annawilde, and Marion) have grown up. Although Avey continues to work, her late husband, Jerome, has left ample provisions for her financial security. Her yearly cruise to the Caribbean is but one measure of her comfortable lifestyle.

Avey does not understand the meaning of her dream, nor can she account for the uncomfortable, bloated feeling she has been experiencing since dessert in the ship's elegant Versailles Room. She momentarily recalls her daughter's despairing comment: "Versailles. . . . Do you know how many treaties were signed there, in that infamous Hall of Mirrors, divvying up India, the West Indies, the world? Versailles?" (47). Historical time again invades the present, and the uneasiness we feel with the above association is manifested in Avey's discomfiture in body. Unaccountably, she experiences a persistent, distended sensation, which, as the novel progresses, becomes a physical symptom of what Barbara Christian terms her spiritual "dis-ease." Marshall ensures that we will not misinterpret this fact when Avey glances in the mirrors that surround the room. She sees a woman tastefully dressed in "beige crepe de Chine and pearls" who carries herself with "the Marian Anderson poise and reserve." This woman, in other words, has the unqualified "look of acceptability." Significantly, Avey abruptly thinks: "She would never be sent to eat in the kitchen when company came!—*I am the darker brother. They send me to eat in the kitchen / when company comes* . . . —lines from the poem Jay used to recite to her and sis on Sunday mornings in Halsey Street" (49).

Here and throughout the novel, Marshall borrows from African-American poetry and blues to make cultural connections and associations that Avey dimly recalls. The italicized lines above from Langston Hughes's poem "I, Too" illustrate Avey's obvious recognition of Western values, but they are clearly assimilated at the expense of her Africanness. The mirror image comes to represent a distancing, a lack of recognition or identification with the African-American woman who is Avey herself. Sudden remembrances of things past—even commonplace things—now carry for her new and complex meanings she has never before considered. The very same Versailles Room, for instance, with its crystal, tapestries, and damask-covered tables—all these things seem foreign to her, even though her dining room at home proudly displays her "special crystal in the china closet, her silverplate—all eighty pieces—in its felt-lined case" (26).

Such strange feelings of displacement invade Avey's consciousness, literally whirling about in her mind without apparent connections. It is no small wonder that this proper, usually predictable matron should seek refuge in the familiar and the certain. In totally uncharacteristic fashion and much to the puzzlement of her two female traveling companions, Avey hurriedly packs her six suitcases and decides to leave the ship at the next port of call. From there, she plans to fly back home. But it is not to her home in New York that she travels. The series of events yet to occur make it clear that she is destined to travel to her ancestral home.

Marshall has been nudging the reader all along toward a philosophical understanding and a new appreciation of the problems inherent in experiencing time from a dual perspective. Although Avey functions, for all intents and purposes, in Western linear time, her thoughts travel in circles to illustrate her subconscious apprehension of synchronic time. Time, in both dimensions, becomes symbolic of separate cultural constructs at odds with each other. To reconcile that conflict, Marshall places Avey in Grenada where, unable to make flight connections, she is forced to stay overnight. Grenada, and later Carriacou, become important locales because both islands are geographically and culturally closer to Africa. It is especially in Carriacou that Avey connects with African rituals that have lain dormant in her consciousness.

As the harried Avey stands on the wharf awaiting a taxi to take her to a hotel, she notices that what had been a small crowd of people around her has grown to include hundreds who seem, by their familiar and intimate manner, to include her in their ranks. They are boarding rickety schooners to travel the short distance to the small island of Carriacou. We discover that the people are "out-islanders," taking the yearly excursion to their homeland. They speak a patois or creole, a mixture of African and French languages. Avey, of course, is unable to understand the language and is somewhat annoyed with their persistent efforts to communicate. Yet fleetingly, she recalls a similar speech spoken by the older people on

Tatem Island. The author again suggests cultural connections through language, even as she underscores what one of Avey's two traveling companions had earlier suggested: "Somethin's deep behind this mess. Somethin' deep" (23). And indeed there is—something so deep and mysterious as to exert upon the protagonist an irresistible magnetic pull toward her still unspecified destination.

The seeming rambling characterization of Avey Johnson thus far is actually developed in the tightly structured framework typical of Marshall's artistry. Book One, for example, is importantly entitled "Runagate," and it is prefaced with the following lines from Robert Hayden's poem of the same title: "and the night cold and the night long and the river / to cross." This epigraph becomes emblematic of the haunting and harrowing experience Avey only begins with the cruise. But Marshall draws an even tighter correlation between the stumbling slave in the poem and the faltering Avey developed in the novel. The water imagery in both the poem and the novel connote a journey (physical and mental) from slavery in the South to freedom in the North. In the novel especially, it suggests the transatlantic passage of Africans to the New World and, in Avey's case, from the New World toward Africa by way of the Caribbean. Like the slave in the poem, Avey "Runs falls rises stumbles on from darkness into / darkness." She plunges as well "into quicksand, whirlpools, mazes" before she can proclaim, "Mean mean mean to be free." Marshall, however, provides an ironic twist, for, as Barbara Christian comments, Avey's "unconscious run for freedom takes her south, physically south to the Caribbean, psychically south to Tatem, South Carolina, while consciously she believes her promised land to be the North, her safe comfortable home in North White Plains." Christian further comments: "Like the Runagate in Hayden's poem, Avey's Great-Aunt Cuney recalls history, this time in the form of ritual, which, like the written poem, has the quality of continuity, for it too can be passed on from one generation to the next."[11] Though Avey sees herself not as a culture bearer nor as a bridge between generations, we begin to sense that some type of continuity is taking hold. Irony is apparent on another level, for in attempting to run from her life Avey is figuratively running toward it.

Once again, Marshall uses architectural imagery to reflect confusion in character when a taxi driver selects what he feels is a suitable hotel for her: "a towering structure of stark white concrete and glass done in a 'ski slope' design, with hundreds of balconies set at a dizzying slant up its sheer face" (80). The architecture here further serves to conjure up for Avey very uncomfortable images of old age and death. Exhausted from the whirl of thoughts that ceaselessly come in snatches, however, she quickly registers, makes plane reservations, and requests that the taxi driver pick her up the next day according to schedule. As she wearily falls asleep, we prepare ourselves for Book Two, "The Sleeper's Wake."

Book Two reenacts the wake for Avey's late husband, Jerome Johnson, and it details the conscious awakening of a woman who has metaphorically slept through the past thirty years or more of her life. She appears to us "like someone in a bad dream who discovers that the street along which they are fleeing is not straight as they had believed, but *circular,* and that it had been leading them all the while back to the place they were seeking to escape" (82, 83, italics mine). In Avey's continuing erratic dreams, the place becomes Brooklyn where she and her husband (then referred to as Jay) spent the first twelve years of their marriage. Marshall paints in this section a truly moving portrait of a young couple with children struggling to get ahead on too little income in a too small flat. Certainly not without hardship, they initially seem able to cope with the problems of racism and poverty because they turn for sustenance to the "nurturing ground" of their culture.

In her depiction of both Avey and Jay, Marshall illustrates the problem inherent in accepting Euro-American values that displace those of traditional African culture. Their lives are torn asunder by the sacrifices they feel they must make, but they are sacrifices that are far too costly. The author takes us back to the cramped, cold apartment on Halsey Street in Brooklyn, where we listen with Jay to the music of Coleman Hawkins, The Count, Lester Young, The Duke, and others. And on some days, we listen to the blues of such greats as Ida Cox, Ma Rainey, Bill Broonzy, or Mamie Smith. On a Sunday afternoon, we hear the spirituals harmonized by the Southerneers, the Fisk Jubilee Choir, or the Five Blind Boys. We might even overhear Jay dramatically reciting to Avey and the enraptured children "The Creation," by James Weldon Johnson, or a poem or two by Langston Hughes.

Jay Johnson is intelligent, loving, reliable—the most positive male figure Marshall has created to date. It is critical to the novel and to Jay's characterization that he actually believes in the Ibo myth repeated to him by his wife. In fact, during the early years of their marriage, Jay and Avey looked forward to their annual bus ride to Tatem, South Carolina, where they would, in effect, commemorate the sacred ground from which the "unrecorded, uncanonized miracle" took place. Privately, he exudes what Amiri Baraka calls "that strong nigger feeling," exemplified in the small rites mentioned above and the scandalous talk he engaged in during lovemaking. Marshall's language is especially beautiful when she describes the physical union between Avey and Jay. Turning to African imagery, she writes that

as they are joined in love, they are surrounded by Erzulie, Yemoja, Oya—
"a pantheon of the most ancient deities." But with the struggle to get
ahead, to "succeed" in the modern world, a drastic change occurs.

One of the most memorable scenes in the novel forecasts this change.
Avey is pregnant with a third and unwanted child, which, because of their
limited means, she tries to abort. She is disgruntled with their poor living
conditions and constantly complains, though she knows that economic
opportunities for blacks are limited and far between. Jay has been working two and sometimes three jobs just to make ends meet. Avey becomes
shrewish and unkempt and, as she grows bigger and bigger with child,
she imagines Jay's attraction to other women. More accurately, she
projects other women's understandable attraction to the steady Jay. The
tension builds until Avey explodes with the rage borne of deprivation,
self-pity, and loneliness: *"Goddamn you, nigger, I'll take my babies and go!"*

This defiant outburst becomes an avenue by which Marshall can explore the other side of poverty, the Saturday night drama enacted by thousands of African-American women as they retrieve "delinquent" husbands
caught up in the tensions created by poverty and racism. Avey becomes,
for a moment, the exact replica of "the half-crazed woman" she quietly
disdained—the one who left her children in the less than adequate apartment to scour the bars before the pay envelope had vanished. The one
whose "voice—loud, aggrieved, unsparing—did violence to the stillness
as she herded the man, stumbling along in surly compliance just ahead of
her, back down Halsey Street." The one who, with tears in her eyes, "quietly begged [Avey] not to turn her back on them, not to forget those like
herself stranded with men who just wouldn't do right" (107–9). Here and
elsewhere are indications that Avey has emotionally separated herself from
her kin—her community as well as her people.

We certainly understand Avey's frustration, but we also know that Jay
is neither a derelict nor a spendthrift. In fact, he has only one small van-
ity, "a moustache modeled after the one sported by his father around
World War I." It provided that "rakish" look that made him so attractive. "It was also, Avey sensed, a shield as well, because planted in a thick
bush above his mouth, it subtly drew attention away from the intelligence
of his gaze and the assertive, even somewhat arrogant arch to his nostrils,
thus protecting him. And it also served to screen his private self: the man
he was away from the job" (93).

However, partially goaded by Avey's complaints, Jay no longer gives
attention to his private self. In his struggle to gain economic freedom and
security, the music and the poetry stop. The problems associated with
their home and work environments make inevitable the angry confronta-

tion Marshall describes. With one child screaming in the background and another assuming the role of referee, an abrupt silence falls and Jay is caught between two forces pulling him in opposite directions:

> All of a sudden, in the interminable silence, there could be heard the faint scraping of his shoe on the floor and one foot could actually now be seen moving back. One foot and then the other and he would have taken the first (and she was convinced) irreversible step toward the door.
>
> Before the step could be completed, he stopped short with a kind of violence, the other current asserting its hold on him.
>
> He drew himself up, tensing every muscle of his body to the point where it was clearly painful and he was trembling. Having steeled both his body and his will, he stepped forward, Jay stepped forward, and the sound of his tears as he held her and Sis, the strangeness of it in the small rooms, brought Annawilde's shrill cry to a startled halt for a moment. (111)

Shortly after this confrontation Jay shaves his moustache.

The significance of that moment is not to register fully until Avey is in Grenada, for in her semiconscious state she knows that Jay, in fact, had left. Replacing him was the more somber and relentlessly driven Jerome, who, in exchange for the White Plains address, literally worked himself to death. His hard-won and growing career left no time to cultivate "those small rites, an ethos they held in common, [which] had reached backed beyond [Avey's] life and beyond Jay's to join them to the vast unknown lineage that had made their being possible. And this link, these connections heard in the music and in the praisesongs of a Sunday: '. . . *I bathed in the Euphrates when dawns were / young . . .*' had both protected them and put them in possession of a kind of power" (137).

It is significant that the line italicized above from Langston Hughes's "The Negro Speaks of Rivers" names the source of African-American heritage. The entire passage, in fact, suggests that without an active acknowledgment and appreciation of African cultural roots, blacks fall prey to spiritual barrenness leading to personal disintegration and disconnectedness. Indeed, as Busia comments, it is a rupture "tantamount to a repetition in . . . private life, of that original historical separation."[12] Therefore, in this extended section of the novel, Avey mourns not the death of the rigid and compulsive Jerome but the more sensitive and culturally attuned Jay. She also mourns her own cultural loss. In bereavement, she struggles to answer the question so many upwardly mobile African-Americans ponder:

> Would it have been possible to have done both? That is, to have wrested, as they had done over all the years, the means needed to rescue them from

Halsey Street and to see the children through, while preserving, safe-
guarding, treasuring those things that had come down to them over the
generations, which had defined them in a particular way. The most vivid,
the most valuable part of themselves! (139)

As she did in *The Chosen Place, the Timeless People,* Marshall offers an answer:

> Awareness. It would have called for an awareness of the worth of what
> they possessed. Vigilance. The vigilance needed to safeguard it. To hold it
> like a jewel high out of the envious reach of those who would either de-
> stroy it or claim it as their own. And strength. It would have taken
> strength on their part, and the will and even cunning necessary to with-
> stand the glitter and the excess. To take only what was needed and to run.
> And distance. Above all, a certain distance of the mind and heart had
> been absolutely essential. *". . . Her body she always usta say might be in
> Tatem, but her mind, her mind was long gone with the Ibos."* (139)

To make that connection between the mind and the body, between herself and the Ibos, Avey must undergo a rite of passage that includes confession, cleansing, and confirmation. Velma Pollard remarks that Marshall
"avoids the hackneyed Christian/Western symbol of cleansing by baptism
(water and blood). The rituals that are really important in parent African
societies are birth and death."[13] Keeping with her objective to reclaim African cultural traditions, Marshall clearly prioritizes the rituals of birth
and death, but I would add that rather than avoiding Christian symbols
of baptism, Marshall incorporates them to reflect African-American syncretism of Western religion. This approach makes the rituals of Avey's
rebirth accessible to at least one grouping of the diasporan people.

Certainly another grouping of African peoples can find accessible the images and symbols in Book Three, "Lavé Tête." Marshall introduces the book
with the following *Vodun Introit* from Haiti: "*Papa Legba, ouvri barrière pou'
mwê.*" She includes an effective translation from Randall Jarrell: "*Oh, Bars of
my body, open, open.*" These verses signal the first step toward Avey's rebirth.
She becomes receptive to sorting out and clarifying the barrage of impressions that have plagued her from the beginning. And to take us all the
way back to her physical beginning, Marshall skillfully interweaves childhood memories with Avey's current actions and thoughts. We see that
after Avey's prolonged night of grieving the past, her mind is now "like a
slate that has been wiped clean, a *tabula rasa* upon which a whole new
history could be written" (151). Avey, in fact, becomes childlike, examin-
ing as if for the first time the small marine life, the sky, the palm trees on
the island. Memories constantly jostle her mind, leaving her unaware of

the time (importantly, she had forgotten her watch) or of the distance she had traveled during her morning walk. The distance, we begin to see, covers miles as well as years and forecasts the physical cleansing that Avey must undergo before she can become fully restored to her proper axis.

That movement toward restoration is guided and facilitated by Lebert Joseph, an old man who owns the rumshop upon which the exhausted Avey stumbles. His agelessness, his timelessness, is described in terms of indestructibility: "He was one of those old people who have the impression of having undergone a lifetime trial by fire which they somehow managed to turn to their own good in the end; using the fire to burn away everything in them that could possibly decay, everything mortal. So that what remains finally are their cast-iron hearts, the few muscles and bones tempered to the consistency of steel needed to move them about, the black skin annealed long ago by the sun's blaze and thus impervious to all other fires; and hidden deep within, out of harm's way, the indestructible will: old people who have the essentials to go on forever" (161).

Lebert Joseph, with "lines etched over his face like the scarification of a thousand tribes," turns out to be one of the out-islanders busily preparing to go on the excursion to Carriacou. Although he is visibly annoyed by Avey's intrusion, something about her causes him to engage in conversation. He even recounts, as if sacred testimony, his family history, "going on like some Old Testament prophet chronicling the lineage of his tribe" (163). We overhear his explanation of the meaning of the excursion, an annual reunion primarily dedicated to family and to the remembrance of the "Old Parents," the "Longtime People." He might have been speaking directly to Avey of Great-Aunt Cuney when he states: "I tell you, you best remember them! . . . If not they'll get vex and cause you nothing but trouble. They can turn your life around in a minute, you know. All of a sudden everything start gon' wrong and you don' know the reason. You can't figger it out all you try. Is the Old Parents, oui. They's vex with you over something" (165).

To assuage the anger of the Old Parents and to ask forgiveness for any offense committed, the outlanders perform a ritual called "Pa 'done mwê," or "The Beg Pardon." Lebert Joseph tells Avey of the practice of placing for the dead a roasted ear of corn on a plate next to a lighted candle, then performing the libation (sprinkling rum outside the house). Finally, comes the Big Drum or the Dance of the Nations, during which descendants of the various tribes acknowledge (through learned movements) their ancestry. Marshall makes more and more apparent the cultural connections between the people of Carriacou and Africa, but Avey sees herself as a tourist, an outsider to such strange conventions. And much to the dismay and bereavement of the old man, she, like so many other blacks scattered throughout the world, cannot name her tribal origins.

It is important to note that during all of his conversation with Avey, Lebert Joseph does not inquire of her name; rather, he asks of her ethnicity, suggesting the overriding importance of her collective kinship rather than her personal identity.[14] In fact, her kinship with the old man seems a foregone conclusion when she finds herself confessing to Joseph. She recounts her dream of Great-Aunt Cuney and her subsequent plans to fly back to New York. But the old man, Marshall writes, "already knew of the Gethsemane she had undergone last night. . . . His penetrating look . . . marked him as someone who possessed ways of seeing that went beyond mere sight and ways of knowing that outstripped ordinary intelligence (*Li gain connaissance*) and thus had no need for words" (172).

Marshall's language is deliberate. With the Christian reference to Gethsemane, she again alludes to Avey's holy pilgrimage. More pronounced, though, are connections with Africa—particularly with the vision and wisdom of the Ibos whom Cuney revered. In many respects, Lebert Joseph becomes Cuney's counterpart: as she is Avey's spiritual mother, he is Avey's spiritual father; as she entreats Avey to come to a consecrated place, he entreats Avey to travel to another sacred shrine in Carriacou. And just as Avey feels in her dream of Great-Aunt Cuney a magnetic pull, she now feels, without the man ever touching her, the man "gently but firmly" taking her by the wrist. Likenesses to Great-Aunt Cuney are also apparent when Joseph performs for Avey a dance called the Juba, a name that the widow vaguely recalls. "'*We di la wen Juba,*' he sang, and his voice also sounded more youthful. Moreover, it had taken on a noticeably feminine tone. The same was true of his gestures. The hand snapping the invisible skirt back and forth, the thrusting shoulders, the elbow flicking out—all were movements of a woman" (179). Androgynous qualities are clearly incorporated into Joseph's characterization just as they were earlier incorporated into Cuney's. Significantly, Joseph's changing forms in height as he shifts from his short leg to his longer leg, brings to mind Legba, the African god of the Crossroads. Avey is, in fact, at the crossroads of her life, and Marshall provides her with the guidance and protection of a living figure. But first Avey must take the second step toward rebirth.

The passages describing the excursion are filled with associations that Avey can now consciously make. The festive colors donned by the out-islanders on the wharf remind her of the bright, colorful clothing worn by her family and others as they took their annual boat rides up the Hudson to Bear Mountain. Marshall invokes connections through imagery of the umbilical cord:

> As more people arrived to throng the area beside the river and the cool morning air warmed to the greetings and talk, she would feel what seemed to be hundreds of slender threads streaming out from her navel and from the place where her heart was to enter those around her. And the threads went out to not only people she recognized from the neighborhood but to those she didn't know as well, such as the roomers just up from the South and the small group of West Indians whose odd accent called to mind Gullah talk and who it was said were as passionate about their rice as her father. (190)

In the preceding quotation, the cord extends from Avey, but in the following passage, the cord extends from others toward her:

> She visualized the threads as being silken, like those used in the embroidery on a summer dress, and of a hundred different colors. And although they were thin to the point of invisibility, they felt as strong entering her as the lifelines of woven hemp that railed out into the water at Coney Island. If she cared to she could dog-paddle (she couldn't swim) out to where the Hudson was deepest and not worry. The moment she began to founder those on shore would simply pull on the silken threads and haul her in. (191)

Marshall suggests that Avey is not a single individual sufficient unto herself but a member of "a huge wide confraternity" that both nurtures and protects. As a child, Avey intuitively recognized her inclusion with a people, but over the years she has suppressed her group identity. With her disconnection from kin, she has not only dishonored the story of the Ibos but also fled from the destiny named holy by her maternal forebears.

Critical to Marshall's message is that Avey must cross over water. The schooner, significantly named the *Emmanuel C* is "scarred and battered," boasting up front "the crudely carved figurehead of a *saint* on the bow. . . . Only the *crucifix* in its hand had by some miracle remained intact. This it held out over the water as though it were a *divining rod* that had once led the way to a *rich lode of gold*" (193, italics mine). Its sails, though dingy and patched to Avey's eyes, are suddenly "transformed into sails that called to mind those huge, ecclesiastical banners the Catholics parade through the streets on the feast days of the saints. And not understanding why, she catches herself thinking: it had been done in the name of the Father and of the Son" (195). Christian imagery becomes more culturally directed when Avey, seated among the older women on the boat, makes a mental transference to the elder women of the African-American church:

They were—she could have sworn it!—the presiding mothers of Mount Olivet Baptist (her own mother's church long ago)—the Mother Caldwells and Mother Powes and Mother Greens, all those whose great age and long service to the church had earned them a title even more distinguished than "sister" and a place of honor in the pews up front. From there their powerful "Amens" propelled the sermon forward each Sunday. Their arms reached out to steady those taken too violently with the spirit. And toward the end of the service when the call went out: "Come/Will you come . . . ?" and the sinners and backsliders made their shamefaced calvary up to the pulpit, it was their exhortations which helped to bring them through. (194)

Echoes of Aunt Cuney's plea at Ibo Landing unmistakably signal that Joseph will guide Avey toward another hallowed ground.

Marshall masterfully inserts another of Avey's childhood memories: a sermon on the Resurrection of Christ. Complete with the intonations and gestures of the African-American preacher and the call-and-response of the congregation, the message concerns "the shameful stones of false values." And as the preacher exhorts sinners to "call on the Lord," his rocking motion is juxtaposed against the rocking motion of the boat. Just as Avey the child "could feel her breakfast and the chocolate Easter egg she had eaten after Sunday School sloshing around like a great sour wave inside her," Avey the older woman is "startled out of her dream with her hand to her mouth" (203). Suddenly released is the "strange oppressive fullness," which had been with her since the start of her journey. To her added horror, she also loses control of her bowels. In graphic terms, the author suggests that a physical purging is necessary for a spiritual cleansing. This becomes even more evident as the women assisting her repeatedly whisper, "Bon!"

In the privacy of the deckhouse to which she has been escorted, Avey dimly brings to consciousness the image of a slave ship: "She was alone in the deckhouse. That much she was certain of. Yet she had the impression as her mind flickered on briefly of other bodies lying crowded in with her in the hot, airless dark. A multitude it felt like lay packed around her in the filth and stench of themselves, just as she was. Their moans rising and falling with each rise and plunge of the schooner, enlarged upon the one filling her head. Their suffering—the depth of it, the weight of it in the cramped space—made hers of no consequence" (209). With this reference to the middle passage, Marshall symbolically retraces the transport of Africans to the New World to establish their common, historical, and binding connection.

For Avey, other subconscious connections through space and time become consciously binding in the final book, "The Beg Pardon," which is
prefaced by the following:

> "Ultimately the only
> response is to hold the event
> in mind; to remember it."
>
> Susan Sontag

And remember Avey does, just as the timeless people of *The Chosen Place*
remember a history inscribed with pain but also with a meaning vital to
the survival whole of herself and her larger family. Marshall continues to
weave the recurring dream of Great-Aunt Cuney with various other childhood memories to indicate that in a synchronic state of mind, Avey becomes receptive to buried impulses. In discovering and acknowledging
cultural connections, she is empowered—indeed, self-possessed. Once she
has arrived on the island, however, her cultural possession must be confirmed.

In this regard, Marshall includes in Book IV the "laying on of hands,"
a religious ritual common in African-American and other cultural practices that combines the sensual with the process of spiritual rebirth.
Joanne V. Gabbin writes: "Some identify the practice with one of the gifts
of the Spirit that Paul speaks of in Corinthians. Thus it is associated with
the healing power of Christ as he lays his hands on sufferers and they are
cured. Others see the practice as central to the African concept that *the
body and spirit are one*" (italics mine).[15] In the novel, this ritual is performed
by Lebert Joseph's daughter, Rosalie Parvey, who, like Athena in Greek
mythology, so resembles her father in appearance and manner that she
"might have sprung whole from his head, a head-birth without benefit or
need of a mother; an idea made flesh" (216).

Mrs. Parvey, also a widow, stands vigil during the night "like a votary
beside the bed," and in her fitful sleep, Avey alternately envisions her as one
of the significant women—including her great-aunt—in her life. Mrs.
Parvey seems to have that special way of seeing and knowing—*li gain
connaissance*—and is able to soothe Avey. She bathes and anoints the weakened woman in a slow, methodic fashion, periodically punctuating the
silence with "what sounded like a plainsong or a chant." Avey allows herself to remember the weekly scrubbings her great-aunt administered to
her as a child in Tatem. And during the application of a light oil, she is
soothed by the kneading and stretching of her limbs (something Avey herself used to do to her own children when they were infants to "see to it
that their bones grew straight"). Marshall comments that Rosalie Parvey

"was oblivious to everything but the sluggish flesh she was working between her hands as if it were dough she had baked that morning or clay that had yet to be shaped and fired" (223). The entire process suggests a merging of the physical with the spiritual to create a new being. Thus, Avey's response is given in terms of sexual release and conception: "The warmth, the stinging sensation that was both pleasure and pain passed up through the emptiness at her center. Until finally they reached her heart. And as they encircled her heart and it responded, there was the sense of a chord being struck. All the tendons, nerves and muscles which strung her together had been struck a powerful chord, and the reverberation could be heard in the remotest corners of her body" (224).

The musical metaphor in this passage resounds in another powerful chord at the Big Drum later that night. For now, however, her mind continues "to swing like a pendulum gone amok from one end of her life to another . . . dwelling in any number of places at once and in a score of different time frames" (232). Interestingly, Lebert Joseph also seems to modulate within and between time periods. On and off, he seems afflicted with a nervous tick like a "metronome swinging to and fro." And mysteriously older than his ninety years, he is suddenly in need of a walking stick. At other moments, he shifts to his good leg and briskly moves forward, "throwing off at least a thousand years" (233).

All these time frames coalesce at the dramatic climax of the novel when Marshall vividly details the rituals of the "Beg Pardon" and the "Dance of the Nations," which Lebert Joseph described earlier. As in the previous rituals, the ceremonies are performed with religious seriousness as the call (or theme) is chanted and the response of the community is spontaneously delivered "as if to shore up" the single voice of the introit. Marshall records not only the preliminary acts of libation but also the style of dancing (reminiscent of the marchers during Carnival in *The Chosen Place, the Timeless People* and harking back to the Ring Shout that Avey observed with Cuney). It is a movement "designed to stay the course of history."

Marshall indisputably and firmly roots her vision worldwide as she indicates that the "Pa 'done mwê" extends to the outmost reaches of the African diaspora. The "supplicants" kneel in an *unbroken* circle, pleading and petitioning "not only for themselves and for their friends and neighbors present in the yard, but for all their far-flung kin as well—the sons and daughters, grands and great-grands in Trinidad, Toronto, New York, London" (236). Though sitting on the sidelines, Avey also begs forgiveness, for she now understands that her Great-Aunt Cuney had been beckoning her all along to seek the rebirth of her heritage, to claim the role that Cuney's grandmother had so long ago preordained.

To underscore this point, Marshall describes the Dance of the Nations as, one after the other, the various tribes proclaim their beginnings: Temne, Banda, Arada, Cromanti, Chamba. The last dance of the ritual is set aside for the Creoles who, because of "separation and loss," cannot identify their tribes. The lively music is interrupted with a reverberating, plaintiff note from the drums:

> And the single, dark, plangent note . . . , like that from the deep bowing of a cello, sounded like the distillation of a thousand sorrow songs. For an instant the power of it brought the singing and dancing to a halt—or so it appeared. The theme of separation and loss the note embodied, the unacknowledged longing it conveyed summed up feelings that were beyond words, feelings and a host of subliminal memories that over the years had proven more durable and trustworthy than the history with its trauma and pain out of which they had come. After centuries of forgetfulness and even denial, they refused to go away. The note was a lamentation that could hardly have come from the rum keg of a drum. Its source had to be the heart, the bruised still-bleeding innermost chamber of the collective heart. (244, 245)

Because the creole dance reflects a collective experience, everyone joins in as the dance continues. Almost involuntarily, Avey is drawn into the circle as well, performing the steps with deft agility. Had not Jay often said, *"Girl, you can out-jangle Bojangles"*?

To confirm Avey's rebirth, the old man is the first to bow and the others follow suit, singing a praisesong to the widow. It is a song that acknowledges Avey's tribal distinction as well as her cultural inclusion. When asked her name by an elderly, admiring woman who, because of wispy hairs on her chin, is associated with "Tiresias of the dried dugs," Avey replies as her Great-Aunt Cuney had taught her so long ago: not with simply "Avey," or even "Avey Williams," but always "Avey, short for Avatara."

At the close of the novel, Avey indeed becomes an avatar (spirit incarnate), for she assumes her messianic role—her mission of old—to continue the storytelling legacy of Great-Aunt Cuney and Cuney's grandmother. As she leaves for New York, she vows to keep her culture alive by describing to her grandchildren not only the Ibo Landing but also the excursion, the music on Halsey Street, and the poetry. She will tell it all. And if by chance the same taxi driver comes to take her to the airport, she will tell him as well. Marshall concludes: "Her territory would be the street corners and front lawns in their small section of North White Plains. And the shopping mall and train station. As well the canyon streets and office buildings of Manhattan. She would haunt the entranceways of the skyscrapers. And wherever she spotted one of them amid the crowd, those young, bright, fiercely articulate token few for whom her generation had worked the two and three jobs, she would stop them" (255). And she will quote for them what her namesake had said: "Her body . . . might be in Tatem but her mind, her mind was long gone with the Ibos."

In *Praisesong for the Widow,* Marshall emphasizes African cultural similarities, not to minimize obvious distinctions between black peoples of the diaspora but to encourage a spiritual return to African roots. "In order to develop a sense of our collective history," she says, "I think it is absolutely necessary for black people to effect this spiritual return. As the history of people of African descent in the United States and the diaspora is fragmented and interrupted, I consider it my task as a writer to initiate readers to the challenges this journey entails."[16] We see this reiterated in *Praisesong for the Widow.* We see in *Praisesong* as well the message that has become the hallmark of her fiction since the beginning of her career: the human need to find one's personal identity and to establish one's cultural affiliation and allegiance. In *Praisesong* she further suggests that the search has no age or geographical limitations. Like the African griots of old, Marshall brings to her art the freshness and vitality of a master storyteller dedicated to keeping alive traditional values. Maintaining the exacting aesthetic standards of her ancient forebears, she sings praises to all mankind for the marvelous human potential to succeed in unifying the spiritual with the physical.

Chapter Seven

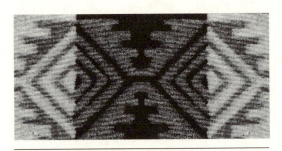

Transformation and Re-creation of Female Identity in *Daughters*

The title of Marshall's most recent novel obviously reveals her focus in the text on women, but the many relationships the author describes extend beyond biological connections between mother and child. As I will later discuss, they include "other-mothers" and "community other-mothers," both of whom respond to the well-being of children outside their nuclear families. In *Daughters* (1991), Marshall also explores relationships between women as sister/friend and presents an unusually sensitive portrait of the "other" woman, most aptly described in the Caribbean vernacular as the "outside woman" or the "keep-miss." While most of these relationships are female centered, they remain, in one way or another, connected to men. In fact, the novel develops its primary theme through the compelling story of a father-daughter relationship, even as it delves into the more general subject of black female–black male relationships. In short, we follow the lives of several women who are, to borrow a phrase from Alice Walker, "in love and trouble." But characteristic of Marshall's fiction is its wide scope, which incorporates several other considerations. In *Daughters* these include Marshall's previous concern with the spread of Western imperialism to newly formed nations, the continuing destructive effects of capitalism upon the poor and disempowered, and the responsibilities incumbent on the black middle class. Given the expansive nature of this complex and probing novel, I will comment briefly on all of the above, but I will emphasize the four or five female characters who figure most prominently.

These women, I shall argue, contribute to the transformation and re-creation of the novel's heroine. They make it possible for the protagonist to evolve into a self-defining female identity who, in the most laudatory of terms, becomes what Toni Morrison terms "a woman good enough even for the respect of other women."[1]

Marshall creates in *Daughters* the changing and complex parameters of a female persona living and growing in the two worlds that have formed her: the Caribbean and the United States. She indicates that the outline of the novel came about in Pirandello-like fashion some eight years ago when she attended an Alvin Ailey Company dance performance in New York City. On the printed program was an epigraph to one of the dances:

> Little girl of all the daughters,
> You ain' no more slave,
> You's a woman now.

This epigram, Marshall goes on to say, "triggered . . . a story about a group of women who had been waiting backstage in my mind, waiting for me to find the right story for them"[2] While *Daughters* centers around Ursa-Beatrice, significantly named after both her American and Caribbean grandmothers, Marshall says it is also "about all the women who have an impact on her life, about the linkages of Black women. *Daughters* uses all of their voices—Caribbean, urban—giving the book a sense of the power these women achieve through language."[3] Here are echoes of Marshall's earlier acknowledgment of women as preeminent crafters of the spoken word. Yet the female power we find in the novel stems from more than language. Women come to effect power through a partial acceptance of and a simultaneous resistance to traditional cultural practices. Such give-and-take allows for the emergence of changing definitions of gender. It further creates new paths toward personal and collective liberation within a community of women as true intimates.

Perhaps this gradual transformation is reflected in Marshall's initial comments about *Daughters.* In a telephone interview conducted shortly after the novel's release, the author stated that Ursa-Beatrice Mackenzie "is someone I've been waiting to write about since I was her age—my early thirties—but the other books always got in the way."[4] From one standpoint, the other books may have facilitated the creation of Ursa. If we consider *Praisesong for the Widow,* Ursa-Beatrice might very well be an example of "one of those young, bright, fiercely articulate token few for whom [Avatara Johnson's] generation had worked the two and three jobs." She is an educated, politically astute, professional woman who has the ability and the opportunity to move upward on the socioeconomic scale. Ursa-

Beatrice might also be a revisiting and rewriting of Selina Boyce of *Brown Girl, Brownstones.* No longer the young girl in search of her cultural identity, the more mature heroine in *Daughters* is reasonably comfortable with her multicultural background. She is certainly one who has been firmly grounded in both her African-Caribbean and African-American cultures. *Daughters* harkens back to *Brown Girl, Brownstones* in other ways. Clive Springer, Selina's beleaguered lover, resurfaces in Lowell Carruthers, Ursa's lover. But even more suggestive of Selina is Ursa's relationship with her father, Primus Mackenzie. This "primal" father figure is reminiscent of Deighton Boyce in *Brown Girl, Brownstones,* for Marshall again paints a mixed but loving portrait of a male parent. With this retrospective view, it is not altogether surprising that Marshall thought of her new novel as a mechanism through which she could, at long last, work out ambivalent feelings about her own father.[5] Quite tellingly, the book is dedicated to her father, Samuel Burke, and to her brother, Frank.

Beyond bringing closure to a personal dilemma that has haunted her most of her life, Marshall brings to the novel a closure of another sort. She presents in *Daughters* a review and possibly a culmination of her preoccupation with an African cultural past to suggest new directions for its cultural future. She seems to call for the creation of a new, transformative identity, which, while culturally focused, is self-defined and ever-evolving. Careful to develop sensitive portraits of both male and female characters, the artist takes into account differences created by historical era, age, ethnicity, and social class. These factors are central to the way in which she structures the novel around political events. These factors are also central to the way she views changing roles for black women in particular. Indeed, by contextualizing Ursa's story within the boundaries of the feminine, Marshall inscribes female authority by virtue of female subjectivity. Women, in the final analysis, become active agents who can be enablers, clearing a space for liberation across culture and gender.

To create an "intimacy between context and consciousness," Marshall gives each character in *Daughters* a distinctive voice in separate chapters. Their voices, however, overlap in the four books that subdivide the novel to create a spiraling effect associated with transcendence and re-formation. Book I, "Little Girl of All the Daughters," introduces the adult Ursa and, through her reflections, the major characters in the novel. The geographical setting is New York City, Ursa's second home, but we travel through her thoughts to the place of her early childhood, the island of Triunion, so named because of its three former colonizers (England, France, and Spain). Book II "Constellation," moves directly to Triunion, where we continue to follow Primus Mackenzie's career as a leading politician. We also listen to the voices of the several women who make up the galaxy of his as well as Ursa's life. Book III, "Polestar," depicts the corruption and power of Western politics both in the Caribbean and the United States. Book IV, "Tin Cans and Graveyard Bones," resolves some of the major political, social, and personal problems raised in the novel and moves toward recovery. It is important to note that, rather than being truncated or artificial divisions, the books of the novel radiate and resonate upon each other. This reflexive, meandering approach, which she employed in earlier novels, allows Marshall to open up again a larger historical, political, and cultural panorama to illustrate how the past is reinscribed in the present. The structure further emphasizes the interrelatedness of the women in Ursa's life to gradually unveil how she is daughter to each.

The story proper covers only two months as we follow the aftermath of Ursa's second abortion. Curiously, the pain of the procedure has not yet taken hold. "Maybe whatever it is," she continually thinks, "is still there." Like the protagonist in *Praisesong for the Widow,* Ursa is bombarded with memories that take the reader along on a journey through time and place. With some guilt, she thinks of her biological mother, the American-born Estelle, who now lives in Triunion. Estelle had any number of miscarriages ("slides," as they were called in Triunion) before returning to the States to give birth to her only child. Ursa's thoughts wander to her "other-mother," Celestine, who helped raise her. This Triunion woman no doubt would have reprimanded, *"Mal eleve!* You should have had it, *oui,* and sent it down for me to raise!"[6] Ursa's also thinks of Astral Forde, her father's "keep-miss" (mistress) and the manager of his hotel. "Wha' the rass!" might be Miss Forde's response to the predicament of "the Mistress Ursa." She might have advised the young woman as her friend had advised her: "Throw down little dirt when you leave the place so the child won't come back to hag your spirit" (126). Emotionally estranged and physically isolated from these women, the troubled Ursa shifts her thoughts to her African-American sister/friend, Vinceretta (Viney) Daniels, who later is outraged that Ursa has chosen to keep secret for a week that afternoon visit to the abortion clinic. It is Viney who sums up the problem at hand:

> "You remind me of a cat with a string of some bones from a graveyard tied to its tail when it comes to your folks. And I don't only mean your parents but Celestine and especially Miss Stone-face [Astral Forde]. All that stuff about them and that island that stays on your mind. . . . The cans and bones keep up such a racket you can't hear your own self, your own voice trying to tell you which way to go, what to do with your life. You can't hear Ursa. You know what you're gonna have to do with all that stuff, don't you?' *Her hand, held ramrod straight, came up and then swiftly down, slicing the air."* (112, italics mine)

Both here and in the abortion scene that opens the novel, the author represents literally and symbolically Ursa's need to sever those psychological and emotional ties.

Beyond the clear distinction between female voices, the reader will note here a shift in the author's use of umbilical cord imagery. In *Praisesong for the Widow,* Marshall used the symbol to represent her thematic focus upon the individual's need to keep taut familial and communal ties. In *Daughters* she changes her angle of vision to suggest that sometimes these ties can be so personally constricting as to disable. Without a conscious, willful act of cutting these ties, another sort of bondage may set in: "the bondage of the mind and heart."[7] To illustrate the latter, the author develops a portrait of the man who for Ursa is both nemesis and idol. Repeatedly she conjures up her father's overpowering image:

> He used to stand at the edge of the swimming pool everyone said he had installed more for her than for the guests at the so-called hotel he owns, keeping an eye on her while she made like a little chocolate Esther Williams in the water. His shoulders in the shirt-jac suit he wore on Sundays—their day to go to the pool—would look to be a mile wide above her. His head with the high domed forehead she had inherited, and that had earned him the nickname PM when he was a boy, would appear larger than the sun. Sometimes, as she glanced up and found she couldn't see the sun or even a blue patch of sky because of his being in the way, she'd do a sudden flip, annoyed, pull the water like a blanket over her head and dive to the bottom of the pool and sit there. Just sit in the wavery blue sunlit silence until the last bubble of air floated up from her lips and disappeared and her lungs ached to breathe in anything, even the blue water. She did it to impress, tease and frighten him a little. She always surfaced with a grin and a wink. Then to get back into his good graces, she'd do more minilaps than they had agreed on for the day. (9–10)

The same annoyance, coupled with her desire to please, continues to trouble the seemingly independent Ursa. Her struggle to break free of her father's hold translates into the process of self-liberation. Importantly, however, her father's place in her life and imagination eclipses Ursa's emotional connection and identification with the women in her life; it is Primus who communicates with her regularly. Ursa even reserves in the compartment of her headboard a special place for his correspondence to keep the "sound of his voice on paper within easy reach" (44).

Complicating Ursa's struggle are political allegiances. To unravel what become multiple layers of meaning, Marshall once again turns to myth. Functioning much like the legend of Cuffee Ned in *The Chosen Place, the*

Timeless People and the story of the Ibos in *Praisesong for Widow*, *Daughters* presents the account of Congo Jane and Will Cudjoe. They were "co-leaders, conspirators, lovers, consorts, friends"—vanguards of the Triunion slave rebellion. The story had been passed down orally among the islanders of how the slaves, from one estate to the next, banded together in defiance of the tyranny of the "Big Three." "The French up this way, the Spanish to the south, and the English everywhere else. *Gallia est omnis divisa in partes tres*" (138). The rivaling powers had fought over "twenty-three wars in two centuries" in efforts to lay claim to one little island. Distracted by their own fighting, the colonizers were caught by surprise when the quashies (slaves) revolted. Once Triunion obtained home rule, the ruling party erected a monument, ostensibly to show strong nationalism. Four stone figures were carved out on a pedestal to commemorate the event:

> To the left . . . stood the old man from Gran' Morne they called Pere Bossou, the conch shell he had used as a bugle raised to his lips. To the right, brandishing the sword he had taken off a conquistador he had slain on the long march up from Spanish Bay was eighteen-year-old Alejandro, the youngest of the four. And in between the oldest and the youngest, striding just a little ahead of them, came the two co-leaders, coconspirators, lovers, consorts, friends: he, Will Cudjoe, a cutlass in one hand, a stolen musket in the other and a bandage made of the finest Alençon lace around his head; she, Congo Jane, also doubly armed and wearing draped around her shoulders, the ends crisscrossing her chest like bandoliers, the shawl—Jane's famous shawl—that had supplied the bandage for the gunshot wound on Will Cudjoe's forehead. (138)

Marshall illustrates here the various national identities that make up the population of the island to underscore the global dispersal of African peoples. And, once again, she provides a historical account of unified resistance against oppression. But we observe a persistent political reality, for the monument was significantly placed in the distant district of Morlands "so as not to offend the white people in town" (140).

Especially relevant to one of her major concerns in *Daughters*, Marshall presents a historical precedent for mutual support between black women and black men. One of Ursa's fondest childhood memories is of standing on her mother's shoulders so that she could touch the toes of the stone figures. "'*Stretch all the way up,*' Estelle had instructed, '*and touch Congo Jane's toes, Ursa-Bea. Go ahead, stretch!* . . . *And make sure to touch Will Cudjoe's toes while you're at it. You can't leave him out.*' . . . *Warmed by the sun, their toes had felt alive as her own*" (13–14). Congo Jane and Will Cudjoe—"You couldn't call her name without calling his. They had been that close." Not until

Ursa was old enough to understand was she told about Jane's shawl, which had hidden a breast "[t]orn to shreds by the nine knotted tails on the whip." During the rebellion, "Jane had snatched the shawl off the woman who owned her, to save it from being bloodied, and draped it around herself. Laying claim to it as long overdue compensation for the loss she had suffered when she was no more than eleven" (pp.138–39).

Many years later when Ursa attended college in the United States, the story of mutual support between the sexes remained alive. In fact, she proposed to write her senior thesis on "the relatively egalitarian, mutually supportive relations that existed between the bondmen and women" (11). Remembering that her professor had once said that "all history no matter who writes it is only factual fiction at best," she would use as her sources "the slave narratives and oral histories, the old plantation records, Aptheker, the Angela Davis article. Why not? They were just as valid as the scholarly texts" (12). Ursa still rankles at the rejection of her proposal and even considers writing the study as a second master's degree. "By the end of *Daughters*," as Susan Fromberg Schaeffer states, "Ursa acts out rather than writes down what she has learned, but first she must radically revise her original conception."[8] Important to that new conception is the author's weaving throughout the novel a polyvocal female narrator, which enables the reader to see beyond the heroine's limited perceptions. We can thus appreciate more fully the woman-centered community that Ursa initially rejects. We see as well the conflicts between men and women that sometimes obstruct female bonding.

By historicizing and politicizing the major characters, Marshall makes more accessible and immediate the central issues of the novel. What initially appears to be the ideal female-male relationship is captured in the courtship and subsequent marriage of Estelle Harrison and Primus Mackenzie. Their early relationship mirrors the closeness and support of Congo Jane and Will Cudjoe, for they share the dream of nation-building and work together to effect reform in Triunion. They even spend their honeymoon on the campaign trail as Primus seeks re-election to his seat as a member of the House. As the favorite son of the impoverished Morlands District where he grew up, his political position is virtually assured. However, the ruling Democratic National Party (DNP) controls the government with its wealth and power. The "Do-Nothings," as the PM calls them, support little to improve conditions in his black-majority district. As we survey those conditions, snapshots become double exposures: the "trash" houses that line the hills of Triunion are superimposed against the run-down housing available to the poor in Harlem or Brooklyn. The problems that plague urban America—the drugs and violence, the squalor and disease—also plague rural Triunion.

Marshall presents ugly details of the corruption in business and government that stymies the growth of black communities. Contemporary politics are "at play" when blacks in the United States as well as in the West Indies are displaced from their homes to make room for a highway constructed for the use of the privileged to circumvent dilapidated neighborhoods. Ursa cannot separate the landscape when later in the novel she drives past an inner-city neighborhood in the States: "Dresden, she said to herself and then immediately changed it to Beirut" (p.296). For a number of years Primus is committed to revolutionary change and, along with Estelle, works tirelessly against overwhelming odds. But with the sight of the U.S. Navy "armed to the teeth" to oversee fraudulent election procedures, his spirit is defeated. Like Mayor Sandy Lawson, his African-American counterpart in Midland City, New Jersey, he is gradually co-opted by the wealthy and the powerful.

Marshall presents two separate accounts of black men of potential political leadership buttressed by the strong moral consciences of black women. Marginalized by race and gender, both Estelle MacKenzie and Mae Ryland understand the dual oppression they and other black women face. Armed with a sense of social responsibility, however, they work to the best of their considerable abilities to bring about change. Estelle, a former school teacher, initiates various projects in Morlands to instill cultural pride and to improve working conditions, especially for women. She voices her opinions at political rallies and, to her husband's embarrassment, disrupts government parties in protest against policies and programs of no value to the majority population of the island. She is clearly a Congo Jane in her own right, and Primus is thankful that she will "see to it that this country boy in his donkey cart keeps to the straight and narrow." In confirmation, Estelle "held up a pair of small, clenched, buff yellow fists that she had turned upwards. To show him the grip she intended keeping on the reins" (p.133). But her grip slackens with the runaway gallop of her husband's personal ambitions.

We learn much about Estelle's character through her letters to her "home-folks" back in Connecticut. What is omitted is also significant. Making use of the epistolary form, Marshall continues to reveal similarities between the Caribbean and the United States. She also reveals the growing momentum of the Civil Rights era, which is gradually taking hold on the island. But the majority of the people in Triunion still struggle for the essentials of survival. Of the market women who begin their workday before dawn, Primus Mackenzie muses aloud to his wife:

> "Nobody realizes it, but those are some of the best business minds in the world you see walking about these dark roads at night. Never been near a

schoolhouse, most of them, yet the ladies can buy and sell you in a minute if you're not careful. They belong on Wall Street. . . . Or here running the Ministry of Finance instead of the jackasses we now have. But what to do? They were born the wrong color, the wrong sex, the wrong class, and everything else on a little two-by-four island that doesn't offer anybody any real scope." (143)

Although Marshall reveals the autonomy these women maintain in their limited spheres, it is precisely because Triunion is so limited that Estelle decides early on to send Ursa-Bea back to the States. She intends for her daughter to be exposed to other options for women—to become independent and assertive in the continuing struggle for communal progress.

In more ways than one, Ursa is to take Estelle's "place at the barricades." Like her mother and uncle before her, she attends Weaver High so she can learn how to "walk the walk and talk the talk" (224). And each time she returns for a visit to Triunion, Estelle is pleased to see "a new edge and quickness to [Ursa's] walk and gestures. A way of looking at and listening to you, as if to say, I'm listening to more than just the words. A subtle, necessary wariness. 'Damn!' she would forget herself and say, and Estelle heard Hartford's North End" (228). And each time Ursa returns, she detects a change in her parents' relationship.

As noted above, Estelle omits important information in her letters back home.[9] She makes no mention of her husband's infidelity and the upheaval it causes in her personal life. Nor does she comment on her frustration with Primus's political dealings. Unquestionably, she presents herself as a model of stoicism and self-reliance, but because of her cultural isolation and precarious marital situation, Estelle is emotionally damaged. One cannot overlook her erratic and sometimes self-destructive attempts to gain her husband's attentions. As the novel opens, Ursa has stayed away for four years, struggling to make sense of contradictions that become increasingly apparent in her life and in the lives of those she loves. She, in effect, is staging a silent protest against the growing corruption in her beloved father and the puzzling behavior of her misunderstood mother.

Broadening and deepening her thematic concerns, Marshall describes how a similar corruption affects the political career of the African-American mayor, Sandy Lawson. Once again, another black woman—Mae Ryland/Miz Ryland/Mother Ryland/The Coalition Lady—is the force behind Lawson's initial triumph. In a clear African-American voice, she reveals much about herself and her community as she warms up an audience during Lawson's mayoral campaign:

"The Lord didn't see fit to give me no babies of my own but I got me more grands and great-grands than I can count. And they are your grands too"—

pointing with a small forefinger. . . at the audience. . . . . "Never mind what
mess they might be into or how much stuff they on or how much you'd like
to disown them sometime, they still all of us grands. Who else we got? So
I'm looking for you to be down to the polls come November eleventh, cause
it ain't just Sandy you gon be voting for but all these grands out here look
like they trying to do away with theirself and us too. Think about it." (281)

Mother Ryland need not think long about resigning from her appointed
position as liaison person when, as in Triunion, an expressway is routed
through part of the black community. But she refuses to give up just yet.
She confides to Ursa: "Maybe we need to let him run with it for a while
till he sees for himself what those folks downtown are up to. He's young.
Maybe he can learn." Mae Ryland, and later Estelle, are nonetheless prepared to act for the good of the community-at-large:

> "But if we find he can't learn and keeps on doing like he's doing"—her
> tone has suddenly changed; her face has tightened—"if we see he just
> ain't no *use* no kinda way, we'll vote his little gap-toothed self outta here
> the same way we voted him in, and find us another grand. And if that one
> don't do right neither, we'll vote his butt out too, and just keep on till we
> find us the right one. . . ." (299)

Repeating a major concern in many of her novels, Marshall targets the
black middle-class as morally responsible for the welfare of their communities. In *Daughters* she presents several characters who have benefited from
the social and political struggles of the fifties and sixties. Clearly Primus
and Estelle Mackenzie are two. The next generation of the black middle-
class is represented through Ursa MacKenzie, Viney Daniels, and Lowell
Carruthers. All three are college-educated professionals. All three are potential members of what Ursa despairingly terms the YRUMs—the
Young and the Restless Upwardly Mobiles. Through a quick succession
of flashing images, Marshall describes the restlessness which, in part,
stems from the frenetic lives the middle-class leads in the fast-paced, competitive world that is New York. The restlessness is also attributed to the
pursuit of luxuries and selfish indulgences that only the relatively successful can afford. Marshall is careful to explain the vulnerabilities and temp-
tations to which members of this class may fall—particularly as the various characters respond to the debilitating effects of racism and sexism in
their personal and professional lives. Nonetheless, she insists upon a strong
moral imperative: that for the sake of communal progress, black men and
black women must stand together in mutual support.[10]

What becomes clear in *Daughters* is that mutual support entails mutual struggle. This is a lesson that both Ursa and Viney come to under-

stand. After her five-year relationship with the parasitic Willis Jenkins, Viney explains to Ursa in metaphoric terms:

> "The world is on fire out here," my granddaddy used to say, "and we need everybody that can tote a bucket of water to come running." He used to say that all the time, talking about the situation of Black Folks in this country, you know, and the need for all of us to stand up and be counted. To be useful. And one day I took a good look at Willis Jenkins and knew he was not one of those Folks. He might be bright, talented, good to look at, great in bed, someone who knew how to talk the talk to get over, but he really wasn't useful. Because Willis Jenkins wasn't about to tote so much as a thimbleful of water anywhere, for anybody, not even for himself if his own patch of woods was on fire. (102)

With "the flat of her hand [coming] down like a scalpel, severing the air," Viney states quite literally, "If thy right hand offend thee!" (102)

Only a few years older than Ursa, Viney is a refreshingly frank and assertive woman whom Ursa can count on for unsolicited advice. So it had been in their college years when Viney, one of the RAs in charge of the freshman dorm, first detected Ura's foreign accent. Originally from Petersburg, Virginia, Viney herself felt like a foreigner at the small New England college. "But I learned to deal," she confesses to Ursa. "Had to! . . . I just trained myself to save the 'y'alls' and such for Folks with a capital F—and to use 'you' singular *and* plural with everybody else, including the siddities. If you ever need it, I'll teach you how to deal too. Just hang with me" (65–66). And hang they did. "Here comes the long and short of it," their friends would say to acknowledge Viney's long-legged five feet nine inches next to Ursa's four eleven and three-quarters. If you see one you *gots* to see the other" (66). Their physical contrast is supplemented and complemented by their distinctive voices. Note, for instance, how the author conveys similarity in meaning and experience even when the characters themselves misunderstand:

> "Hey girl, hey sistuh, how ya doin'? / And the other: 'Hey soully-gal, how yuh keepin'?' / One: 'It's a bitch out here having to deal with these men *and* the white folks, ain't it?' / The other: 'It's true. Still here, bes' proof.'"

Yet, here and elsewhere, the author advances her theme of the connectedness between women of African descent. Viney's physical description serves this purpose especially well: "She could be a dancer—a Judith Jamison in 'Cry' . . . or a high fashion model—some Imam being shot in silhouette—or a market woman in Triunion, getting ready with that hand on her hip to haggle you to death over the price of her mangoes. Dancer, model, market woman. Viney could be all three" (61). In referencing African-American, Caribbean, and African women, Marshall underscores diasporan linkages. These links are forged and soldered as we intermittently follow the lives of Ursa and Viney, single professional women meeting the demands of their high-paying jobs and frantically searching for elusive black mates. Through the parties and the night clubs, through temporarily satisfying liaisons with men, through Ursa's first abortion and Viney's pregnancy, both remain a source of mutual strength.

Reciprocal support is illustrated most poignantly in the scene in which Viney comes close to committing suicide. It is a scene reminiscent of one in Gloria Naylor's *The Women of Brewster Place* (1982) where Mattie Michael bathes Luciela Turner and rocks her back to life after the death of Ciel's child and her husband's abandonment. In *Daughters,* Ursa gentle rocks Viney as the latter, "with thickened waist . . . and breasts that were twice their normal size," dangles from the ledge of a swimming pool:

> [Ursa] heard it then; a deep, racking sound that could have come only from the source of the river. Viney's head remained thrown back, her arms rigid along the gutter, her flooded gaze on the banked lights overhead, but her body had begun to heave with a sound like the tearful raging of a mute. 'Oh, Viney don't'—holding her tighter, cradling her all the more, while the racking sound and the heaving went on and on, growing stronger, until soon she could feel it beginning to drain the body dangling like a plumb line over the edge of the pool. (78)

Ursa holds on until "the last of the river had dried." And that river, we know, represents heartache—heartache with which Ursa, for different reasons, is familiar but which she stubbornly disavows.

In describing female vulnerability to men, Marshall does not ignore female power. Viney, for example, goes on to build a comfortable life in Brooklyn for herself and her precocious son, Robeson. She sends him to a private school and instills in him the importance of his African-American heritage. Robeson's middle-class status, however, does not spare him the outrage of police brutality against black boys in general. When only nine years old, he is falsely arrested by a white officer, handcuffed, and taken to a police station. Marshall deftly illustrates in this episode how readily young children become unwitting victims of "legal" authority, and the reader is made all too aware of the possible—indeed, probable—consequences of Robeson's verbal "resistance." Fortunately, Viney has the contacts and the financial means to follow through on a "clear case of unlawful arrest and the abuse and intimidation of a minor." She recognizes, however, the many blacks who have no such resources. In a reflective tone, she considers why so many black mothers seemingly mistreat their children: "[M]aybe they're not just being too strict or taking out their frustrations on the kids. . . . Maybe it's their way of teaching them how to behave around the Pirellis out here. That might be part of it. So they'll know better than to go up in some white cop's face talking about their constitutional rights and running the risk of being blown away" (329).

Further illustrating the theme of the need for mutual support between black men and women, Viney recalls a childhood activity of cutting out and dressing boy and girl paper dolls from a book: "When I'd cut out one doll there'd be this empty outline left next to the one I hadn't gotten to yet. That's what the hole next to me today felt like, the outline, the space where some decent, halfway-together black man should have been. Okay, someone with a few problems—who doesn't have a few?—but with enough there for you to work with. Someone useful" (330–31). Viney is certainly aware of her ability to manage on her own, but the ideal is to fill in the "blank space." And Robeson, too, feels the absence of the male figure.

With Viney's story Marshall depicts the strength required of so many single mothers. While she emphasizes that it is a strength which is nurtured by the love of women for each other, the author reiterates the urgent need for mutual support between black men and black women. In no way does she minimize the difficulty of this mandate. Through Estelle and Primus's relationship and several other female-male relationships in the novel, Marshall shows that matters of the heart often interfere with or altogether impede the positive reinforcement of couples. Ursa herself seems stuck in a relationship. *Stasis* is the word Viney uses to describe the love affair between Ursa and Lowell Carruthers. "Stasis . . . meaning stagnation, meaning at a standstill, meaning going absolutely nowhere as in constipation. Stasis" (89). To remain in any unsatisfactory situation is certainly not characteristic of Ursa, who, as a matter of principle, abruptly resigns from her position as Associate Director of Research, Special Markets at the National Consumer Research Corporation. Promoting whiskey, beer, and cigarettes "was a way of doing in Folks, so she walked." Further indicating her immersion in African-American culture, Ursa repeats a segment of a line from one of her uncle's favorite blues songs: "I'd ruther drink muddy water and sleep in a hollow log than work another day for NCRC" (90). In one of her rare correspondences to Ursa, Estelle sends a telegram consisting of the word "HOORAY!" Before finding free-lance work with the foundation that underwrote the Lawson campaign, Ursa sells nearly all of her possessions to live, as Lowells put it, "like a peon in one room."

Through Lowell Carruthers, Marshall sensitively presents the portrait of a financially successful, highly educated African-American male, daily contending with the racism of the business world. His job, she writes, "has raised a frown like a permanent welt between his eyebrows, eaten away at his hairline so that at thirty-eight he looks almost the age of the PM" (57). Caught between a rock and a hard place, Carruthers's preference is to establish a college recruiting program for black youth, but he is afraid to risk venturing out on his own. Returning to the architectural imagery so prominent in her fiction, the author best captures Carruthers's character through a description of his living room. It reminds Ursa of

> a display room of furniture in a department store. Everything's that neat, that arranged, that organized. Not a book or a record album leans out of place in the huge wall system that rises from the floor to the ceiling between the windows that overlook the city. Not a speck of New York's gritty fallout is ever to be seen on the dust cover to the stereo, on the glass-topped coffee table, the windowsills or anywhere else. The thoughtfully hung prints and few abstract originals are never so much as a fraction awry. But then, startling you, one of the prints rises above the neatness and the cordoned-off, unlived-in look of a display room to dominate the walls and the entire living room. It's a Romare Bearden collage of a mother, a midnight black mother with a domed forehead similar to her own, reading to a child by the light of a kerosene lamp like the kind still used in Morlands. (259–60)

Masterfully, Marshall once again links African-American and African-Caribbean cultures. And as she continues, we admire another dimension of his African heritage: "Ursa always sits facing the collage. It serves to remind her—because she's always forgetting—that this too is Lowell. Just as is the framed photograph of his three nephews on an end table, his sister's children with whom he has spent nearly every other weekend since their father was killed in Viet Nam. A devotion she resents at times, although it remains one of the things about him she still likes" (260). Here, of course, is a reference to the extended family, which both Ursa and Carruthers hold in deep reverence.

In her development of Carruthers's character, Marshall is equally concerned with depicting the personal and social factors that impede supportive relations between black men and women. The reader understands Carruthers's innermost yearning to be of use in the larger black struggle. Along with him, we acknowledge that he is handicapped by his extreme caution. We further understand why he questions whether or not his project can still make a difference in "the mean streets which have gotten even meaner." He clearly believes in the need for black men and women to return to the kind of thinking that Congo Jane and Will Cudjoe enjoyed. Yet, devastated by the failure of his first marriage and needing the security of a well-paying job, he is paralyzed. Even more important to his self-esteem is Ursa's complete absorption with the other man in her life—the PM. In an angry confrontation he accurately discloses: "Everything's about him!"

> "Her quitting her job, for a starter. It wasn't only that the cigarette and whiskey surveys had gotten to her. She was also trying to stand up to De Lawd. To stop always doing what pleased him. She'd never admit it, but that was behind it. The same with her going back to school again. What does she need with another master's? De Lawd. It's not only about a paper she never got to write because of some racist professor, it's about Pappa-daddy as well. Another degree to make up to him for having left the job. To get back in his good graces again" (266)

Confirming what Viney had earlier summarized, he shouts, "You need to come out from under certain people. Quit letting them run your life by remote control. You need to say Stop! in the name of love." (269). With this reference to the lyrics of a popular African-American song, Marshall returns her focus to Ursa's personal dilemma. The PM's prominence in Ursa's life limits her potential for intimacy. Because she cannot admit to her own vulnerability, her growth toward womanhood is stunted.

We follow throughout the novel the separate dilemmas of other women intimately connected to the PM, a man who seems able "to charm the devil himself." Celestine Marie-Claire Bellegarde, whose full name suggests her long-standing role as guard and keeper of the Mackenzie household, adores his mere presence. To Estelle's dismay, "not only does she appear almost before [the PM] calls her, but she seems to know what he wants without him having to say" (166). As for 'ti Ursa (little Ursa), who is "everything like him, oui," Celestine has a similar devotion. The author includes Celestine's portrait to illustrate the traditional African role of "other-mothers."

Patricia Hill-Collins defines "other-mothers" as reflections of "both a continuum of West African cultural values [around the centrality of family] and functional adaptations to race and gender oppression." Boundaries of motherhood, Hill-Collins continues, become "fluid and changing" as black women care for children outside their biological connections.[11] Celestine has certainly observed a precedent in her previous relationship with Mis-Mack, the PM's mother. The latter, in fact, might also be seen as a "community other-mother," one who feels "accountable to all the black community children."[12] Mae Ryland represents her African-American counterpart. All three women serve to expand the Euro-American definition of "mother" to include women "who create, nurture, and save life in social and psychological as well as physical terms."[13] Still mourning Mis-Mack's death, Celestine fondly recalls how the older woman had taken her in at the age of eight. Starved to the point where even her hair had changed color, Celestine's undersized body yet retained her absolutely straight legs "like gateposts." As she did with many others, Mis-Mack granted the orphan a place in her household. But Celestine had felt special. "Mis-Mack had trusted her, had depended on her, had *chosen* her. . . . It was like Mis-Mack had been waiting all along for her to come. Special" (345).

Many memorable passages devoted to Celestine are richly punctuated with Creole expressions, which give her voice a fresh vitality and power. In reference to Estelle, whose American ways are beyond understanding, she sighs, "*mes amis!* He [the PM] has a cross to bear in the *blanche neg'*, *oui*. A cross" (199). Though never voicing her objections, she frequently disapproves of Estelle's mothering style:

> "Every chance she gets she drags off the pretty dresses [the PM] buys for her [Ursa] and every piece of gold and puts her in a overall like she's go-ing to weed in a canefield. She's not raising the child proper. Letting her call her and the PM by their first names. . . . The creole is *Quel betise!* whoever heard of such a thing? And she don't want me to do for the child, *oui*. . . . 'There's not going to be a soul to wait on her hand and foot when she goes to live in the States.' Already rushing the child off to America and she only just came into the world yesterday." (197)

Celestine continues her silent disapproval by upbraiding Estelle for allow-ing a gang of "fowl yard children" to play with '*ti* Ursa: "Is that any com-pany to play with the PM child?" We understand that Estelle's actions teach Ursa community building, sharing, and social responsibility. We further understand that due to her ethnicity, education, and placement in time, Estelle is inevitably influenced by Euro-American notions. In many ways she personifies the transformation of African culture as it interfaces with other cultural dynamics. Celestine's cultural isolation prevents a similar integration. Yet Marshall emphasizes female community, for Celestine and Estelle grow to accept and respect each other. The bond between them is only strengthened by their mutual love for Ursa.

But Marshall wishes both to praise and critique Celestine. Her posi-tion as "other-mother" certainly contributes to Ursa's development as a woman. In symbolic tribute, Ursa later braids her hair like "a heraldic wreath around her head" as Celestine had always worn hers (388). In her service to others, nonetheless, Celestine nurtures no sense of self. The grand affair of Celestine's heart is mentioned only in passing when, late in the novel, she surveys the room where for years she slept on a pallet next to her young charges. She smiles as she remembers the older Primus sneaking back into the room to be with her. "And not as some little seven and eight-years old boy, but the PM grown and a man" (348). As for the PM's long-standing affair with Astral Forde, Celestine glibly remarks, "And what if the woman is his Keep-miss? Show me the man in this place that don't have one and sometimes more than one. This ain't America where they must do things different" (198).

Marshall suggests again cultural differences in female attitudes and expectations of men. Although Estelle threatens to leave when she learns of her husband's extramarital affair, she reluctantly but gradually accepts the "arrangement." The reader wonders along with the adult Ursa: "Why didn't you, why don't you just leave him? Nobody stays and takes shit anymore. That's passé" (255). We know that Ursa is very much like her mother when in the next breath she wonders, "And why, goddammit, did you have to make me like you so I can't say *later* for Mr. Carruthers— never mind there're one or two things I still like about him. Just bless him and release him and split" (255).

There is no releasing or splitting for Astral Forde, who for some thirty-odd years has sustained an extramarital affair with the PM. The author includes in *Daughters* a sympathetic portrait of the "outside woman" to investigate yet another example of female relationships with men. Astral, a Creole woman from the Spanish Bay district, is a "wild dog puppy," or born out of wedlock. Her "fowl yard tongue" is more than ample compensation for her silence as a child, purportedly struck speechless by evil means. A minor character explains: "That wife of the mechanic fella from Spanish Bay paid good money to put you so when she found out he was licking about with your mother when he came to work in the sugar mill during crop season" (176). Determined to improve her status, Astral gradually rises from the extreme poverty of the island to relative comfort. Because of her high (light) color and her long, luxuriant hair, she attracts men of various positions of power before she is installed as the "keep-miss" manager of the small hotel the PM owns. Her position is not completely gratuitous, though, for after training in hotel management, Astral runs the business with the strict efficiency of an ill-tempered CEO in a major corporation:

> "You call this bathroom clean?
> "You call this bed made proper?
> "You call these sheets washed?
> "Who the rass told you to put spoons to the left when you setting a table? . . .

"What the bloody hell is happening with the cooking oil, Millicent?
Every time I look another gallon's finished and you're asking for more.
You must be drinking it one, or taking it home to sell?" (207)

Astral is attracted to the PM because he is one of "the great people,
them!"—the kind with whom she fantasizes marriage and social eleva-
tion. Beyond fantasy, however, is a deep love enhanced by a cultural bond:
"To besides, there wasn't no need for a lot of talk between them. No need
to be always explaining their explanatories. They were both from the same
little two-by-four place, after all, and knew how things were done here,
were said here: the unspoken that lay not only behind the words spoken
but in a look, the wave of a hand, a cut-eye, a suck-teeth. You talking to
the other person but without having a word to say. So much in common
between them" (188).

Astral certainly knows that despite the PM's gifts—"gift offerings to
delight, to honor, to appease"—despite the passionate lovemaking, the
PM's public and private allegiance is to his wife. In moments of honest
reflection, she even considers that Estelle could be a woman-friend: "She
looked like she'd be an easy person to talk to, somebody you could ask
about all kinds of things" (183). However, notions of class attitudes and
behaviors, combined with her rage and jealousy, prevent Astral from pur-
suing such thoughts. Instead she concentrates on her "self-absorbed universe." Even in her conversation with her only woman friend, who lays
dying in the government "horse-pital" (where one is guaranteed not to
leave . . . alive), Astral is consumed with herself. We come to understand
that her single-mindedness and her irascible manner disguise her childhood fear of homelessness, of "finding herself out on the road." Particularly when the PM considers selling his hotel to invest in a government
scheme, Astral is inconsolable. To be sure, Astral wishes to protect the
PM's investment, but she is also driven to protect her personal interests.
Toward the end of the novel, Estelle confesses to her daughter that she
herself does not understand why she put up with that "other woman":
"What happened to my ego, my pride? Why is it that all I've felt for Miss
Forde for years now is sympathy and a little curiosity? What's the woman
like? How could she put up with someone who's never taken her any-
where, never spent a night with her? I doubt if your father's ever sat down
and had a meal with her. How could she take that?" (387). In retrospect,
Estelle knows the answer: Astral Forde was really married to the place she
herself named the Miles Tree Colony Hotel.

In terms of Astral's relationship with the protagonist, the author returns to Ursa's childhood. Every Sunday after her swim at the hotel pool,
the PM insisted that Astral bring a towel and the soursop juice Ursa loved

as a child. Astral secretly resents this particular chore: "He seems to think I like standing there watching her as much as him. Like she's some child belonging to me" (211). The reader may recall a similar sentiment expressed by Celestine, who openly marvels at little Ursa's features "as if they all had been formed in the secrecy of her own flesh" (194). Because of their love for the PM, both women seem to become vicarious mothers to the child who is his very reflection.

Ursa and Astral share other connections. Both sucked their thumbs as children. Though under very different circumstances and for very different reasons, both have had abortions. And it is certainly from Astral that Ursa inherits the "fowl-yard tongue" she occasionally uses. Most importantly, Ursa's relationship with Astral teaches her by example the emptiness of life when the pursuit of material security outweighs the fulfillment of personal needs.

With Estelle's urging at the end of the novel that Ursa visit Miss Forde, the author offers another view of relationships between women. Marshall does not explicitly endorse polygamy, but she does suggest at least a tentative understanding of shared partnerships between men and women. Of the PM's treatment of Astral, Ursa empathizes: "He didn't mean to insult you, Astral. You know that. What he would have liked, I guess, was for all of us to be together in one happy compound. He was born on the wrong continent" (405). Perhaps what the author really suggests here is that women become more empathetic with each other in situational relationships with men. If we consider Ursa's lack of understanding of her parents' relationship and perhaps Estelle's misunderstanding of the depth of her daughter's love for the PM, Marshall may be more indirectly suggesting that, rightly or wrongly, individuals make choices according to their personal needs. Furthermore, personal choices may sometimes be "no one else's business." This is the thought that Ursa entertains when she reconsiders the relationship between her parents, whose two profiles come to resemble "bas-relief heads on a medallion or a specially minted commemorative coin" (356). But it does become Ursa's business to perform the one act her mother cannot. At re-election time, she returns to the island, importantly at Estelle's written request, and "silently offer[s] herself for whatever would be required of her" (363).

What is required of Ursa is the task of delivering to the PM's opponent the previously uncirculated prospectus that outlines the development of a resort on public lands in the Morlands District. It is a scheme that would potentially net personal gain for her father, but it would bring no benefit to his constituents. With Ursa's decisive move to abort her father's plan, she fulfills her destiny to become useful to at least one of her communities. Additionally, she also offers her father a chance for rebirth. (The recently formed Independent Party, headed by a new Congo Jane and Will Cudjoe, has offered him the status of "honorary head and principal adviser.") With Ursa's act also comes her new openness to a community of women as trusted confidantes, advisors, and friends. We note, as a case in point, that she and her mother discuss their love lives for the first time. Finally, with Ursa's act comes the pain of womanhood, for she experiences the physical dis-ease anticipated since the novel's beginning. Lying naked on her bed, she welcomes the soreness and discomfort that cut across "the well of her stomach," for it also announces the birth of her self. Symbolically, Ursa has finally cut her ties to her father. While she will always retain her resemblance to the PM, that resemblance will no longer "overshadow those parts of her face that took after no one but herself. That were simply Ursa" (408). No longer operating by "remote control," she is free to chart and navigate the stars that will make up her own self-defined galaxy.

Paule Marshall in all of her fiction to date has insisted that African peoples take a journey back through history and time to retrieve those traditional values which have sustained black peoples throughout the diaspora. While *Daughters* journeys backward to review yet another aspect of that history, it also shifts forward, suggesting that movement toward wholeness incorporates change. As is strikingly apparent, star imagery dominates *Daughters.* Even the names of the central female characters evoke the radiating influence women can exert in the universe. The novel also suggests that as self-contained entities, women may also be inwardly directed, determining their own separate spheres of existence. The naming of the protagonist is especially relevant in this regard. Ursa makes reference to Ursa Major ('*ti* Ursa, Ursa Minor) with its prominent feature, the North Star. The latter, of course, is a traditional symbol in African-American literature of physical and spiritual freedom. Beatrice, a name that connotes blessedness, serves to underscore the nature of the protagonist's transformation. Together the names honor maternal forebears and simultaneously claim a dual heritage. And together the names announce the re-creation of a larger female identity. For Marshall, this re-creation telescopes back to a communal, specifically woman-centered African source. Geographical and temporal positioning are clearly important to this re-creation, signaling both symbolic rootedness and soil for growth. Through the author's development of Ursa as instrumental in the political change hoped for by the novel's end, Marshall perhaps projects a new focus for her fiction to come. In *Daughters* she unquestionably augurs new roles for modern women—perhaps as stars in the politically and culturally changing universe. In any event, Ursa's story celebrates a shared past even as it looks forward to a shared future. That future promises another stellar performance by one of America's most gifted and prophetic literary artists.

Notes

Introduction: Anatomy of an Aesthetic— The African Cultural Base

1. Barbara Christian, *Black Women Novelists: The Development of a Tradition, 1892–1976* (Westport, Conn.: Greenwood Press, 1980), 80.
2. Stuart Hall, "Cultural Identity and Diaspora," in *Identity, Community, Culture, Difference,* ed. J. Rutherford (London: Lawrence and Wishart, 1990), 225.
3. I borrow this term from Benedict Anderson, *Imagined Communities: Reflections on the Origin and Spread of Nationalism,* rev. ed. (London: Verso Press, 1991).
4. See Geneva Smitherman, *Talkin' and Testifyin': The Language of Black America* (Boston: Houghton Mifflin, 1977); J. L. Dillard, *Black English: Its History and Usage in the United States* (New York: Random House, 1972); Joseph E. Holloway, ed., *Africanisms in American Culture* (Bloomington: Indiana Univ. Press, 1990).
5. Paule Marshall, "Shaping the World of My Art," *New Letters* (Autumn 1973): 103, 104.
6. Paule Marshall, "From the Poets in the Kitchen," in *Reena and Other Short Stories* (Old Westbury, N.Y.: Feminist Press, 1983), 8–9.
7. Levy-Bruhl qtd. in Janheinz Jahn, *Muntu: An Outline of the New African Culture,* trans. Marjorie Grene (New York: Grove Press, 1961), 97.
8. Basil Davidson, *The African Genius: An Introduction to African Social and Cultural History* (Boston: Little, Brown, 1969), 163.
9. For an in-depth study of oral art as literature, see Ruth Finnegan, *Oral Literature in Africa* (Oxford: Clarendon Press, 1970).
10. Robert Bone, review of Marshall's *Brown Girl, Brownstones, New York Times,* 30 Nov. 1959, 54.
11. Finnegan, *Oral Literature in Africa,* 11.
12. Ibid., 12.

13. John S. Mbiti, *African Religions and Philosophies,* rev. ed. (New York: Anchor Books, 1970), 21.

14. Davidson, *The African Genius,* 162.

15. Mbiti, *African Religions and Philosophies,* 3.

16. Ibid., 143.

17. Bonnie Barthold, *Black Time: Fiction of Africa, the Caribbean, and the United States* (New Haven: Yale Univ. Press, 1981), 101.

18. Filomina Chioma Steady, "African Feminism: A Worldwide Perspective," in *Women in Africa and the African Diaspora,* ed. Rosalyn Terborg-Penn, Sharon Harley, and Andrea Benton Rushing (Washington, D.C.: Howard Univ. Press, 1987), 6.

19. Niara Sudarkasa, "The Status of Women in Indigenous African Societies," in *Women in Africa and the African Diaspora,* ed. Terborg-Penn, Harley, and Rushing, 35.

20. Ibid., 36.

21. Ibid., 25.

22. Lillian Ashcraft-Eason, "West African Culture, Women, and the Transatlantic Slave Trade" (work in progress).

23. Karla Holloway, *Moorings and Metaphors: Figures of Culture and Gender in Black Women's Literature* (New Brunswick, N.J.: Rutgers Univ. Press, 1992), 30.

1. Challenging the American Norm: The Gendered Sensibility in "The Valley Between"

1. "The Valley Between" was originally published in the now defunct *Contemporary Reader.* After having been out of print for close to thirty years, it was reprinted in *Reena and Other Stort Stories* (Old Westbury, N.Y.: Feminist Press, 1983), 13–24.

2. Headnote to "The Valley Between" in *Reena and Other Short Stories,* 15.

3. bell hooks, *Ain't I a Woman: Black Women and Feminism* (Boston: South End Press, 1981), 177.

4. Interview by author, 21 May 1990, Richmond, Va.

5. Ibid.

6. Ibid.

7. "The Valley Between," in *Reena and Other Short Stories,* 13–24.

2. Beyond *Bildungsroman*: Constructions of Gender and Culture in *Brown Girl, Brownstones*

1. See Christian, *Black Women Novelists;* Susan Willis, *Specifying: Black Women Writing the American Experience* (Madison: Univ. of Wisconsin Press, 1987); Susan Stanford Friedman, "Women's Autobiographical Selves: Theory and Practice," in *The Private Self: Theory and Practice in Women's Autobiographical Writings,* ed. Shari Benstock (Chapel Hill: Univ. of North Carolina Press, 1988); Mary Helen Washington, afterword to first Feminist Press edition of Marshall's *Brown Girl, Brownstones* (Old Westbury, N.Y.: Feminist Press, 1981).

2. Alexis DeVeaux, "Paule Marshall: In Celebration of Our Triumph," *Essence,* May 1979, 98.

3. Kimberly Benston, "Architectural Imagery and Unity in Paule Marshall's *Brown Girl, Brownstones,*" *Negro American Literature Forum* 9 (Fall 1975): 69.

4. Interview by author, 21 May 1990, Richmond, Va.

5. Qtd. in DeVeaux, "Paule Marshall," 124.

6. Ibid.

7. *Brown Girl, Brownstones* (Chatham, N.J.: Chatham Bookseller, 1959), 4. The page numbers of subsequent references are noted parenthetically in the text.

8. Marshall, "From the Poets in the Kitchen," 6.

9. Qtd. in Henry Louis Gates, Jr., *The Signifying Monkey: A Theory of African-American Literary Criticism* (New York: Oxford Univ. Press, 1988), 81–82.

10. Benston, "Architectural Imagery," 68.

11. Qtd. in DeVeaux, "Paule Marshall," 98.

12. Marshall, "From the Poets in the Kitchen," 8.

13. Ibid.

14. Ibid., 5.

15. G. O. Bell, review of *Brown Girl, Brownstones, Bim* 8, no. 30 (1960): 134–36.

16. Benston, "Architectural Imagery," 68.

17. Ibid.

18. W. E. B. DuBois, *The Souls of Black Folk* in *Three Negro Classics* (New York: Avon Books, 1968), 215.

19. Deborah Schneider, "A Search for Selfhood: Paule Marshall's *Brown Girl, Brownstones,*" in *The Afro-American Novel since 1960,* ed. Peter Bruck and Wolfgang Karrer (Amsterdam: B. R. Grüner, 1982), 65.

20. Rosalie Riegle Troester, "Turbulence and Tenderness: Mothers, Daughters, and 'Other Mothers' in Paule Marshall's *Brown Girl, Brownstones,*" *SAGE: A Scholarly Journal on Black Women* 1, no. 2 (1984): 14.

21. Mbiti, *African Religions and Philosophies,* 267.

22. Eugenia Collier, "The Closing of the Circle: Movement from Division to Wholeness in Paule Marshall's Fiction," in *Black Women Writers (1950–1980): A Critical Evaluation,* ed. Mari Evans (Garden City, N.Y.: Anchor Press, 1983), 302.

23. Ibid.

24. Marshall, "Shaping the World of My Art," 103.

25. Barbara Christian, "Paule Marshall," in *African-American Writers,* ed. Valerie Smith, Leah Baechler, and A. Walton Litz (New York: Scribner's Sons, 1991), 289–304.

26. Troester, "Turbulence and Tenderness," 14.

27. John P. Davis, ed., *The American Negro Reference Book* (Englewood Cliffs, N.J.: Prentice-Hall, 1966), 69.

28. John Cooke, "Whose Child? The Fiction of Paule Marshall," *CLA Journal* 24 (Sept. 1980): 7.

29. Collier, "The Closing of the Circle," 303.

30. Missy Dehn Kubitscheck, "Paule Marshall's Women on Quest," *Black American Literature Forum* 21, no. 1–2 (Spring-Summer 1987): 51.

31. Friedman, "Women's Autobiographical Selves," 51.

3. Cultural Expansion and Masculine Subjectivity: *Soul Clap Hands and Sing*

1. Christian, "Paule Marshall," 233.
2. Interview by author, 21 May 1990, Richmond, Va.
3. Headnote to "Brooklyn" in *Reena and Other Short Stories,* 51.
4. Bulletin from the Virginia Kirkus Service, 1 July 1961.
5. Ihab Hassan, "A Circle of Loneliness," *Saturday Review,* 16 Sept. 1961, 30.
6. Marcia Keiz, "Themes and Style in the Works of Paule Marshall," *Negro American Literature Forum* 9 (Fall 1975): 72.
7. Qtd. in DeVeaux, "Paule Marshall," 72.
8. Darwin T. Turner, introduction to *Soul Clap Hands and Sing* (Washington, D.C.: Howard Univ. Press, 1988), xlvi.
9. Interview by author, 21 May 1990, Richmond, Va.
10. Headnote to "Brooklyn," 51.
11. Interview by author, 21 May 1990, Richmond, Va.
12. For this observation, I am grateful to my colleague, Thadious M. Davis.
13. Qtd. in DeVeaux, "Paule Marshall," 123.
14. Turner, introduction to *Soul Clap Hands and Sing,* xxiv.
15. *Soul Clap Hands and Sing,* 4. The page numbers of subsequent quotations are noted parenthetically in text.
16. In her headnote to the Feminist Press edition of "Barbados," Marshall explains that while she was in Barbados revising *Brown Girl, Brownstones,* her landlord actually hired a young servant girl to cook and clean. "She never said two words to me either. (I changed this though when I got around to writing about her.)," 51–52.
17. Headnote to "Brooklyn," 27.
18. Interview by author, 21 May 1990, Richmond, Va.
19. Qtd. in Lloyd W. Brown, "The Rhythms of Power in Paule Marshall's Fiction," *Novel: A Forum on Fiction* 7, no. 2 (1974): 165.

4. Maturation and Multiplicity in Consciousness: The Short Stories

1. DeVeaux, "Paule Marshall," 133.
2. Roy S. Bryce-LaPorte, introduction to *Black People and Their Culture: Selected Writings from the African Diaspora,* ed. Linn Shapiro (Washington, D.C.: Smithsonian Institution, 1976), n.p.
3. Turner, introduction to *Soul Clap Hands and Sing,* xxix, xxx.
4. Patricia Hill Collins, "The Social Construction of Black Feminist Thought," *Signs: A Journal of Women in Culture and Society* 14, no. 4 (1989): 755.
5. "Reena," *Harper's,* no. 225 (Oct. 1962): 156. The page numbers of subsequent quotations will be noted parenthetically in the text.
6. Barthold, *Black Time,* 27.
7. Marshall agrees in the headnote to the Feminist Press edition of "Reena" that the story is a "mixed bag technically" and that she has "never been comfortable with it because of that." She further comments: "Since I'd never attempted an article before and thought of myself as strictly a fiction writer, I told them [*Harper's*] I'd try doing a kind of story-essay" (71).

8. Toni Morrison poignantly develops this idea in her 1972 novel, *The Bluest Eye.*

9. In *The Chosen Place, the Timeless People* (New York: Harcourt, Brace and World, 1969), Marshall uses earrings of a similar style to symbolize the inner conflict of Merle Kinbona. This symbol appears as well in the novella "Merle."

10. Barthold, *Black Time,* 27.

11. Mbiti, *African Religions and Philosophies,* 32.

12. Washington, afterword to *Browngirl, Brownstones,* 314.

13. Barthold, *Black Time,* 130.

14. Paule Marshall, "Some Get Wasted," in *Harlem: Voices from the Soul of Black America,* ed. John Henrik Clarke (New York: New American Library, 1970), 136. The page numbers of subsequent quotations are noted in the text.

15. Dirty Dozens: "A very elaborate game traditionally played by black boys, in which the participants insult each other's relatives, especially their mothers. The object of the game is to test emotional strength. The first person to give into anger is the loser." (Definition cited in Clarence Major, *Dictionary of Afro-American Slang* [New York: International, 1970], 46.) By extension, Marshall's characters test their emotional strength and resilience in their continuous struggle for survival.

16. John Wideman, "The Black Writer and the Magic of the Word," *New York Times,* 28 Jan. 1988, 28.

17. Paule Marshall, headnote to "To Da-duh: In Memoriam," in *Reena and Other Short Stories,* 95.

18. Paule Marshall, "To Da-duh: In Memoriam," in *Black Voices: An Anthology of Afro-American Literature,* ed. Abraham Chapman (New York: New American Library, 1968), 207. The page numbers of subsequent quotations are noted in the text.

19. Marshall inserts this information to record a common experience for workers in the Caribbean who, of economic necessity, traveled outside their homelands to earn livelihoods for themselves and to support their families. A similar reference is made in *The Chosen Place, the Timeless People* when Vereson Walkes returns home from the United States.

20. Lloyd Brown, "The American Image in British West Indian Literature," *Caribbean Studies* 11, no. 1 (1971): 33.

21. Ibid.

5. Changing the Present Order: Personal and Political Liberation in *The Chosen Place, the Timeless People*

1. Marshall, "Shaping the World of My Art," 110–11.

2. Christian, *Black Women Novelists,* 135.

3. Christian, "Paule Marshall," 237.

4. Ibid.

5. Ibid.

6. *The Chosen Place, the Timeless People.* The page numbers of subsequent quotations are noted parenthetically in the text.

7. Mbiti, *African Religions and Philosophies,* 24.
8. Hortense Spillers, *"Chosen Place, Timeless People:* Some Figurations on the New World," in *Conjuring: Black Women, Fiction and Literary Tradition,* ed. Marjorie Pryse and Hortense Spillers (Bloomington: Indiana Univ. Press, 1985), 162.
9. Marshall later develops Merle's story as a novella. See "Merle" in *Reena and Other Short Stories.*
10. Constance Sutton, letter to Chamba Media Foundation in support of movie translation of *The Chosen Place, the Timeless People,* Nov. 29, 1980.
11. Spillers, *"Chosen Place, Timeless People,"* 160.
12. Lizabeth Paravisini-Gebert, *"The Chosen Place, the Timeless People:* Race, Colonial Power and the Absence of Sisterhood," unpublished essay, 2–3.
13. Spillers, *"Chosen Place, Timeless People,"* 173n.
14. John Cooke, "Whose Child?" 14.
15. Paravisini-Gebert, *"The Chosen Place, the Timeless People,"* 13–14.
16. To Welch's objection that Marshall presents a skewed vision of the power of the upper-class white woman, I suggest that Harriet's characterization is authentic. Such an assessment does not obviate the white male as the "primary holder of power." In the novel, Harriet clearly relies upon Chester Heald for her financial backing. Certainly in the context of the historical relationship between black and white women, Harriet's portrayal is valid. She attempts to use her considerable economic power to control Merle, her unquestioned "inferior." Even so, Marshall does not disregard nor does she minimize the sexism that distorts the lives of both women. One of her objectives in writing the novel is to explore how several forms of oppression are compounded or mitigated by individual attitudes and behaviors of women. See Sharon Welch, *A Feminist Ethic of Risk* (Minneapolis: Fortress Press, 1990), 188n.
17. Welch, *A Feminist Ethic,* 58.
18. Ibid., 60.
19. Qtd. in DeVeaux, "Paule Marshall," 126.
20. John Reilly, "Paule Marshall," in *Contemporary Novelists,* ed. James Vinson (New York: St. Martin's Press, 1976), 913.

6. Recognition and Recovery: Diasporan Connections in *Praisesong for the Widow*

1. This idea I borrow from Velma Pollard who writes of a "subterranean essence." She notes that Edward Braithwaite uses the term *submarine unity.* See Pollard's "Cultural Connections in Paule Marshall's *Praisesong for the Widow," World Literature Written in English* 25, no. 2 (1985): 285, 286.
2. Qtd. in DeVeaux, "Paule Marshall," 131.
3. Abena P. A. Busia, "What Is Your Nation? Reconnecting Africa and Her Diaspora through Paule Marshall's *Praisesong for the Widow,"* in *Changing Our Own Words: Essays on Criticism, Theory, and Writing by Black Women,* ed. Cheryl A. Wall (New Brunswick, N.J.: Rutgers Univ. Press, 1989), 198.
4. *Praisesong for the Widow* (New York: Putnam's Sons, 1983), 39. The page numbers of subsequent quotations are noted parenthetically in the text.
5. Mbiti, *African Religions and Philosophies,* 28.

6. Ibid., 29.

7. Keith A. Sandiford, "Paule Marshall's *Praisesong for the Widow:* The Reluctant Heiress, or Whose Life Is It Anyway?" *Black American Literature Forum* 20, no. 4 (1986): 377.

8. Ibid., 374.

9. Ibid., 376.

10. Ibid.

11. Barbara Christian, "Ritualistic Process and the Structure of Paule Marshall's *Praisesong for the Widow,*" in *Black Feminist Criticism: Perspectives on Black Women Writers* (New York: Pergamon Press, 1985), 151.

12. Busia, "What Is Your Nation?" 197.

13. Pollard, "Cultural Connections," 296.

14. Sandiford, "Paule Marshall's *Praisesong for the Widow,*" 386.

15. Joanne V. Gabbin, "A Laying On of Hands: Black Women Writers Exploring the Roots of Their Folk and Cultural Tradition," in *Wild Women in the Whirlwind: Afro-American Culture and the Contemporary Literary Renaissance,* ed. Joanne M. Braxton and Andrée N. McLaughlin (New Brunswick, N.J.: Rutgers Univ. Press, 1990), 247.

16. Qtd. in "Return of a Native Daughter: An Interview with Paule Marshall and Maryse Condé," trans. John Williams, *SAGE: A Scholarly Journal on Black Women* 3, no. 2 (1986): 52.

7. Transformation and Re-creation of Female Identity in *Daughters*

1. Toni Morrison, *Tar Baby* (New York: New American Library, 1981), 281.

2. Qtd. in Shirley M. Jordan, "*Daughters:* The Unity That Binds Us," in *American Visions,* Oct. 1991, 38.

3. Qtd. in Elsie B. Washington, "Paule Marshall: Merging Our Cultures," in *Essence,* Oct. 1991, 48.

4. Qtd. in Rosemary L. Bray, "Ursa Reveals Herself," review of *Daughters, New York Times Book Review,* 27 Oct. 1991, 3.

5. Interview by author, 21 May 1990, Richmond, Va.

6. Paule Marshall, *Daughters* (New York: Atheneum, 1991), 86. The page numbers of subsequent references are noted paranthetically in the text.

7. Qtd. in Bray, "Ursa Reveals Herself," 3.

8. Susan Fromberg Schaeffer, "Cutting Herself Free," review of *Daughters, New York Times Book Review,* 27 Oct. 1991, 3.

9. For this observation, I am indebted to my graduate student, Ann Khaddar.

10. Schaeffer, "Cutting Herself Free," 310, 129.

11. Patricia Hill-Collins, *Black Feminist Thought: Knowledge, Consciousness, and the Politics of Empowerment* (New York: Routledge, 1990), 119.

12. Ibid., 129.

13. Ibid., 131.

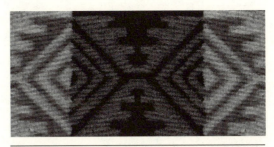

Selected Bibliography

Works by Paule Marshall

"The Valley Between." *The Contemporary Reader* 1, no. 2 (Aug. 1954): 46–57.

Brown Girl, Brownstones. New York: Random House, 1959; Chatham, N.J.: Chatham Bookseller, 1971; Old Westbury, N.Y.: Feminist Press, 1981. (Dramatic adaptation presented on CBS Television Workshop, Apr. 1960.)

Soul Clap Hands and Sing. New York: Atheneum, 1961; Chatham, NJ: Chatham Bookseller, 1971; Washington, D.C.: Howard Univ. Press, 1988. (Collection includes "Barbados," "Brooklyn," "British Guiana," and "Brazil.")

"Reena." *Harper's,* no. 225 (Oct. 1962): 155–63.

"Return of the Native." In *Freedomways* 4 (Summer 1964): 358–66.

"The Negro Woman in America." *Freedomways,* 1st quarter (1966).

"To Da-Duh: In Memoriam." *New World Magazine,* 1967. Reprinted in *Black Voices: An Anthology of Afro-American Literature.* Ed. Abraham Chapman. New York: New American Library, 1968. Rpt. in *The Heath Anthology of American Literature* 2. Ed. Paul Lauter. Lexington, Mass.: D. C. Heath and Co., 1990.

The Chosen Place, the Timeless People (Originally entitled *Ceremonies at the Guest House.*) New York: Harcourt, Brace and World, 1969; London: Longman, 1970; New York: Avon, 1976; New York: Vintage Books, 1984.

"Some Get Wasted." In *Harlem: Voices From the Soul of Black America.* Ed. John Henrik Clarke. New York: New American Library, 1970. 136–45.

"Fannie Lou Hamer: Hunger Has No Color Line." *Vogue,* June 1970, 126–27.

"Shaping the World of My Art." *New Letters,* Autumn 1973, 97–112.

"Shadow and Act." *Mademoiselle,* June 1974, 82–83.

"The Making of a Writer: 'From the Poets in the Kitchen.'" *New York Times Book Review,* 9 Jan. 1983, p. 3.

Praisesong for the Widow. New York: Putnam's Sons, 1983; New York: Penguin, 1984.
Reena and Other Short Stories. Old Westbury, N.Y.: Feminist Press, 1983. (Collection includes "From the Poets in the Kitchen," "The Valley Between," "Brookyln," "Barbados," "Reena," "To Da-duh: In Memoriam," and "Merle.")
"Islanders of Bed-Stuy: The West Indian Zest to 'Buy House' Rejuvenates a Community." *New York Times Magazine,* 3 Nov. 1985, 179–82.
Daughters. New York: Atheneum, 1991; New York: Plume, 1992.

Criticism and Reviews

Barksdale, Richard K. "Castration Symbolism in Recent Black American Fiction." *College Language Association Journal* 4 (June 1986): 400–413.
Bell, G. O. Review of Paule Marshall's *Brown Girl, Brownstones. Bim* 8, no. 30 (1960): 134–36.
Benston, Kimberly. "Architectural Imagery and Unity in Paule Marshall's *Brown Girl, Brownstones.*" *Negro American Literature Forum* 9 (Fall 1975): 67–76.
Bond, Jean Carey. "Allegorial Novel by Talented Storyteller." *Freedomways* 10 (1970): 76–78.
———. "Masterpiece Reissued." Review of *Brown Girl, Brownstones. Freedomways* (2nd Quarter 1982): 110–12.
Bone, Robert. Review of Paule Marshall's *Brown Girl, Brownstones. New York Times,* 30 Nov. 1959, 54.
———. Review of *The Chosen Place, the Timeless People.* New York Times. 30 Nov. 1969.
Brathwaite, Edward K. "The Love Axe/I: Developing a Caribbean Aesthetic, 1962–1964." *Bim* 16, no. 61 (1977): 53–65.
Brathwaite, Edward L. "Rehabilitations." *Critical Quarterly* 13 (Sept. 1971): 175–83 .
———. "West Indian History and Society in the Art of Paule Marshall's Novels." *Journal of Black Studies* 1 (Dec. 1970): 225–38.
Bray, Rosemary L. "Ursa Reveals Herself." Review of *Daughters. New York Times Book Review,* 27 Oct. 1991, 3.
Bröck, Sabine. "Transcending the 'Loophole of Retreat': Paule Marshall's Placing of Female Generations." *Callaloo* 10, no. 1 (1987): 79–90.
Brown, Lloyd W. "The Rhythms of Power in Paule Marshall's Fiction." *Novel: A Forum on Fiction* 7 (Winter 1974): 159–67.
———. "The Calypso Tradition in West Indian Literature." *Black Academy Review* 2, no. 1–2 (1971).
———. "The American Image in British West Indian Literature." *Caribbean Studies* 11, no. 1 (1971): 30–45.
Busia, Abena P. A. "What Is Your Nation? Reconnecting Africa and Her Diaspora through Paule Marshall's *Praisesong for the Widow.*" In *Changing Our Own Words:*

Essays on Criticism, Theory, and Writing by Black Women, ed. Cheryl A. Wall (New Brunswick: Rutgers Univ. Press, 1989). 196–211

Christian, Barbara. *Black Women Novelists: The Development of a Tradition, 1892–1976.* Westport, Conn.: Greenwood Press, 1980.

————. "Ritualistic Process and the Structure of Paule Marshall's *Praisesong for the Widow.*" *Callaloo* #18, vol. 6, no. 2 (1983): 74–84.

————. "Paule Marshall." In *Dictionary of Literary Biography.* Vol. 33, ed. Thadious M. Davis and Trudier Harris, 161–70. Detroit: Gale Research, 1984.

————. "Paule Marshall." *African-American Writers.* Ed. Valerie Smith, Leah Baechler, and A. Walton Litz. 1991. New York: Collier Books, 1993. 225–39.

————. *Black Feminist Criticism: Perspectives on Black Women Writers.* New York: Pergamon Press, 1985.

Collier, Eugenia. "The Closing of the Circle: Movement from Division to Wholeness in Paule Marshall's Fiction." In *Black Women Writers (1950–1980): A Critical Evaluation.* Ed. Mari Evans. Garden City, N.Y.: Anchor Press, 1983. 295–315.

Cooke, John."Whose Child? The Fiction of Paule Marshall." *CLA Journal* 24, no. 1 (1980): 1–15.

DeVeaux, Alexis. "Paule Marshall: In Celebration of Our Triumph." *Essence,* May 1979, 70.

deWeever, Jacqueline. *Mythmaking and Metaphor in Black Women's Fiction.* New York: St. Martin's Press, 1991.

Denniston, Dorothy L. "Early Short Fiction by Paule Marshall," *Callaloo* #18, vol. 6, no. 2 (1983): 31–45. Reprinted in *Short Story Criticism.* Detroit: Gale Research, 1990.

————. "Paule Marshall." In *American Women Writers* 3. Ed. Lina Mainiero and Langdon Faust, 125–27. New York: Frederick Ungar, 1981.

Eko, Ebele. "Beyond the Myth of Confrontation: A Comparative Study of African and African-American Female Protagonists." *Ariel: A Review of International English Literature* 17, no. 4 (1986): 139–52.

Friedman, Susan Stanford. "Women's Autobiographical Selves: Theory and Practice." In *The Private Self: Theory and Practice in Women's Autobiographical Writings.* Ed. Shari Benstock. Chapel Hill: Univ. of North Carolina Press, 1988. 34–62

Gabbin, Joanne A. "A Laying On of Hands: Black Women Writers Exploring the Roots of Their Folk and Cultural Tradition." In *Wild Women in the Whirlwind: Afra-American Culture and the Contemporary Literary Renaissance.* Ed. Joanne M. Braxton and Andrée Nicola. McLaughlin, N.J.: Rutgers Univ. Press, 1990, 246–63.

Giddings, Paula. "A Special Vision, a Common Goal." *Encore American Worldwide News* (23 June 1975): 44–48.

Gikandi, Simon. "Modernism and the Masks of History: The Novels of Paule Marshall." In *Writing in Limbo: Modernism and Caribbean Literature.* Ithaca: Cornell Univ. Press, 1992.

Harris, Trudier. "No Outlet for the Blues." *Callaloo* #18, vol. 6, no. 2 (1983): 57–67.

Hassan, Ihab. "A Circle of Loneliness." *Saturday Review,* 16 Sept. 1961.

Holloway, Karla. *Moorings and Metaphors: Figures of Culture and Gender in Black Women's Literature*. New Brunswick: Rutgers Univ. Press, 1992.

Hull, Gloria T. "To Be a Black Woman in America: A Reading of Paule Marshall's 'Reena.'" *Obsidian: Black Literature in Review* 4, no. 3 (1978): 5–15.

Jordan, Shirley M. "*Daughters:* The Unity That Binds Us." *American Visions* (Oct. 1991).

Kapai, L. "Dominant Themes and Techniques in Paule Marshall's Fiction." *CLA Journal* 16 (Sept. 1972): 49–59.

Keiz, Marcia. "Themes and Style in the Works of Paule Marshall." *Negro American Literature Forum* 9 (Fall 1975).

Kubitscheck, Missy Dehn. "Paule Marshall's Women on Quest." *Black American Literature Forum* 21, no. 1–2 (Spring-Summer 1987): 43–60.

LaSeur, Geta. "One Mother, Two Daughters: The Afro-American and the Afro-Caribbean Female Bildungsroman." *The Black Scholar* 17, no. 2 (1986): 26–33.

McClusky, John, Jr. "And Called Every Generation Blessed: Theme, Setting, and Ritual in the Works of Paule Marshall." In *Black Women Writers (1950–1980): A Critical Evaluation*. Ed. Mari Evans. Garden City, N.Y.: Anchor, 1983. 316–34.

Ogunyemi, Chikwenye Okonjo. "The Old Order Shall Pass: The Example of 'Flying Home' and 'Barbados.'" *CLA Journal* 3 (Mar. 1982): 303–14.

Nazareth, Peter. "Paule Marshall's Timeless People." *New Letters* 40, no. 1 (1973): 113–31.

———. *The Third World Writer: His Social Responsibility*. Nairobi, Kenya: General Printers, 1978.

Pannill, Linda. "From the 'Workshop': The Fiction of Paule Marshall." *Melus: The Journal of The Society for the Study of the Multi-ethnic Literatures of the United States*. (Summer 1985): 63–73.

Pollard, Velma. "Cultural Connections in Paule Marshall's *Praisesong for the Widow*." *World Literature Written in English* (Autumn 1985): 285–98.

Reilly, John. "Paule Marshall." In *Contemporary Novelists*. Ed. James Vinson. New York: St. Martin's Press, 1976. 849–50.

Sale, Faith. "Editing Fiction Editors on Editing." In *Editors on Editing*. Rev. ed. Ed. Gerald Gross. New York: Harper and Row, 1985, 186–99.

Sandiford, Keith. "Paule Marshall's *Praisesong for the Widow*: The Reluctant Heiress; or, Whose Life Is It Anyway?" *Black American Literature Forum* 20 (Winter 1986): 371–92.

Schaeffer, Susan Fromberg. "Cutting Herself Free." Review of *Daughters*. *New York Times Book Review*, 27 Oct. 1991, 3.

Schneider, Deborah. "A Search for Selfhood: Paule Marshall's *Brown Girl, Brownstones*." In *The Afro-American Novel since 1960*. Ed. Peter Bruck and Wolfgang Karrer. Amsterdam: B. R. Grüner, 1982, 53–73.

Sealy, Karl. Review of Paule Marshall's *Soul Clap Hands and Sing*. *Bim* 9, no. 35 (1962): 225–28.

Serebnick, J. "New Creative Writers." *Library Journal* 84 (June 1959).

Skerrett, Joseph T., Jr. "Paule Marshall and the Crisis of Middle Years." *Callaloo* #18, vol. 6, no. 2 (1983): 68–73.

Spillers, Hortense J. *"Chosen Place, Timeless People:* Some Figurations on the New World." In *Conjuring: Black Women, Fiction and Literary Tradition.* Ed. Marjorie Pryse and Hortense J. Spillers. Bloomington: Indiana Univ. Press, 1985. 155–75.

Stoelting, Winnifred. "Time Past and Present: The Search for Viable Links in *The Chosen Place, the Timeless People." CLA Journal* 16, no. 1 (1972): 60–71.

Sutton, Constance. Letter to Chamba Media Foundation, 29 Nov. 1980.

Talbert, L. Lee. "The Poetics of Prophecy in Paule Marshall's *Soul Clap Hands and Sing." MELUS* 5 (1977): 49–56.

Talmor, Sascha. "Merle of Bourne-hills." *Durham University Journal* 80, no. 1 (1987): 125–28.

Thompson, Robert Ferris. *Flash of the Spirit: African and Afro-American Art and Philosophy.* New York: Vintage Books, 1984.

Troester, Rosalie Riegle. "Turbulence and Tenderness: Mothers, Daughters, and 'Other-Mothers' in Paule Marshall's *Brown Girl, Brownstones." SAGE: A Scholarly Journal on Black Women* 1, no. 2 (1984): 14.

Turner, Darwin T. Introduction to *Soul Clap Hands and Sing.* Washington, D.C.: Howard Univ. Press, 1988.

Wade-Gayles, Gloria. "The Truths of Our Mothers' Lives: Mother-Daughter Relationships in Black Women's Fiction." *SAGE: A Scholarly Journal on Black Women* 1, no. 2 (1984): 8–12.

Walcott, Derek. "A Story of Lust in Four Lands." *Trinidad Guardian,* 12 Sept. 1962.

Wall, Cheryl A., ed. *Changing Our Own Words: Essays on Criticism, Theory and Writing by Black Women.* New Brunswick: Rutgers Univ. Press, 1989, 196–211.

Waniek, Marilyn Nelson. "Paltry Things: Immigrants and Marginal Men in Paule Marshall's Short Fiction." *Callaloo* #18, vol. 6, no. 2 (1983): 46–56.

Washington, Elsie B. "Paule Marshall: Merging Our Culture." *Essence* (Oct. 1991).

Washington, Mary Helen. "Black Women Image Makers." *Black World* 23 (Aug. 1974): 10–18.

———. Afterword to first Feminist Press edition of Marshall's *Brown Girl, Brownstones,* 1981.

———. "I Sign My Mother's Name: Alice Walker, Dorothy West, Paule Marshall." In *Mothering the Mind: Twelve Studies of Writers and Their Silent Partners.* Ed. Ruth Perry and Martine Watson Brownley. New York: Holmes and Meier, 1984.

Waxman, Barbara Frey. "The Widow's Journey to Self and Roots: Aging and Society in Paule Marshall's *Praisesong for the Widow." Frontiers: A Journal of Women Studies* 9, no. 3 (1987): 94–99.

Welch, Sharon D. "Memory and Accountability." In *A Feminist Ethic of Risk.* Minneapolis: Fortress Press, 1990, 49–64.

Wilentz, Gray. *Binding Cultures: Black Women Writers in Africa and the Diaspora.* Bloomington: Indiana Univ. Press, 1992.

Williams, John. "Return of a Native Daughter: An Interview with Paule Marshall and Maryse Conde." *SAGE: A Scholarly Journal on Black Women* 3, no. 2 (1986): 52–53.

Willis, Susan. "Describing Arcs of Recovery: Paule Marshall's Relationship to Afro-American Culture." In *Specifying: Black Women Writing the American Experience.* Madison: Univ. of Wisconsin Press, 1987. 53–82.

Background Sources

Anderson, Benedict. *Imagined Communities: Reflections on the Origin and Spread of Nationalism.* Rev. ed. London: Verso Press, 1991.

Asante, Molefi, and Karimu Welsh Asante, eds. *African Culture: The Rhythms of Unity.* Trenton, N.J.: Africa World Press, 1990.

Ashcraft-Eason, Lillian. "West African Culture, Women, and the Transatlantic Slave Trade" (work in progress).

Augier, F. R. *The Making of the West Indies.* London: Longmans, 1960.

Baker, Houston A. *The Journey Back: Issues in Black Literature and Criticism.* Chicago: Univ. of Chicago Press, 1980.

———, ed. *Reading Black: Essays in the Criticism of African, Caribbean, and Black American Literature.* Monograph Series, No. 4. Univ. of Pennsylvania, Afro-American Studies Program and Cornell Univ., Africana Studies and Research Center, 1976.

Barksdale, Richard, and Kenneth Kinnamon, eds. *Black Writers of America.* New York: Macmillan, 1972.

Barrett, Leonard. *Soul Force African Heritage in Afro-American Religion.* New York: Doubleday, 1974.

Barthold, Bonnie. *Black Time: Fiction of Africa, the Caribbean, and the United States.* New Haven: Yale Univ. Press, 1981.

Bastide, Roger. *African Civilisations in the New World,* translated by Peter Green. New York: Harper and Row, 1971.

Baugh, Edward. *Critics on Caribbean Literature: Readings in Literary Criticism.* New York: St. Martin's Press, 1978.

Blassingame, John. *The Slave Community: Plantation Life in the Ante-bellum South.* New York: Oxford Univ. Press, 1975.

Blauner, Robert. "Black Culture: Myth or Reality?" In *Afro-American Anthropology: Contemporary Perspectives.* Ed. Norman E. Whitten, Jr., and John Szwed. New York: Free Press, 1970.

Bone, Robert. *The Negro Novel in America.* New Haven: Yale Univ. Press, 1958.

Bracey, John, and August Meier, eds. *Black Matriarchy: Myth or Reality?* Belmont, Calif.: Wadsworth, 1971.

Brathwaite, Edward K. *Contradictory Omens: Cultural Diversity and Integration in the Caribbean.* Mona, Jamaica: Savacou, 1974.

Broderick, Francis, and August Meier. *Negro Protest Thought in the Twentieth Century.* Indianapolis: Bobbs-Merrill, 1966.

Brown, Lloyd W. "The American Image in British West Indian Literature." *Caribbean Studies* 11 (Apr. 1971).

Butterfield, Stephen. "The Calypso Tradition in West Indian Literature." *Black Academy Review* (Spring–Summer 1971).

Cannon, Katie G. *Black Womanist Ethics.* Atlanta: Scholars Press, 1988.

Carr, W. I. "The West Indian Novelist: Prelude and Context." *Caribbean Quarterly* 11, no. 1–2 (1965).

Clarke, John Henrik, ed. *Marcus Garvey and the Vision of Africa.* New York: Random House, 1974.

Collins, Patricia Hill. "African-American Women's Quilting: A Framework for Conceptualizing and Teaching African-American Women's History." *Signs: A Journal of Women in Culture and Society* 14 (Summer 1989).

———. "The Social Construction of Black Feminist Thought." *Signs: A Journal of Women in Culture and Society* 14, no. 4 (1989): 745–73.

———. *Black Feminist Thought: Knowledge, Consciousness and the Politics of Empowerment.* New York: Routledge, 1990.

Collymore, Frank. "Is There a West Indian Literary Culture?" *The Bajan* (Dec. 1963).

Cook, Mercer, and Stephen Henderson. *The Militant Black Writer in Africa and the United States.* Madison: Univ. of Wisconsin Press, 1969.

Cook, Mercer, ed. *Modern Black Novelists: A Collection of Critical Essays.* Englewood Cliffs, N.J.: Prentice-Hall, 1971.

Coulthard, G. R. "Rejection of European Culture as a Theme in Caribbean Literature." *Caribbean Quarterly* 5, no. 4 (1959).

Davidson, Basil. *The African Genius: An Introduction to African Social and Cultural History.* Boston: Little, Brown, 1969.

Davis, John P., ed. *The American Negro Reference Book.* Englewood Cliffs, N.J.: Prentice-Hall, 1966.

Dillard, J. L. *Black English: Its History and Usage in the United States.* New York: Random House, 1972.

DuBois, W. E. B. *The Souls of Black Folk* in *Three Negro Classics.* New York: Avon, 1968.

Ellison, Ralph. *Shadow and Act.* New York: New American Library, 1953.

Fanon, Frantz. *Black Skin, White Masks.* Translated by Charles Markham. New York: Grove Press, 1967.

———. *Wretched of the Earth.* Translated by Constance Farrington. New York: Grove Press, 1965.

Finnegan, Ruth. *Oral Literature in Africa.* Oxford: Clarendon Press, 1970.

Fisher, Dexter, ed. *The Third Woman: Minority Women Writers of the United States.* Boston: Houghton Mifflin, 1980.

Ford, Nick A. *The Contemporary Negro Novel.* College Park, Md.: McGrath, 1968.

Foster, Frances. "Changing Concepts of the Black Woman." *Journal of Black Studies* 3 (June 1973).

Franklin, John Hope. *From Slavery to Freedom: A History of Negro Americans.* New York: Vintage Books, 1969.

Frazier, E. Franklin. *The Negro Family in the United States.* Revised and abridged. Chicago: Univ. of Chicago Press, 1966.

Gates, Henry Louis, Jr. *Figures in Black: Words, Signs and the "Racial Self."* New York: Oxford Univ. Press, 1987.

————. *The Signifying Monkey: A Theory of African-American Literary Criticism.* New York: Oxford Univ. Press, 1988.

Gayle, Addison, Jr. *The Way of the New World: The Black Novel in America.* New York: Anchor Press/Doubleday, 1975.

Genovese, Eugene D., and Stanley Engerman, eds. *Race and Slavery in the Western Hemisphere.* Princeton: Princeton Univ. Press, 1975.

Gutman, Herbert G. *The Black Family in Slavery and Freedom, 1750–1925.* New York: Pantheon Books, 1976.

Hall, Stuart. "Cultural Identity and Diaspora." In *Identity, Community, Culture, Difference.* Ed. J. Rutherford. London: Lawrence and Wishart, 1990.

Handler, Jerome S. *Plantation Slavery in Barbados: An Archeological and Historical Investigation.* Cambridge: Harvard Univ. Press, 1978.

Harris, Trudier. "No Outlet for the Blues," *Callaloo* #18, vol. 6, no. 2 (1983): 57–67.

Harris, Wilson. "History, Fable, and Myth in the Caribbean and Guianas." *Caribbean Quarterly* 16, no. 2 (1970).

————. *Tradition, the Writer, and Society: Critical Essays.* London: New Beacon, 1967.

Herskovits, Melville. *Acculturation: The Study of Culture Contact.* New York: J. J. Augustin, 1938.

————. *Continuity and Change in African Culture.* Chicago: Univ. of Chicago Press, 1962.

————. *The Myth of the Negro Past.* Boston: Beacon Press, 1941.

Holloway, Joseph E., ed. *Africanisms in American Culture.* Bloomington: Indiana Univ. Press, 1990.

Hooks, Bell. *Ain't I a Woman: Black Women and Feminism.* Boston: South End Press, 1981.

Huggins, Nathan, and Martin Kilson. *Key Issues in the Afro-American Experience.* New York: Harcourt, Brace, Jovanovich, 1971.

Jahn, Janheinz. *Muntu: An Outline of the New African Culture.* Translated by Marjorie Grene. New York: Grove Press, 1961.

————. *Neo-African Literature.* Translated by Oliver Coburn and Ursula Lehrburger. New York: Grove Press, 1969.

James, C. L. R. *West Indian Nations: A New History.* New York: St. Martin's Press, 1973.

————. *West Indian Story.* London: Longmans, 1960.

Jones, LeRoi, and Larry Neal, eds. *Black Fire: An Anthology of Afro-American Writing.* New York: William Morrow, 1968.

Jones, LeRoi. *Home: Social Essays.* New York: William Morrow, 1972.

King, Bruce, ed. *West Indian Literature.* Hamden, Conn.: Archon Books, 1979.

Knight, Franklin W. *The Caribbean: The Genesis of a Fragmented Nationalism.* New York: Oxford Univ. Press, 1978.

Lamming, George. "On West Indian Writing." *Revista* 2 (Summer 1975): 149–62.

————. "The West Indian People." *New World Quarterly* 2, no. 2 (1966).

————. "The Negro Writer and His World." *Caribbean Quarterly* 5 (Feb. 1958).

Larson, Charles R. *The Emergence of African Fiction.* Bloomington: Indiana Univ. Press, 1972.

Levine, Lawrence W. *Black Culture and Black Consciousness: Afro-American Folk Thought from Slavery to Freedom.* Oxford: Oxford Univ. Press, 1977.

Levi-Strauss, Claude. *Myth and Meaning.* New York: Schocken Books, 1979.

Livingston, James T. *Caribbean Rhythms: The Emerging English Literature of the West Indies.* New York: Washington Square Press, 1974.

Mbiti, John S. *African Religions and Philosophies.* Rev. ed. New York: Anchor Books, 1970.

Mintz, Signey W., and Richard Price. *An Anthropological Approach to the Afro-American Past: A Caribbean Perspective.* Philadelphia: Institute for the Study of Human Issues, 1976.

————. *Caribbean Transformations.* Chicago: Aldine, 1974.

————. *Slavery, Colonialism, and Racism.* New York: Norton, 1974.

Moore, Gerald. *The Chosen Tongue: English Writing in the Tropical World.* London: Longmans, 1969.

Moses, Yolanda. "Female Status, the Family and Male Dominance in a West Indian Community," *Signs* 3 (Autumn 1977).

Ngugi, Wa Thiong'O. *Homecoming: Essays on Caribbean and African Literature, Culture and Politics.* London: Heinemann, 1972.

Perry, Ruth, and Martin Watson, eds. *Mothering the Mind.* New York: Holmes and Meier, 1984.

Price, Richard, ed. *Maroon Societies: Rebel Slave Communities in the Americas.* New York: Anchor Press/Doubleday, 1973.

Ramchand, Kenneth. *The West Indian Novel and Its Background.* London: Faber and Faber, 1970.

Reid, Ira De A. *The Negro Immigrant: His Background, Characteristics and Social Adjustments, 1899–1937.* 1st AMS edition. New York: AMS Press, 1968.

Schorer, Mark, ed. *Society and Self in the Novel.* New York: Columbia Univ. Press, 1956.

Schraufnagel, Noel. *From Apology to Protest: The Black American Novel.* Deland, Fla.: Everett/Edwards, 1973.

Sertima, Ivan Van. *Caribbean Writers.* London: New Beacon Press, 1968.

Shapiro, Linn, ed. *Black People and Their Culture: Selected Writings from the African Diaspora.* Washington, D.C.: Smithsonian Institution, 1976.

Singh, Amritjit. "Social Background of the West Indian Novel." *Black Orpheus* 4 (Oct. 1956).

Smitherman, Geneva. *Talkin' and Testifyin': The Language of Black America.* Boston: Houghton Mifflin, 1977.

Staples, Robert. *An Introduction to Black Sociology.* New York: McGraw-Hill, 1976.

————. *The Black Woman in America.* Chicago: Nelson Hall, 1973.

Tembo, Mwizenge S. "The Concept of African Personality: Sociological Implications." In *African Culture: The Rhythms of Unity.* Ed. M. K. and K. W. Asante. Trenton, N.J.: African World Press, 1990.

Terborg-Penn, Rosalyn, Sharon Harley, and Andrea Benton Rushing, eds. *Women in Africa and the African Diaspora.* Washington, D.C.: Howard Univ. Press, 1987.

Turner, Darwin T. *Black American Literature: Essays.* Columbus, Ohio: Merrill, 1969.

Turner, Lorenzo. *Africanisms in the Gullah District.* Chicago: Univ. of Chicago Press, 1949.

Vinson, James, ed. *Contemporary Novelists.* London: St. James Press, 1976.

Whitlow, Roger. *Black American Literature: A Critical History.* Chicago: Nelson Hall, 1973.

Whitten, Norman E., and John Szwed. *Afro-American Anthropology: Contemporary Perspectives.* New York: Free Press, 1970.

Wickham, John. "A Quality of Intimacy." *Bim* 9, no. 36 (1963): 266–73.

———. "The Arts in Barbados and in the Caribbean." *Caribbean Background* 4 (1972).

———. "West Indian Writing." *Bim* 13, no. 50 (1970): 68–80.

———. "Some Women in West Indian Fiction." *Barbadienne,* 1975, 21–22.

———. "The Artist as an Agent in the National Development Process." *Bajan,* 28 Dec. 1976.

Wideman, John. "The Black Writer and the Magic of the Word." *New York Times,* 24 Jan. 1988, p. 28.

Williams, Aubrey. "The Predicament of the Artist in the Caribbean." *Caribbean Quarterly* (Mar.-June 1968).

Wynter, Sylvia. "Novel and History, Plot and Plantation," *Savacou* 5 (June 1971).

———. "Reflections of West Indian Writing and Criticism." *Jamaican Journal* 4 (Dec. 1968) and 1 (Mar. 1969).

Index